CHOOSING THE TORY LEADER

CHOOSING THE TORY LEADER

CONSERVATIVE PARTY LEADERSHIP ELECTIONS FROM HEATH TO CAMERON

TIMOTHY HEPPELL

Tauris Academic Studies
LONDON • NEW YORK

Published in 2008 by Tauris Academic Studies, an imprint of I.B.Tauris & Co Ltd
6 Salem Road, London W2 4BU
175 Fifth Avenue, New York NY 10010
www.ibtauris.com

In the United States of America and in Canada distributed by Palgrave Macmillan
a division of St. Martin's Press, 175 Fifth Avenue, New York NY 10010

International Library of Political Studies 19

ISBN: 978 1 84511 486 2

A full CIP record for this book is available from the British Library
A full CIP record is available from the Library of Congress

Library of Congress Catalog Card Number: available

Printed and bound in India by Thomson Press India Limited
From camera-ready copy edited and supplied by the author

CONTENTS

LIST OF TABLES

ACKNOWLEDGEMENTS

I would like to express my gratitude to colleagues in the Department of Politics at the University of Huddersfield, both present and past, for their support of my research. Notable thanks are owed to Professor Valerie Bryson for the advice that she has offered. I also offer my appreciation to Dr Georgina Blakeley, Dr John Craig, Professor Brendan Evans, Dr Christopher Gifford, Dr Sarah Hale, Michael Hill, Dr Derek Lynch and Dr Peter Woodcock.

I acknowledge my gratitude to Professor Andrew Taylor, from the University of Sheffield, who offered suggestions on the original book proposal and who also provided the preface to the book. I should also note my appreciation for the comments and suggestions offered by Dr Matt Beech from the University of Hull.

Two other people are worthy of consideration. First, I am indebted to Elizabeth Munns at I.B.Tauris for her guidance throughout. Second, this publication would not have been possible without the expertise of Susan Smith of the University of Huddersfield, who ensured that the manuscript was presented to the publishers in the appropriate format.

On a personal level I would like to thank my parents, Irene and Neil, and my family for their support, which has enabled this book to be completed. Without their support this would not have been possible. I dedicate this book to my wife Gayle and our son Matthew.

2007   Dr Timothy Heppell

PREFACE

The Conservative Party dominated British politics during the twentieth century, a time in which Britain became a mass democracy, fought two world wars, established a welfare state, experienced relative decline, lost an empire and joined Europe. Few, if any parties have demonstrated such an ability to ride the political storms. The Conservative Party's ability to prosper in so turbulent a domestic and international environment has seldom ceased to fascinate academics who have struggled to identify the reasons for this success.

The explanations usually entail a combination of factors such as the party's supposed lack of an ideology that permits it to speedily and easily adapt to changed political circumstances. Other factors identified have included the strength of social deference in British political culture and the party's mastery of the arts, some of them black, of the political manipulation of a mass democracy. Another factor identified has been the party's ability to identify and sustain leaders able to reconcile the competing demands of the party activist and the median voter and articulate a convincing narrative.

Historically, the role of leadership has been seen as a particularly important aspect of Conservative political success. Only the leader has the right to pronounce authoritatively what constitutes Conservatism in any particular period. This is not to say that the leader has complete freedom to determine what constitutes the party's narrative, the leader has to reconcile multiple competing definitions of Conservatism and from this create a dominant narrative that satisfies the party and the electorate. This means that a party leader who successfully does so enjoys considerable latitude and freedom; the leader that fails to do so, or who loses the magic touch, can expect to be ruthlessly cast aside. The importance of the leader and the style of leadership for the Conservative Party cannot, therefore, be underestimated.

There is a considerable biographical literature on party leaders. All, from the most to the least successful, have their biographies and these provide an important resource for scholars but if we are to understand the complexity of party leadership and the dynamics of leadership politics in the party then comparative studies of cases is essential. This book provides such an analysis and is therefore to be welcomed.

Whilst common elements in the various leaders of the party can be identified and examined, the modern party leadership dates only from 1963 and the controversies provoked by Harold Macmillan's resignation and manipulation of the succession in favour of Alec Douglas Home. The creation of a leadership election process, despite changes in electoral formula and counting rules, created a new pattern of leadership politics that sheds a bright light on the internal politics and culture of the Conservative Party. As until relatively recently being party leader also meant becoming Prime Minister, this electoral process had major implications for governance. Heppell's book provides a detailed analysis of Conservative leadership politics from 1963 to the present.

The book is important not just because it considers each case of leadership election since 1963, but because it locates these instances in the wider development of Conservative politics. The study of leadership is difficult because, of course, each leader is, by definition, *sui generis*, but each leader has to deal with a broadly similar syndrome at whose core is the need to secure election. This, of course, is the main measure whereby leaders are judged and ranked. This is another reason why Heppell's book is important.

Looming over this is, of course, the leadership of Margaret Thatcher. Whoever followed Mrs Thatcher, thereby benefiting from her ouster, would have experienced serious problems but John Major found the Thatcher legacy, when coupled with the collapse of the party's statecraft in the early-1990s, to be unmanageable. The Conservative Party has lost elections, and lost them badly, in the past but not in recent history has the party suffered such an extended period of electoral and political failure as it has experienced since 1997. Never before has the Conservative Party had so many leaders in so short a period of time. Given the importance of effective leadership to the party and to electoral politics, the election of Hague, Duncan Smith and Howard raise fascinating and important questions about why the party selected leaders that proved so unsuitable and unattractive in electoral terms. These elections allow Heppell to explore the meshing of internal party considerations and the external electoral considerations, given that the leader is expected to bridge these arenas. The period after 1997 indicates how difficult a path Conservative leaders have to tread and it may be that the emergence of David Cameron sees the party recovering. Whether this is the result of Cameron's election or the failures of the Blair governments, or a combination, is a different question.

Heppell's book is to be welcomed because it provides both an overview and a detailed analysis of the politics of leadership in the Conservative Party but it goes further. It examines what mass democracy requires of its leaders and as such it contributes significantly to the study of leadership in democracies.

Andrew Taylor
Professor Politics
University of Sheffield

INTRODUCTION

The process that a political party uses to select their party leader, and the outcome of that selection process, will critically effect perceptions of the electoral appeal of the party. For the Conservatives, the process of leadership determination has historically been designed towards producing an outcome which addressed three essential needs: first, a party leader who could enhance the electoral appeal of the party; second, a party leader who would unify the party, on the basis that divided parties are electorally unattractive and divisiveness would impede governing effectiveness should they acquire office; and, third, a party leader who will demonstrate political and governing competence (Bogdanor, 1994:94).

These dilemmas of process and outcome did not seem to be too problematic to the Conservatives prior to the era of formally electing their party leader. Between 1885 and 1965, from when Lord Salisbury acquired the party leadership to when Alec Douglas-Home resigned from it, the Conservatives had only ten party leaders. With the exception of the short-lived tenure of Austen Chamberlain between 1921 and 1922, all of the other party leaders, Arthur Balfour, Andrew Bonar Law, Stanley Baldwin, Neville Chamberlain, Winston Churchill, Anthony Eden and Harold Macmillan, also served as Conservative Prime Ministers.

The Conservatives maintained their proximity to power from the age of Salisbury to Douglas-Home, as they occupied office, either singularly or in coalitions, for fifty-seven years of that eighty year period. Their claim to be the natural party of government flowed from this unparalleled capacity for voter mobilisation; a capacity which was seen to flow from their pragmatism (and political adaptability) and their internal unity and loyalty. Culturally hierarchical and inclined towards veneration of the party leader, the obsessive desire of the Conservatives was to sustain or manufacture new forms of political statecraft: i.e. the art of winning elections (the politics of support) and the art of governing effectively (the politics of power) (Bulpitt, 1986:19-39).

In observing their record of electoral and governing success, Bogdanor would note that the process through which they determined their party leadership, through un-codified processes of consultation, had played a pivotal role in their record of electoral success (Bogdanor, 1994:96). The Bogdanor assertion is critical. It assumes a correlation between the process of selection (i.e. the un-codified processes of consultation amongst elites through which a new leader emerged), and the cultural characteristics of a party of government: political pragmatism, internal unity and loyalty to the party leader.

The abandonment of the un-codified process of consultation, through which a new party leader emerged, would indirectly contribute to a cultural revolution within the party. This cultural revolution occurred through three stages. First, there was the initiation of limited internal democracy in 1965. This involved the establishment of formal processes for electing the party leadership from within the parliamentary Conservative Party. Second, there was an extension of internal democracy from leadership *election* procedures alone to formalised leadership *ejection* procedures in 1975. Third, there was the extension of democracy to the mass membership in 1998. This led to the establishment of a hybrid system, in which Conservative parliamentarians screened candidates until only two remained, and those two were then presented to the mass membership in a one member, one vote ballot.

If we examine the forty year period since the inception of internal democracy an *increasing* instability of party leadership is evident. The first party leadership election was conducted in July 1965, when Edward Heath was elected as their first democratic leader. The second party leadership election occurred in February 1975, when Margaret Thatcher was elected in succession to Heath. No further elections occurred until 1989, meaning that in the first twenty-four years of internal democracy only two elections were conducted to determine the party leader.

In the sixteen year period between 1989 and 2005, a further seven party leadership elections have been conducted. Thatcher defeated the challenge of Anthony Meyer in 1989 before the challenge of Michael Heseltine fatally wounded her during the 1990 leadership contest, causing her withdrawal from the second ballot, which John Major subsequently won. In 1995 Major voluntarily initiated a party leadership election by resigning as party leader and then immediately standing as a candidate in the vacant contest, in which he defeated John Redwood to retain (regain) the party leadership. When Major eventually resigned he was succeeded by William Hague who was elected party leader in the immediate aftermath of the electoral meltdown of 1997. By the time of the next party leadership election, after the electoral rejection of 2001, the party membership was involved in the election procedures. The victor in this succession battle was Iain Duncan Smith who two years later became a victim of new procedures for removing an unpopular and incompetent party leader. A vote of confidence by Conservative parliamentarians removed Duncan Smith from the party leadership, and he was succeeded by Michael Howard in the autumn of 2003, who was the only candidate to stand. The seventh and final party leadership election in this sixteen year period saw David Cameron become party leader, after Howard had resigned in the wake of a third successive electoral defeat in 2005.

We can argue that this cultural revolution within the Conservative Party has, over the longer-term, contributed to an increasing instability surrounding the party leadership; to a growing predilection for initiating party leadership elections; and to an increasing propensity for debating the processes of how to elect the party leader. This leadership instability demonstrates that the relationship between the leader of the Conservative Party and the parliamenttary Conservative party is dependent upon the capacity of the incumbent leader to achieve electoral success. This conditionality frames their security of tenure. If the incumbent is an electoral asset to the Conservative Party, then their authority as party leader will be enhanced which will aid their pursuit of the major dimensions of statecraft, i.e. successful party management, political argument hegemony, governing competence and a winning electoral approach. If the incumbent is perceived to be an electoral liability then this will impede their capacity to successfully pursue the major dimensions of statecraft. The most problematic aspect for a party leader viewed as an electoral liability will be party management. If they are an electoral liability then their authority will be eroded as the ties of loyalty are broken and their insecurity of tenure will be intensified and speculation about removing them will intensify.

Attempting to understand and explain the nature of this party leadership instability provides the rationale for this book. The aim of the book is to offer a chronologically and thematically driven overview of all of leadership elections that have occurred since the Conservative Party adopted formal democratic mechanisms for electing their party leader. Put simply, this book aims to address the eternal succession dilemmas of who was chosen as the new party leader; how the succession process was determined (i.e. what procedures were utilised); and why the victors were chosen. These are the types of dilemmas that scholars of British political history should be engaging with. However, despite this we have to recognise that leadership selection remains an under-researched aspect of British political history and Conservative Party political history.

There are a number of excellent texts on the history of the Conservative Party, the most notable of which are by Blake, Charmley, Gilmour and Garnett, Evans and Taylor, and Ramsden.[1] However, although these offer commendable historical and conceptual analysis of Conservative Party politics, including the post-1965 period, they make limited references to the means by which successive leaders of the Conservative Party actually acquired the party leadership. The books by Fisher and Shepherd,[2] and the chapter by Bogdanor in the edited volume by Seldon and Ball are party leadership centered. However, although they evaluate how and why party leaders have acquired the party leadership, much of their evaluation is pre-1965 and thus pre internal democratization. Furthermore, due to the time in which they were researched and published they are in need of updating, as they do not address five of the nine post-internal democratization electoral contests.

There are a number of excellent texts which include evaluations of the methods by which British political parties determine the leadership of their parties. Punnett, Stark and Watkins[3] have all offered illuminating appraisals of party leadership determination. However, these works are in need of updating, and, furthermore, there are significant methodological differences between these books and this book. For example, all of the aforementioned texts adopt a comparative perspective. The need to analyze the Labour Party (in the case of Punnett and Watkins) and the Liberals / Liberal Democrats in the case of Stark, reduces the capacity to focus on the internal machinations of the Conservative Party. In addition, the methodological approach of this book differs from the approaches adopted by Punnett, Stark and Watkins. These books do not offer discrete evaluations of individual Conservative Party leadership contests, rather they offer a more thematic approach. For example, Stark has a comparative chapter structure, focusing on the candidates in elections, their campaigning strategies, and the outcomes and impacts, whereas Punnett devotes only two chapters to the Conservative Party with one chapter based on pre-1965 and one chapter based on post-1965 up to 1990.

What is required is one historical narrative and analytical evaluation of the Conservative Party leadership elections that have occurred from the inception of internal democracy and the election of Heath to the most recent election of Cameron. Addressing this gap in the academic literature explains the chronological structure of the book. Whilst chronologically structured, the book attempts to offer a thematic approach. This dual approach will involve each chapter offering a historical narrative of the events that precipitated the electoral ballots; the candidates, the campaigning period, and the outcome; before offering a thematically driven evaluation of how and why the victor was elected.

Although the purpose of this book is to evaluate Conservative Party leadership selection in the era of internal democracy, it is important to understand what factors contributed to the inception of internal democracy. Chapter two addresses this by evaluating the war of the Macmillan succession in the autumn of 1963. It will argue that the traditional process through which a new party leader emerged (through undemocratic customary processes of consultation amongst elites) was discredited, due to the manipulative manner in which Harold Macmillan attempted to skew the process away from R. A. Butler and in favour of Alec Douglas-Home, then Lord Home.

That the outcome was disadvantageous to the Conservative Party, as they were saddled with an anachronistic party leader devoid of electoral appeal, intensified the criticism of the process. The nature of the emergence of Douglas-Home had been a failure of process and outcome, and had left the Conservative Party with a party leader devoid of legitimacy and thereby authority. The chapter will demonstrate how the disputed war of the Macmillan succession would create the catalyst for the inception of limited internal democracy and the election of the next leader of the Conservative Party.

Chapter three will offer an evaluation of the leadership election of 1965, through which Edward Heath overcame the pre-contest favourite Reginald Maudling, and marginal candidature of Enoch Powell, to become the first democratically elected leader of the Conservative Party. Before evaluating the election of Heath, the chapter will examine the transition from the customary processes of the magic circle to the formalised election procedures of a parliamentary ballot. Having considered the reasons why Douglas-Home resigned shortly after the inception of internal democracy, the chapter will evaluate the candidates, the campaigning period, and the parliamentary ballot. It will suggest that Heath emerged victorious due to a combination of his superior campaigning strategy and his rapid upwards career trajectory during their brief period in opposition. The emphasis on timing and career trajectory, aligned to campaigning approaches, will neatly dovetail into the primary insight of the leadership election: unlike future leadership elections, it was largely devoid of ideological considerations and the contest was conducted with a degree of harmony and decorum which would be lacking in latter years. The chapter will conclude by arguing that the outcome appeared to validate the process, which in turn legitimated the shift to internal democracy. In doing so, it will observe that the absence of any provision for removing a party leader who was an electoral liability, was not identified as a concern at this stage.

Chapter four will offer a historical appraisal of how Heath was deposed as leader of the Conservative Party in February 1975, following a challenge to his party leadership by Margaret Thatcher, who then proceeded to annex the party leadership in a second ballot. Considerable attention will be devoted to the circumstances surrounding the removal of Heath, with particular emphasis placed on how and why the rules governing leadership elections were adapted to permit an annual challenge to the incumbent leader. The remainder of the chapter will explore the formal challenge initiated by Thatcher and will examine the reasons for her subsequent success. It will suggest that her acquisition of the party leadership can be attributed to two explanations. The traditionalist explanation will argue that her ascent was the unintended consequence of having to remove Heath – i.e. she was an *accidental* leader and her support was the by-product of a *negative* support base. The revisionist explanation will argue that although there is legitimacy to the traditionalist explanation, the election of Thatcher was a consequence of ideological factors – i.e. after the failure of Heathite Conservatism, Conservative parliamentarians wanted an ideological shift to the right.

Chapter five will examine the means by which Thatcher was forcibly removed from the leadership of the Conservative Party and replaced by John Major. The chapter will argue that the easily dismissed lightweight challenge of Anthony Meyer in the autumn of 1989, actually increased the viability of the heavyweight challenge of Michael Heseltine in the autumn of 1990. Having examined the campaigning period and interpreted the inconclusive first ballot, the chapter will highlight how Thatcher felt compelled to resign before the second ballot, in order to prevent Heseltine succeeding her and to ensure that a Thatcherite would succeed her and preserve the ideology of Thatcherism.

When considering the second ballot, in which Major defeated Heseltine and Douglas Hurd, it will be argued that ideology was central to the outcome and that Major would be a default leader of the Conservative Party because of this. The default thesis will argue that his acquisition of the leadership of the Conservative Party was not the by-product of a groundswell of pro-Major Conservative parliamentarians proactively seeking his advancement to propel him into power. Rather the vast majority of his support came from Conservative parliamentarians whose preference was still Thatcher and had voted for her continuance only days earlier. Major may have been the choice of the Thatcherite right but he was not their first choice. Moreover, the fact that those Thatcherites gravitated towards him was due to their desire to prevent her nemesis, Heseltine, from acquiring the leadership of the Conservative Party. Collectively, the chapter will argue that he was the second choice of the Thatcherites (after Thatcher) and that his support was not the product of a pro-Major vote, but rather an anti-Heseltine vote. Moreover, the chapter will conclude by arguing that Major was not in absolute terms a Thatcherite. The support base around which he had acquired the leadership Conservative Party had misunderstood his ideological motivations: this would fatally undermine his authority over the parliamentary Conservative Party and his legitimacy as party leader.

Chapter six will evaluate the put up or shut up strategy that Major adopted in 1995 to retain his position as leader of the Conservative Party. The chapter will demonstrate that Major suffered from a crisis of legitimacy and authority, and how this was creating an insecurity that was immobilising his party leadership and premiership. The main objective of the analysis will be to determine whether Major derived any benefits for himself or the Conservative Party flowing from his defeat of John Redwood. In doing so, it will challenge the vote of confidence thesis that became accepted as the dominant interpretation in the immediate aftermath of the election contest. In disputing this interpretation it will offer a persuasive critique of the put up or shut up strategy which will argue the following. First, that the contest between Major and Redwood was a fundamentally unequal contest and that claims that it amounted to a resounding triumph for Major were spurious. Second, that the strategy offered no tangible benefits to the Conservative Party as it served to institutionalize not resolve their internal conflict, and thus it acted as a disruptive rather than a therapeutic process. Finally, it will argue that the rationale for initiating the contest was only partially successful – i.e. it enhanced the security of tenure of Major till the end of the Parliament, but it did not contribute to the re-acclamation of his authority over the parliamentary Conservative Party or his legitimacy as party leader.

Chapter seven will consider the leadership election of June 1997, in which William Hague was elected as the new party leader in preference to the candidatures of Kenneth Clarke, John Redwood, Peter Lilley and Michael Howard. Having examined the campaign period and the multiple ballots that followed, the chapter will argue that Hague would suffer from a multiplicity of legitimacy problems flowing from the means by which he had acquired the party leadership. It will argue that like Major his ascent was default in nature due to the following factors: first, the fact that the best candidates were not available; second, the fact that of the candidates available there was a desire to prevent Clarke from obtaining the party leadership and Hague emerged by default as the best ABC candidate (i.e. anybody but Clarke); third, the fact that despite being of the Thatcherite Eurosceptic right he had not secured the legitimate endorsement of these factions, which had split between Redwood, Lilley and Howard, rather than for Hague; and fourth, the delayed endorsement of Thatcher, which was brought about out of political necessity, served to re-emphasise the shallowness of his political support.

Chapter eight examines the leadership election of 2001, which was the first to occur under the 1998 leadership rules that included the mass membership of the Conservative Party in the democratic process. Having examined the rationale for the new leadership election procedures and the reason why Hague resigned, the chapter will then attempt to explain the rise of the quiet man of British politics, Iain Duncan Smith. The evaluation of the parliamentary stage of the leadership election will examine how the assumed party membership run off between the two heavyweight candidates, Michael Portillo and Kenneth Clarke, failed to materialise. Having examined the divisive and prolonged party membership campaign the chapter will conclude that Duncan Smith emerged as a default leader on the back of negatively induced votes. His position, as one of the first two candidates from the parliamentary ballots, was derived from a stop Portillo faction of social conservatives, who mobilised socially conservative sentiment to prevent the socially liberal Portillo being presented to the party membership. His subsequent party membership victory was tainted by the perception that a predominantly Eurosceptic party membership voted for him by default, in order to prevent the pro-European Clarke from assuming the party leadership. The chapter will conclude that the election of Duncan Smith, after an elongated and divisive process, was to demonstrate that a failed process had produced a flawed outcome. It will argue that Duncan Smith was the fortunate benefactor of an inherently failed set of procedures to determine the succession. Those failed procedures that enabled Duncan Smith to emerge with a very weak parliamentary basis of support, would ensure that he commenced his party leadership tenure with minimal legitimacy and authority amongst his parliamentary colleagues.

Chapter nine seeks to explain the bizarre events of autumn 2003 in which the parliamentary Conservative Party evicted Duncan Smith from the party leadership. It will argue that the Duncan Smith had assumed the party leadership on an inherently weak mandate, and that his disputed legitimacy had brought the new leadership election procedures into disrepute. Moreover, the disputed means of acquisition was compounded by the weaknesses of his political leadership style. The chapter will argue that Duncan Smith had a leadership credibility problem derived from his poor political image, the incoherence of his policy narrative, the ineptitude of his party management, his inability to exploit the weaknesses of a second term Labour government, his own reputation of rebelliousness, and the fear that the scale of his electoral limitations could plunge the Conservatives into third party status behind the Liberal Democrats. The chapter will argue that the confluence of these factors prompted dissidents within the parliamentary Conservative Party to utilise the new vote of confidence rules to brutally evict him. It will then examine how Conservative parliamentarians circumvented the need to consult with the party membership by agreeing that only one candidate should be put forward, Michael Howard, thus creating a modern equivalent of an old style emergence.

Chapter ten of the book will concentrate on the protracted leadership election of 2005. In evaluating the two-stage electoral process – the first amongst Conservative parliamentarians and the second amongst the party membership – the chapter will attempt to explain the unexpected triumph of the arch-modernizer, David Cameron. The chapter will evaluate the prolonged resignation of Howard and his failed attempt to alter the leadership election procedures, before examining the credentials of the four candidates vying for the succession. It will postulate that the Cameron candidature brought together moderate Eurosceptics with social liberals in alliance of modernising forces that Portillo had sought but failed to advance four years earlier. The chapter will suggest that the election of Cameron indicated that the era of ideological categorisation being the leading determinant for mobilising support for *or* against candidates appeared to be ending. It will argue that the mass membership gravitated towards the ideological nebulousness of Cameron and the rhetoric of modernisation because perceptions of voter appeal and leadership style transcended the ideological certainties of the Thatcherite candidature of David Davis. Perhaps this indicated that the Conservatives were finally learning from the mistakes of the post-Thatcherite era, and had elected a modernising pragmatist, whose objective was power and for whom dogma was an impediment to that objective?

Having explained the rationale for the book and how it will be structured, it is necessary to note three qualifying comments relating to the parameters of the book and the approaches or methodology underpinning it. The first qualifying comment amounts to a reminder of what the book is not. The book is not a definitive history of the Conservative Party over the last four decades. It does not claim to be. It seeks to explore a particular aspect of Conservative Party politics, which has received insufficient attention from the political historians who have offered definitive histories of the Conservative Party. The chapters amount to snapshots of pivotal stages within the history of the Conservative Party over the last forty plus years. As snapshots of pivotal stages they offer considerable detail about short periods of change, crisis or intrigue, as the party has switched from one party leader to another. What the chapters do not offer is detailed appraisals of Conservative Party politics in the periods between leadership elections. It is assumed that the reader already possesses a rudimentary appreciation of the key events and developments within Conservative Party politics between leadership elections. Each chapter does, however, incorporate a brief overview of how and why a leadership election or change would be activated.

The second qualifying comment relates to how we approach the rules governing the election of the leader of the Conservative Party. One of the defining characteristics of the Conservative Party over the last forty years has been their predilection for adapting the rules governing the election of their party leaders. As and when the procedures for the leadership determination have changed they are referred to within the chapters. However, for procedural clarity the appendix includes a definitive guide to the rules governing the election of the party leader.

The final qualifying comment relates to the methodological issues relating to examining the conduct of Conservative parliamentarians in leadership elections. A recurring theme throughout the chapters of this book, and a theme which dominates the conclusion, is the importance of ideology as a determinant of voting behaviour in parliamentary ballots. Whilst it is recognized that other variables, such as experience, competence, age, social background and education, can influence voting behaviour, the emphasis on ideology is justified for the following reason. Political biographies, autobiographies and newspaper cuttings gathered, indicate the dominance of ideology as a voting variable. The consequence has been that candidates have secured votes due to their ideological views, and some candidates have accrued default votes to prevent the ideological views of other candidates prevailing.

This presented a significant methodological challenge. One of the objectives of the book was to analyse the ideological motivations of Conservative parliamentarians when selecting their party leader. However, Conservative parliamentarians would vote in secret ballots. Although some Conservatives would be reluctant to reveal their voting intentions / behaviour, and it is plausible to believe that some may have lied, we can attempt to construct listings of voting behaviour in leadership elections. As leadership elections became more regular and media coverage of them more detailed, it was possible to utilise extensive newspaper listings of voting behaviour for each of the leadership elections from 1990 onwards. Such newspaper based listings, which were cross-referenced from a range of different newspapers, give extensive listings of voting behaviour. Each Conservative parliamentarian was also attributed an ideological affiliation within the ideological spectrum of Conservatism. The Norton ideological typology, and findings of the ideological composition of the parliamentary Conservative Party, identified the ideological affiliations of the electorates in the 1975, 1989 and 1990 party leadership election[4] (Norton, 1990a:41-58). My own ideological typology, and findings of the ideological composition of the parliamentary Conservative Party, identified the ideological affiliations of the members participating in the 1995 and 1997 leadership elections, whilst the Hill findings relating to the post-1997 parliamentary Conservative Party ensured that the ideological positioning of each Conservative parliamentarian was known for the 2001, 2003 and 2005 leadership elections[5] (Heppell, 2002:299-324; Hill, 2004; 2007).

The emphasis on ideology as a voting determinant is also intriguing as it is through this theme that our examination of Conservative Party leadership elections can come full circle. Thatcher acquired the party leadership from Heath due to a combination of political circumstance (i.e. the desire to remove Heath) and ideological factors (i.e. the desire of some Conservative parliamentarians to develop further their embryonic neo-liberal ideological project). The subsequent leadership elections were strongly influenced by ideological factors. For example, Major acquired the party leadership due to the support of the economic Thatcherite right, as the economic Tory left split between Heseltine and Hurd. Hague assumed the party leadership due to the support of the Eurosceptic Thatcherite right, as the Europhile Tory left embraced Clarke. Duncan Smith was elevated beyond his natural level as social conservatives could not abide the prospect of the socially liberal Portillo assuming the party leadership, whilst Eurosceptics could not abide the thought of the pro-European Clarke annexing the party leadership.

The methods by which Heath triumphed in the first party leadership election and Cameron triumphed in the most recent party leadership election are similar. Both emerged in contests with a less pronounced emphasis on ideology. Both spouted the nebulous mantra of modernisation, both defied concrete ideological categorisation, both acquired support from a wide spectrum of opinion within Conservative circles rather than an ideologically defined block, and in victory they both appeared to have settled the question of the succession for a generation.

The comparison between Cameron and Heath can be extended to the immediate predecessor to Heath, the widely derided Douglas-Home. Those Conservatives vexed by the emergence of Douglas-Home to the party leadership forty plus years ago placed considerable emphasis on his status as an Etonian, arguing that he was socially unrepresentative and thereby an electoral anachronism. They would be bemused by the exultant reaction amongst Conservatives to the recent election of the Etonian Cameron. His election via the dual franchise of the parliamentary party and the party membership, rather than the contrived magic circle, was fuelled by the belief that Cameron had electoral appeal and could connect with the ordinary voter. After having elected a succession of non-Etonians, the Conservatives had returned to their Etonian traditions. This would have delighted the Etonian Macmillan. His mishandling of the succession crisis of the autumn of 1963 and his obsession with advancing his fellow Etonian, Home, would act as the catalyst for electing the party leader. It would provide the path towards the chaos, intrigue and political theatre that would increasingly dominate and disfigure the Conservative Party over the next forty years.

THE WAR OF THE MACMILLAN SUCCESSION: THE CATALYST FOR ELECTING THE PARTY LEADER

The rationale for this book is to assess each of the leadership elections that the Conservative Party have engaged in since the inception of formal democratic processes in 1965. However, to provide a historical context to these democratic elections for the party leadership it is necessary to consider two questions. First, what leadership selection processes did the Conservatives utilise prior to 1965; and, second, and of greater significance, why did the Conservatives feel it necessary to establish such formal democratic processes? In order to answer these questions, it is necessary to consider the pre-1965 era and more specifically the war of the Macmillan succession, which acted as the catalyst for creating formal election processes.

Prior to 1965, the Conservatives retained a belief in non-democratic processes of consultation amongst party elites, through which a new party leader emerged. This mechanism operated on the following basis. Elites within the Conservative establishment would collectively evaluate the merits of potential leading candidates. Through their deliberations one candidate would emerge. Once elites had agreed on an approved candidate for the succession, that individual would be ritually acclaimed as the new party leader. Although the deliberations that elites engaged in could consider the state of opinion about the potential candidates amongst their parliamentary colleagues, this aspect of the decision-making process was not formalised, nor were the views of Conservative parliamentarians necessarily quantified (Watkins, 1991:194).

Conservative faith in their customary processes of determining the succession did seem to be justified by historical precedent. Between 1885 and 1957 the party leadership would be considered on ten occasions. As indicated in table one below, on seven occasions processes of consultation were hardly required (and were therefore sometimes non-existent) as there was an obvious and agreed successor.[1]

At the turn of the century, the transition from Lord Salisbury to Arthur Balfour was processed without significant deliberation. Balfour was widely accepted as the heir apparent, and he assumed the party leadership and the office of Prime Minister without delay. When Balfour resigned the party leadership in 1911, when the Conservatives were out of government, Andrew Bonar Law assumed the party leadership in the House of Commons. When concerns surrounding his health caused Bonar Law to resign in 1921, Austen Chamberlain assumed the party leadership in the House of Commons. The party leadership tenure of Chamberlain was brought to an abrupt end when the parliamentary Conservative Party voted to abandon the coalition government, which resulted in the resignation of the Liberal Prime Minister, David Lloyd George. As Chamberlain was a coalitionist and this had been defeated, his party leadership was untenable and he resigned. He was replaced as party leader and as Prime Minister in 1922, by Bonar Law who by this time was assumed to be in better health.

When Bonar Law was forced to resign again due to ill-health in 1923, the party leadership and the office of Prime Minister was assumed by Stanley Baldwin. When Baldwin retired as party leader and Prime Minister in 1937, Neville Chamberlain, who had assumed the status of nominal deputy to Baldwin, was immediately appointed by the monarch as Prime Minister and thereupon assumed the party leadership. When the Prime Ministerial tenure of Chamberlain was curtailed in May 1940, Winston Churchill assumed the position of Prime Minister, with Chamberlain remaining as party leader. When Chamberlain was forced to resign the party leadership due to ill-health five months later, there was no alternative to Churchill, who thus became party leader as well. Nearly fifteen years later, Anthony Eden succeeded Churchill as party leader and as Prime Minister. There was no dispute about the succession as for over a decade it had been widely recognised that Eden was the anointed successor to Churchill. When ill-health and the legacy of the Suez crisis caused Eden to resign, Harold Macmillan assumed the party leadership and the office of Prime Minister (Punnett, 1992:30-31; Bogdanor, 1994:70-71; Stark, 1996:13-15).

Therefore, as table one demonstrates, there were only three occasions when the party leadership was *clearly* disputed: i.e. 1911, 1923 and 1957. In the absence of an heir apparent, processes of consultation were deployed in an ad hoc manner, rather than through adherence to formalised processes of consultation. In 1911, neither of the two leading candidates for the succession, Austen Chamberlain and Walter Long, could claim the loyalty of the others supporters. The fear for party elites was that if either were elevated to the party leadership, then they could be divisive party leaders. The undemocratic aspect of the processes of consultation enabled party elites to identify this capacity for division. Party elites then coalesced around Bonar Law, who assumed the party leadership, after Chamberlain and Long were persuaded to stand aside in the interests of party unity (Bogdanor, 1994:72).

Table 1: **Leaders of the Conservative Party and Possible Alternatives 1885 – 1957**

Year	Leader Selected	Alternative Leaders
1885	Lord Salisbury	
1902	Arthur Balfour	
1911	Andrew Bonar Law	Austen Chamberlain, Walter Long
1921	Austen Chamberlain	
1922	Andrew Bonar Law	
1923	Stanley Baldwin	Lord Curzon
1937	Neville Chamberlain	
1940	Winston Churchill	
1955	Anthony Eden	
1957	Harold Macmillan	R. A. Butler

Note:
Until 1922 the Conservatives only had a designated party leader when there was a Conservative Prime Minister or when they were in opposition and they had a former Prime Minister who was still leader of the House of Commons or leader of the House of Lords. When they were in opposition and without a former Prime Minister, the party leadership effectively went into commission. The Conservatives would then have both a leader of the House of Commons and a leader of the House of Lords. Once obtaining office it was the role of the sovereign to determine which of the two should be invited to form and lead an administration. Therefore, it is important to note that Bonar Law (1911-1921) and Austen Chamberlain (1921-1922) were only leaders of the Conservative Party in the House of Commons. The official title of 'Leader of the Conservative and Unionist Party' did not formally exist until it was conferred upon Bonar Law in 1922.

Source: Adapted from Fisher, 1977:198 and Bogdanor, 1994:69-70

When Bonar Law finally resigned due to ill-health in May 1923, the party leadership was again disputed. The marginally favoured candidate for the succession was the peer, Lord Curzon, with the leading alternative being Baldwin. The expectation of the departing party leader, Bonar Law, had been the Curzon would emerge, but he expressed no preference on his behalf. Moreover, elites within the Conservative establishment could not agree on which of the candidates to advocate, thus placing the monarch in a difficult position. Reasons for the subsequent emergence of Baldwin could be either the concern about appointing a peer as Prime Minister,[2] or the intervention of former Conservative Prime Minister, Balfour, who was contemptuous of Curzon, and would thus manufacture arguments designed to advance the case of Baldwin (Blake, 1998:213).

The informality of the processes of consultation was again evident in the disputed succession battle following the resignation of Anthony Eden in January 1957. The succession was to be disputed between R. A. Butler and Harold Macmillan, with Butler assumed to be best positioned to emerge as the successor to Eden.[3] The processes of consultation suggested, however, that Macmillan was perceived to be a more unifying figure than Butler, who was regarded with scepticism amongst a minority of the right of the parliamentary Conservative party. No equivalent anti-Macmillan faction was identified in the course of the customary processes of consultation (Blake, 1998:278).

Having identified the informal processes through which the Conservatives had determined their party leadership, it is necessary to consider the reasons why such procedures were brought to an abrupt end. The rationale for the traditional method of leadership selection was driven by three essential needs: first, they needed to select a party leader who was an electoral asset; second, they needed to select a party leader who would unify the party; finally, they needed a party leader who was perceived to be politically competent.

The war of the Macmillan succession that occurred in the autumn of 1963 resulted in Lord Home (later Alec Douglas-Home)[4] acquiring the party leadership. His elevation to the party leadership failed to adhere to those three essential needs. Douglas-Home had minimal experience of domestic politics, especially economic politics which dominated electoral competition. He lacked voter appeal and was derided by the opposition as an anachronism in an increasingly meteoritic society. Moreover, his emergence as party leader was disputed. Accusations were made that suggested that the processes of consultation were rigged to the advantage of Douglas-Home, whilst his claim to be a unifying compromise candidate was undermined by the public knowledge that leading figures within the Cabinet were deeply angered by his emergence. Understanding the leadership crisis of 1963 is central to understanding the dynamics of leadership determination within the Conservative Party. We can only understand that leadership crisis, and the fact that it acted as the catalyst for formal democratic processes, by evaluating the implosion of the Macmillan era in order to ascertain why he resigned and how the succession process was mishandled.

2.1   The Resignation of Harold Macmillan

The tenure of Macmillan as party leader and Prime Minister, between 1957 and 1963, had constituted one of the high watermarks of Conservatism

(Evans and Taylor, 1996:101). The positivism that had characterised perceptions of the Macmillan government in the era of prosperity explained their third successive electoral victory in 1959 with an enhanced parliamentary majority. It amounted to a personal triumph for Macmillan given the perilous state of party morale when he assumed the party leadership in the aftermath of the Suez Crisis (Blake, 1998:278, 284).

The Macmillan government would degenerate, however, in its third term. That perception of degeneration and indeed decay was all pervasive and incorporated policy formulation (both economic and foreign) and political management. Evidence of economic decline relative to members of the European Economic Community (EEC) led Macmillan to seek entry as a mechanism for economic recovery. The subsequent rejection in January 1963 of the British application for EEC membership destroyed the main pillars of the strategy for economic recovery and the future dynamics of foreign policy (Evans and Taylor, 1996:122). It also damaged the leadership credibility of Macmillan. Moreover, it undermined the intended electoral strategy of the Conservatives in seeking a fourth successive term. Macmillan had hoped to narrate his re-election campaign around the opportunities that could be afforded through membership of the EEC; indeed, he hoped that such a strategy would provide the basis for modernisation, as this reforming mantra was a slogan which was in vogue in political circles at this time (Blake, 1998:289).

Perceptions of economic mismanagement and the association with decline were immensely damaging to an incumbent and long-serving government. In an attempt to demonstrate the renewal of his administration, Macmillan had engaged in a complete reconstruction of his government in the summer of 1962. The intention had been to create an image of a younger and more dynamic Cabinet and government (Evans and Taylor, 1996:125). Macmillan proceeded to dismiss seven ministers from his Cabinet, in a purge which became dubbed 'the Night of the Long Knives'.[5] However, the advancement of younger ministers served paradoxically to highlight the anachronistic image of Macmillan himself. The butchery of his Cabinet created an indelible image of weakness, whilst the ongoing economic difficulties ensured that an image of incompetence and policy failure remained attached to his government. These electoral impediments were then compounded by the image of decadence and scandal that became associated with the Macmillan government, which reached its zenith with the Profumo Affair in 1963.[6]

The cumulative effect of these governing difficulties was a decline in public confidence in the Macmillan Government. By June 1963 there was considerable evidence of dissatisfaction with Macmillan within the parliamentary Conservative Party, especially as the Labour lead in the opinion polls increased[7] (Blake, 1998:290). Indeed, the Conservative Whips' Office estimated that over half of all Conservative parliamentarians wanted Macmillan to resign. Despite these reservations, Macmillan informed the 1922 Executive Committee in July that it was his intention to lead the Conservative Party into the next general election and to attempt to secure a fourth successive term. On the issue of the succession, Macmillan informed them that:

> I appreciate that where there is not an heir apparent, I must be sure that in due course one is forthcoming, and I give you my word that I shall not give up until I know that, by the various proper methods of communications which are open to us, the party will accept a man who may be called as my successor, and accept him with goodwill and with the certain knowledge that their views have been fully assessed and fully taken into account.   (Goodhart, 1973:189)

Ultimately, however, it was the rapid deterioration in his health on October 8th that drained him of his political resolve and led to his decision to resign. He was taken ill with an inflamed prostrate gland, and fearing that he was seriously ill (he believed that he had cancer), he made the decision to resign (on October 9th) and have an operation the following day (Evans and Taylor, 1996:128).

The timing of his departure, in the sense that it coincided with the annual party conference, was regrettable.[8] On the second day of the conference, the Foreign Secretary, the then Lord Home, read a prepared statement to the party conference confirming the resignation of Macmillan. Douglas-Home announced that:

> In these circumstances I hope that it will soon be possible for the customary processes of consultation to be carried on within the party about its future leadership.   (Stark, 1996:17)

2.2   The Lack of an Obviously Acceptable Successor

That the party conference then degenerated into an unofficial and rather unsavoury leadership convention was a consequence of the fact that Macmillan did not have an obviously agreed heir apparent. The leading candidate for the succession was once again Butler. He had twice acted as Prime Minister, he was currently Deputy Prime Minister, he was the most senior ministerial figure within the Cabinet besides Macmillan, and he was the leading intellectual figure of post-war Conservatism (Evans and Taylor, 1996:128). However, Macmillan would not consider the idea of Butler succeeding him.[9] His opposition to Butler embraced three considerations. First, he had reservations about the electoral appeal of Butler. Second, he was concerned as to whether Butler, as an archetypical left-wing Conservative, would be able to unify the party, as he feared Butler would be unacceptable to the right of the parliamentary Conservative Party. Finally, Macmillan felt that Butler was indecisive and lacked the strength of character required to be Prime Minister[10] (Horne, 1989:471; Watkins, 1998:69-70).

In his desire to acquire a viable non-Butler option for the succession, Macmillan, had advanced two leading Conservatives of the next generation, in the shape of Iain Macleod and Edward Heath. However, neither of them had emerged quickly enough to enable Macmillan to endorse them as a viable non-Butler successor (Fisher, 1977:101). It was clear that leftish Macleod was not a viable alternative as he had alienated the right of the parliamentary party, whilst Heath was seen as too inexperienced, although he was seen as a contender in the next succession contest. The only non-Butler candidate within the House of Commons was therefore the Chancellor, Reginald Maudling, although Macmillan also had reservations about his leadership capabilities. Macmillan was seeking a non-Butler and indeed a non-Maudling candidate (Horne, 1989:531).

Circumstances happened to present Macmillan with a wider range of options. Just a few months prior to his resignation, a parliamentary bill had been passed that would enable hereditary peers to renounce their peerages and stand for election to the House of Commons.[11] It was this bill that was to radically alter the war of the Macmillan succession, as a peerage now ceased to be an obstacle to the succession[12] (Blake, 1998:291). This meant that the Lord President and Minister for Science, Lord Hailsham (Quentin Hogg) could be a candidate for the succession. Crucially at this juncture it was not assumed that Lord Home (Alec Douglas-Home) would be a candidate[13] (Blake, 1998:290). As such, the expectation was that it would be a three-way contest between Butler, Hailsham and Maudling, with Macmillan favouring Hailsham.[14]

The two peers would adopt diametric opposite strategies, in terms of how they utilised the peerage amendment to their advantage, when the succession battle commenced that October. Hailsham immediately declared his intention to disclaim his peerage, in order to ensure that he could claim the party leadership and the premiership. Douglas-Home played a longer tactical and duplicitous game. Douglas-Home consistently gave the impression to Cabinet colleagues that the summit of his political ambitions was his current position of Foreign Secretary. On October 8th, two days prior to the eventual resignation of Macmillan, the Cabinet had been convened and with Macmillan excusing himself, the remainder of the Cabinet discussed what to do should Macmillan resign. The Lord Chancellor, Lord Dilhorne, argued that as he would not be a candidate for the succession, he would be willing to conduct the processes of consultation from within the Cabinet. It is at this juncture that Douglas-Home intervened with a comment that can be defined as a tactical masterstroke and morally indefensible. Douglas-Home indicated to his Cabinet colleagues that he could assist Dilhorne as he would not be a candidate for the succession in any circumstances. Tactically it was a masterstroke as it deceived his rivals for the succession[15] (Gilmour and Garnett, 1998:189).

As the war of the Macmillan succession commenced, the conference became an important platform through which aspirants could showcase their leadership credentials (Shepherd, 1996:257). By the end of the conference season, three known aspirants, Maudling, Butler and Hailsham had failed to enhance their prospects, thereby enabling one assumed non-aspirant, Douglas-Home, to enhance his.[16] The biggest loser from an unedifying conference season would be Hailsham. In the immediate aftermath of his resignation it was assumed that Macmillan would be endorsing Hailsham as the best anti-Butler option available to him. However, by attempting to transform the conference into a nomination convention for his candidature, Hailsham succeeded in alienating many Conservative parliamentarians.[17] Sensing the harsh reactions that his candidature would provoke, Macmillan abandoned Hailsham and gravitated towards Douglas-Home as an alternative unity or anti-Butler candidate, even though at this stage few realised that Douglas-Home had designs on the party leadership (Evans and Taylor, 1996:128). The mobilisation of a Douglas-Home candidature was now being actively stimulated (October 11th), despite the fact that only three days earlier (October 8th) Douglas-Home had indicated to his Cabinet colleagues that he would not be a candidate.[18] With the active encouragement of Macmillan, Douglas-Home was now intimating that although he was not seeking sponsorship, he would be willing to serve if that was deemed to be in the best interests of the party. He did not publicly declare that he was a candidate for the succession until the 16th of October. By this time the customary processes of consultation were well advanced and the manipulation would be clearly advantageous to Douglas-Home (Punnett, 1992:40).

2.3   Bias in the Customary Processes of Consultation?

Prior to his resignation Macmillan had discussed in Cabinet the manner in which his successor should be determined. He had secured the agreement of Cabinet that separate processes of consultation should be conducted to assess opinion in four areas: within the Cabinet; amongst junior ministers and the backbench parliamentary party; from constituency chairs; and finally amongst Conservative peers. The convenor of the discussions amongst the Cabinet was to be the Lord Chancellor, Lord Dilhorne. The Chief Whip, Martin Redmayne, would assess opinion amongst junior ministers and the backbench Conservative parliamentarians. The Chairman of the Party, Lord Poole, would provide feedback on the attitudes of constituency chairmen, whilst Earl St Aldwyn would assess the views of the peers. These processes of consultation would be pivotal to Douglas-Home acquiring the party leadership and the premiership, and they would also be subject to widespread accusations of bias (Punnett, 1992:40-41).

The assessment of the views of Conservative peers, who endorsed Douglas-Home, provoked minimal criticism, but the means by which the other three branches of opinion were assessed seemed open to accusations of bias. We can consider first the means by which the views of party activists were calculated. As this point the Conservative Party had two chairs: Lord Poole and Iain Macleod. That Macmillan consulted with Poole rather than Macleod was immensely significant. Macleod was a keen advocate of Butler, so excluding him from the consultation process was important if Macmillan was to secure his objective of preventing Butler assuming the party leadership (Blake, 1998:292). The soundings undertaken by Poole provided Macmillan with only half of the answer that he would have wanted. Poole indicated that party activists were inclined towards Hailsham. That Poole did not indicate Butler was beneficial to the plotting that Macmillan was engaging in. Of additional significance was the finding that Hailsham supporters were opposed to Butler, and moreover that Douglas-Home was the second choice of Hailsham supporters and also the second choice of Butler supporters. The findings of the party activists, whilst of little real consequence (as they were easiest to discount), served a purpose for Macmillan: they demonstrated opposition to Butler and the unifying capacity of a Douglas-Home candidature (Punnett, 1992:41).

It was the methods by which junior ministerial and Conservative backbench parliamentarians were canvassed and cabinet opinion was assessed, that provoked the most resentment. The authenticity of the assessment of backbench opinion conducted by Redmayne, as Chief Whip, was of particular debate. Redmayne, a known supporter of Douglas-Home, was accused of not providing an accurate numerical estimation of support for each of the candidates from amongst Conservative parliamentarians.[19] Rather, by engaging in a convoluted exercise of creative accountancy, he was able to deduce that there was considerable support for Douglas-Home (Gilmour and Garnett, 1998:196-198).

Redmayne manufactured the process through a process of guided democracy which ensured that he got the answer that Macmillan wanted.[20] Conservative parliamentarians were asked three questions:

1. Who should succeed Macmillan?
2. Who would be your second preference?
3. Who would you least like to see as the next party leader and Prime Minister?   (Bogdanor, 1994:76)

The findings that Redmayne provided were immensely beneficial for Macmillan in advocating Douglas-Home. First, when considering first preferences Douglas-Home was the leading candidate. Second, when considering second preferences, Douglas-Home was also the leading candidate, thus suggesting his capabilities as a compromise candidate.[21] Third, of the three leading candidates, Douglas-Home, Butler and Hailsham, it was Douglas-Home who had the fewest number who were opposed to him acquiring the party leadership, thus suggesting Douglas-Home was the unity candidate. Moreover, these initial findings made it clear that Macleod and Heath were not viable successors as they had low first and second preference returns, but also it indicated that Hailsham was not a viable successor because of high level of definite aversions that were expressed against him. When the parliamentarians who had listed as first preferences Hailsham, Macleod and Heath were re-allocated, then Douglas-Home led Butler by eleven and had eighteen fewer definite aversions. Redmayne had provided findings that aided the case for Douglas-Home as the compromise unity based candidate.

Table 2:   The Redmayne Findings: Leadership Preferences in the Parliamentary Conservative Party (October 1963)

Candidate	No of First Preferences	No of Second Preferences	Definite Aversions	Re-allocated Preferences[22]
Lord Home	87	89	30	113
R. A. Butler	86	69	48	104
Lord Hailsham	65	39	78	-
Reginald Maudling	48	66	6	66
Iain Macleod	12	18	1	-
Edward Heath	10	17	1	-

Source: Adapted from Baston, 2004:208

The Redmayne findings were sufficiently persuasive but they were inherently rigged findings. The process amounted to guided democracy. Consultations were not restricted to the three specified questions. An additional fourth question was often asked to Conservatives who needed guidance. The fourth question was loaded. It addressed the issue of a hypothetical deadlock between Hailsham and Butler. If such a hypothetical scenario emerged Conservative parliamentarians were asked whether they would accept Douglas-Home (Bogdanor, 1994:76). The hypothetical question of Douglas-Home as a compromise party leader gave scope for widespread distortion of parliamentary opinion. Conservative parliamentarians, who were canvassed during the processes of consultation, have hinted that expressions of respect for Douglas-Home that they offered in answering this fourth hypothetical question, were then noted as either first or second preferences, and thus distorted their real views. For example, James Prior would later admit that he suspected that he was classed as a Douglas-Home supporter because he expressed no objections to Douglas-Home, when Douglas-Home was actually his third choice, behind Butler, then Hailsham (Prior, 1986:32-33).

Although the process of consultation amongst Conservative parliamentarians was questionable, it was the circumnavigating of the hostility that existed towards Douglas-Home within the Cabinet that would fatally undermine the customary processes for determining the party leadership. Macmillan had delegated the Lord Chancellor, Lord Dilhorne, to assess Cabinet opinion of his successor. Dilhorne was a supporter of Douglas-Home. Adopting a similar approach to that executed by Redmayne, Dilhorne would inform Macmillan that there was Cabinet support for Douglas-Home. He claimed that soundings led him to believe that ten Cabinet ministers endorsed Douglas-Home, three endorsed Butler, four opted for Maudling, and two preferred Hailsham. Macleod, who would later pen a devastating critique of how Douglas-Home had annexed the party leadership by dubious methods, was scathing in his condemnation of the accuracy of the figures produced by Dilhorne. The implausibility of the figures was demonstrated by the fact that Dilhorne was claiming that Macleod was a Douglas-Home supporter. Why would Macleod subsequently refuse to serve in the Douglas-Home Government if he had been a Douglas-Home supporter as Dilhorne claimed? Why would Macleod, when writing in the Spectator[23] in January 1964, question the accuracy of figures that Dilhorne gathered, if he had supported Douglas-Home? If Douglas-Home had been part of the Cabinet majority for Douglas-Home, as Dilhorne claimed privately during the succession battle, why did he not publicly reveal this when criticised so openly by Macleod? As Gilmour and Garnett conclude the fact that Dilhorne did not suggests that he knew his figures were a manipulation[24] (Gilmour and Garnett, 1998:199).

2.4 The Outmanoeuvring of R. A. Butler

Utilising distorted processes of consultation, Macmillan was able to argue that Douglas-Home was the best candidate to become party leader and Prime Minister. Basing his judgement on the findings of his emissaries, with particular emphasis placed on the distorted findings of Dilhorne and Redmayne, Macmillan deduced that although there was support for Butler and Hailsham there was also considerable opposition to both. He concluded that no such antagonism surrounded Douglas-Home and that it was therefore he who should emerge as a unifying compromise candidate. The speed with which Macmillan then attempted to railroad the succession process in favour of Douglas-Home suggests that he knew antagonism towards Douglas-Home did exist.

On the basis of the aforementioned processes of consultation, Macmillan drafted a memorandum arguing the case for Douglas-Home. Macmillan presented his memorandum to the Queen on the morning of the 18th October.[25] Upon his formal resignation, he advised the Queen to send for Douglas-Home and invite him to form an administration (Jeffreys, 2002:132). That Macmillan informed the Queen of his recommendation of Douglas-Home ahead of his Cabinet was deemed to be tactically significant, i.e. it would limit the time in which Cabinet ministers could mobilise their opposition. However, a group of senior Cabinet ministers had anticipated the attempt by Macmillan to bounce the monarch into inviting Douglas-Home to form an administration. This was known by Macmillan. The day before he formally resigned, a significant request by leading Cabinet ministers was rejected. Macleod, Maudling and, most significantly Butler, asked Dilhorne to convene an emergency cabinet meeting to discuss the succession crisis. Dilhorne indicated that he would only acquiesce to this demand with the consent of Macmillan, who made no reply to the telephone message left by Dilhorne (Punnett, 1992:42).

The level of intrigue was reaching a point which was immensely damaging, as a state of leadership paralysis engulfed the Conservative Party. A group of leading Cabinet ministers, including Hailsham, Powell, Macleod and Butler convened in an attempt to impede the emergence of Douglas-Home, and mobilise the alternative case for Butler. Their strategy was to make the prospect of a Douglas-Home premiership non-viable by collectively refusing to serve under him. Resistance to the notion of a Douglas-Home premiership reached its zenith when

> Hailsham and Maudling declared that they would now accept Butler as leader. They concluded that as there were just three public contenders, and two of them had now agreed to serve under the third, Douglas-Home's role as compromise candidate was no longer necessary. Powell and Macleod spoke to Douglas-Home on the telephone and told him that he should not try to form a government.[26]   (Punnett, 1992:43)

Their objections to Douglas-Home appeared briefly to threaten his desire to remain as a candidate. The logic of his emergence as a compromise based unity candidate was increasingly non-viable if he was the focal point of dissent and disagreement (Gilmour and Garnett, 1998:200). Macmillan then stiffened the resolve of Douglas-Home to continue, claiming that 'if we give into this intrigue then there will be chaos,' before telling Douglas-Home to 'go ahead, get on with it' (Fisher, 1977:108).

Although Macmillan had attempted to bounce the Queen into inviting Douglas-Home to form an administration, it was still feasible for Butler to acquire the party leadership and the office of Prime Minister. Butler was now presented with two options. First, he could capitulate by accepting the offer by Douglas-Home to become Foreign Secretary. Or, second, he could refuse and fight for the succession process to be reopened. His refusal would invalidate the mandate on which Douglas-Home was seeking to claim the party leadership. To achieve this objective Butler needed all of his fellow Cabinet dissenters to remain in agreement not to serve under Douglas-Home. If they did then Douglas-Home would have to inform the Queen that he was unable to form an administration (Watkins, 1998:68).

Powell and his associates believed that they had engineered a scenario in which Butler could defy the machinations of the Macmillan, Dilhorne, Redmayne, and of course Douglas-Home. All that was required was for Butler to claim what Powell believed was rightfully his. Powell would melo-dramatically argue that he had given Butler a loaded revolver and all he had to do was assassinate the candidature of Douglas-Home and thereby the plotting of Macmillan, Dilhorne and Redmayne. When an increasingly agitated Powell attempted to persuade Butler to do so and dispute the succession, he received the following meek but polite reaction[27]

Butler: Will it go off with a bang?
Powell: Well RAB…a gun does make rather a bang when it goes off
              …
Butler: Well thank you very much, I don't think I will. Do you mind?
                                                    (Leonard, 2003:509)

Butler had decided to be pragmatic and serve under Douglas-Home, thus ensuring that his nemesis, Macmillan, secured the outcome that he desired. Lord Home renounced his peerage and reverted to Alec Douglas-Home to become Prime Minister. Having obtained a parliamentary seat at a hastily arranged by-election three weeks later, he became the official leader of the Conservative Party.[28]

With Butler agreeing to serve under him and Hailsham and Maudling also agreeing, the only remaining acts of defiance came from Powell and Macleod.[29] Their cumulative weight had been insufficient to prevent Douglas-Home from assuming the party leadership and the premiership. Macleod refused to serve under Douglas-Home due to the low regard in which he held his new party leader. He had a low opinion of the intellectual capacity of Douglas-Home, whom he felt was a right-wing reactionary.[30] Powell refused to serve on a matter of principle: i.e. that he felt that Douglas-Home had lied to the Cabinet when he had indicated to them that he would not be a candidate for the succession (Leonard, 2003:507,509).

Why did Butler capitulate and allow his chance of the party leadership and the premiership disappear? Two plausible explanations have been identified. The first explanation lies in the character of Butler. Essentially he lacked the resolve required to circumnavigate the plotting of Macmillan and demand that the succession process be reopened. Butler wanted the party leadership and the premiership, but he did not want to have to fight for it (Ramsden, 1996:207). This lack of ruthlessness 'was an endearing character in the man...[but]...it was a fatal flaw in the politician' (Fisher, 1977:110). The second explanation lies in the fact that Butler could only acquire the party leadership and premiership in circumstances that would be immensely damaging to the unity and electoral prospects of the party. For an instinctive party loyalist, he could not bring himself to divide the party for short term personal gain. Ramsden identified the dilemma facing Butler if he disputed the succession:

> Once Douglas-Home had been given first try to form a cabinet, his failure could have been brought only through a constitutional crisis involving the monarchy...and with the party split it is inconceivable that a Butler team formed *after* Douglas-Home's public humiliation would have been able to unite the party to win the coming election.
>
> (Ramsden, 1996:207)

The recriminations reverberated around Conservative circles as the Douglas-Home administration limped to electoral defeat in the autumn of 1964. The scale of that bitterness was evident in the observations of Macleod, as noted by Gilmour and Garnett, in which Macleod,

> Claimed that from the very beginning to the end of his premiership Macmillan had been determined that Butler, although incomparably the best qualified of the contenders, should not succeed him, and that the succession had been determined by what amounted to a conspiracy by a magic circle, compromising of Macmillan himself, Dilhorne and Redmayne...Although confirmed publicly by Powell (and later by Butler) Macleod's account seemed at the time to be overdrawn; in the light of later knowledge it is much more convincing.
>
> (Gilmour and Garnett, 1998:196)

2.5 The Customary Processes in Disrepute: A Failure of Process and Outcome

The war of the Macmillan succession constituted a failure of process and a failure of outcome. When examining why the outcome was flawed (i.e. why Douglas-Home was an inappropriate politician to have propelled to the party leadership) it is clear that the role played by Macmillan in the succession process was open to criticism. His influence was apparent throughout as he appeared to dictate the terms of the succession contest whilst convalescing.

It was Macmillan who framed the terms of reference for the processes of consultation. The term 'customary' processes of consultation can be exposed as a misnomer. There were no clearly defined and documented procedures on how soundings should be conducted; previous succession contests had demonstrated that determining the state of opinion was conducted in a flexible or ad hoc manner. It was therefore possible for Macmillan to construct them in a manner that served his interests. By engaging in extensive evaluations of opinion across four sections of the party – the parliamentary party and junior ministers; Cabinet members; peers; and party chairs – it could be claimed that the process was thoroughly conducted (Punnett, 1992:46-47). Such an assertion would be distorting. Macmillan then determined that acceptable political operators should act as his representatives. The notion of the succession process being a fix had validity given that Macmillan wanted Douglas-Home as did Dilhorne and Redmayne. That their respective calculations were so flawed and that the authenticity of their findings did not need to be demonstrated, added fuel to the resentments that were gathering amongst Conservative parliamentarians. The scale and scope of that resentment was eloquently expressed by a junior Conservative parliamentarian, Humphrey Berkeley, who published a memorandum critiquing the post-Macmillan succession contest. He observed that:

> Uncertainty as to who was entitled to be consulted, the absence of any formalised procedure, the fact that those who took soundings both decided who were to be sounded and what weighting was to be given to the opinions of those who had been sounded and – most important of all – the fact that those who took the soundings and made the weighting were the only people to scruntinise the results of this somewhat arbitrary poll, has led to a feeling that this can never happen again. (Berkeley, 1972:158-161)

The reputation that Macmillan derived for cunning and brutality was derived from his obsessive need to impede Butler. It was this obsession that explained his abandoning of Hailsham, his manipulative advancing of Douglas-Home, his refusal to allow the cabinet to reconvene under Dilhorne to reassess the situation, and his desire to railroad the monarch into appointing Douglas-Home before his Cabinet critics could mobilise a viable revolt. Whilst somewhat immoral, Macmillan had not contravened any of the customary processes as their flexibility was so pronounced. His Machiavellian behaviour may have been regrettable and the motivation for his conduct was widely speculated. The chief assumption was that Macmillan had utilised an inherently rigged process to the advantage of a group of socially unrepresentative elites, and to the detriment of more meritocratic and socially representative Conservative parliamentarians. The suggestion was that an elite magic circle of Etonians had manufactured the process at the behest of the Etonian Macmillan to the benefit of the Etonian Douglas-Home (Leonard, 2003:508).

The second aspect worthy of consideration was the outcome. The ascent of Douglas-Home demonstrated the correlation between process and outcome. His ascent was a direct consequence of the process, i.e. had the process been democratic he would not have been the new party leader, as Punnett concludes:

> It is inconceivable that Douglas-Home would have been elected in a secret ballot of Conservative MPs (even if he had made himself available for such an election by disclaiming his peerage at the beginning of the contest). It is even less likely that he would have been elected in an electoral college based on the party conference or in a ballot of party members. It was the informal and unstructured nature of the processes of consultation that allowed a somewhat unlikely candidate to be imposed on a party that was not sure what was happening.   (Punnett, 1992:46)

The imposition of Douglas-Home can be seen as being detrimental to the Conservative Party in two clear ways. The first damaging consequence of his ascent related to the operational effectiveness of the Conservative Party under Douglas-Home. His ascent created an image of a party at war with itself. That perception of disunity was to the electoral advantage of the Labour Party. That sense of disunity was all encompassing as Powell, the figurehead of the Conservative right, and Macleod, the figurehead of the Tory left, were united in their opposition to him. That Douglas-Home could only unite the extremities of left and right in opposition to him, demonstrated the implausibility of him being as a unifying presence within the Conservative Party. His legitimacy was questioned due to the manner of his ascent. As a consequence the authority that he needed to possess over Conservative parliamentarians and over Cabinet colleagues was weakened. He knew, his Cabinet colleagues knew, the Labour opposition knew, and the electorate suspected, that he was presiding over a Cabinet, in which the key players (Butler, Hailsham and Maudling) had been opposed to his ascent. That he presided over a government so wracked with mutual suspicion and distrust was politically debilitating to him and to the electoral prospects of the Conservative Party.

The second damaging consequence of his ascent related to the most important aspect of politics for any Conservative: the acquisition or retention of power. The primary responsibility of any leader of the Conservative Party is voter mobilisation – the politics of support or the art of winning elections. Douglas-Home failed to retain power for the Conservatives. Although he was constrained as his legitimacy as party leader and Prime Minister was disputed, he also failed once he was Prime Minister, to present himself to the electorate as a credible politician worthy of re-election.[31] In an increasingly telegenic and meritocratic era, the media savvy intellectual moderniser, Wilson, was able to outmanoeuvre the anachronistic Douglas-Home.[32] He was an electoral liability rather than an asset and his ineffectiveness on television was a significant impediment to their election campaign in the autumn of 1964 (Leonard, 2003:510). Douglas-Home was aware of his visual and presentational limitations and did make an effort to improve his television appearances. However, his memoirs would reveal the futility of such efforts, as he sought advice from a make up specialist:

Douglas-Home:	Can you make me look better than I do on television?
Answer:	No
Douglas-Home:	Why not?
Answer:	Because you have a head like a skull
Douglas-Home:	Does not everyone have a head like a skull?
Answer:	No

(Home: 1976:203)

The loss of office at the ensuing election was a by-product of a myriad of factors: the cumulative effect of numerous governmental failings in the last Parliament; the time for a change argument after thirteen years of Conservative rule; and the reforming and modernising appeal of Wilson and a remodelled Labour Party. Rather than attribute defeat to these factors, Douglas-Home came to believe that his narrow defeat was due to Macleod and Powell refusing to serve under him, and thus undermining the credibility of his government, and himself as Prime Minister. Therefore, by his own admission, the nature of his own political ascent had been the cause of the political demise of the Conservative Party. Once in opposition he accepted the view that the customary processes of consultation and emergence to ritual acclamation had been irremediably discredited (Leonard, 2003:511).

2.6   Conclusion

The Conservatives entered their re-election campaign with three impediments: first, the bitterness and ill-feeling generated by the war of the Macmillan succession and the damning impression that it had given to the electorate of the party; second, the perception of internal disunity flowing from the refusal of Macleod and Powell to serve under Douglas-Home; and third, the myriad of electoral limitations associated with Douglas-Home himself, from his weak mandate and disputed legitimacy to his inability to transmit the merits of voting Conservative. The customary processes for determining the leadership succession had brought the Conservative Party into disrepute and had led to an outcome that was detrimental to their electoral prospects.

Despite these disadvantages and the governing ineptitude of their third term, the Labour Party entered power with a parliamentary majority of only four. Many came to believe that if Butler had assumed the party leadership and the premiership instead of Douglas-Home, then the Conservatives would probably have won a fourth successive term. Douglas-Home himself would come to admit that with the benefit of hindsight it would have been better if Butler had secured the party leadership and premiership rather than himself, as he felt that he was an unnatural successor (Gilmour and Garnett, 1998:203). Had Macmillan not worked so hard to impede the chances of Butler, then Butler would probably have secured the party leadership.[33] Had he done so then party unity would have been enhanced as his accession would not have resulted in cabinet resignations. Had he done so then the arguments about the method of determining the party leadership would have been avoided and such dramatic terminology as the magic circle would not have entered the lexicon of British politics (Kumarasingham, 2005:14). By his interference Macmillan contributed to the electoral rejection of the Conservatives at the next general election, and the abandonment of the informal processes of consultation for determining the party leadership. Gilmour and Garnett argue that the consequences were massively significant, by suggesting that had Butler

Gained the succession and gone onto the win the 1964 general election, we should have been spared the Wilson years. A fourth election defeat in a row would surely have split Labour. The party realignment that nearly occurred in the 1980s, or the modernising of the Labour Party that eventually took place in the 1990s, would have been completed in the sixties. Labour would not have subsequently moved to the left, nor the Conservatives to the right, and British politics, would not have taken the direction which Harold Macmillan later deplored....In the eighties, Macmillan admitted that it would perhaps have been better if Butler had succeeded him: then we could have won the 1964 general election. By then, Macmillan could not fail to recognise the harm he had inadvertently done to the Conservative Party. By barring Butler's way, he helped turn the 'party of our dreams' into one more like his nightmare: to Macmillan's regret much of the party's leadership had not only repudiated the pragmatic and sensible compromise between the extremes of collectivism and individualism, it had stigmatised the Governments of Macmillan himself and of other Tory Prime Ministers as misguided collaborators with the socialist enemy. Both the Conservative Party and the country had paid a high price for

Macmillan's insistence, in 1963, on holding 'all the strings in his hand, until the very last minute.'   (Gilmour and Garnett, 1998:203)

The war of the Macmillan succession demonstrated that the non-democratic informal processes of consultation were only viable if there was a consensus by all participants to abide by the outcome of the process. Public acceptance of the outcome was central to the perception that any new party leader was legitimate. By publicly questioning the legitimacy of Douglas-Home as their new party leader, Conservatives were in effect admitting that they needed a codified process for determining the succession – i.e. a formal democratic process. In their squabbling for the succession, the Conservatives had ceased to be gentlemen, without yet becoming democrats (Bogdanor, 1994:80; Ramsden, 1996:197). In the fullness of time the customary procedures that had propelled Douglas-Home to the party leadership would be replaced at his behest. Conjuring away the magic circle was intended as a mechanism to prevent disputation surrounding the party leadership, and to ensure that future party leaders were determined by means that would enhance their legitimacy and thereby their authority. The war of the Macmillan succession would act as the catalyst for democratic procedures for determining the election of future leaders of the Conservative Party. The next forty years would not resolve those dilemmas, as questions on how the party leader should be elected and indeed removed would come to dominate. For a party that took so long to deploy democratic procedures it would develop a growing propensity for intra-party elections by the 1990s. It would also demonstrate an increasing tendency for electing default leaders devoid of the necessary legitimacy to enable them to lead effectively; Douglas-Home by democratic means. Before that though there was Heath and Thatcher.

EDWARD HEATH: THE FIRST DEMOCRATIC LEADER OF THE CONSERVATIVE PARTY

The Conservative Party had occupied power for thirteen years when they faced the electorate in the general election of October 1964. Although this period of Conservative governance had embraced one of the high water-marks of Conservative Party politics - the Macmillan era and the politics of prosperity - a series of economic and political problems had engulfed them during the new decade. The evidence of relative economic decline and perceptions of economic mismanagement; the failed application for membership of the European Economic Community; the divisive Cabinet reshuffle; and the scandalous Profumo Affair, had been immensely damaging to them. The confluence of these events served to reinforce an aura of political degeneration which appeared to demonstrate the exhaustion of one-nation Conservatism (Evans and Taylor, 1996:101, 121-135).

This perception of decadence and decay had undermined faith in the party leadership of Harold Macmillan: ultimately, however, it was ill-health that caused him to resign the party leadership. As the previous chapter identified it was his resignation that propelled the Conservative Party into a damaging and debilitating succession process through which Alec Douglas-Home emerged as the new party in October 1963. Once the Conservatives lost the general election of October 1964, debate centred on the continuation of Douglas-Home as party leader and the viability of the customary and undemocratic processes through which party leaders emerged. New rules governing the election of the party leader through a ballot of the members of the parliamentary Conservative Party were established in February 1965. Those rules were quickly put to the test following the resignation of Douglas-Home in July 1965, through which Edward Heath emerged as the first democratically elected leader of the Conservative Party.

3.1   The Resignation of Alec Douglas-Home

The period between losing the general election in October 1964[1] and his resignation as party leader in July 1965, would involve Douglas-Home engaging in a series of decisions which were reflective of the weakness of his authority and legitimacy as party leader. As identified in the previous chapter, the controversial means by which he had acquired the party leadership had been divisive in equal measure: both the figurehead of the libertarian right, Enoch Powell, and the leading articulator of the one-nation left, Iain Macleod, refused to serve in the Douglas-Home government. Their refusal undermined his credibility as the newly installed party leader. This constraint was compounded by the leader of the Labour Party, Harold Wilson, who skilfully portrayed himself as a symbol of inclusive modernisation in contrast to the evident elitist establishment status of Douglas-Home, thus maximising Conservative discomfiture (Evans and Taylor, 1996:130-131).

The evidence of economic decline made the mantra of modernisation and institutional reform appealing, yet the perceptions of the previous Conservative government as the complacent custodians of decline, impeded their capacity to articulate a reforming and modernising agenda (Evans and Taylor, 1996:131). Symptomatic of this perception of elitism and establishment was the mechanism through which the Conservative Party determined their leaders. The undemocratic customary process of consultation amongst elites and subsequent ritual acclamation (i.e. the secretive magic circle) was ultimately disadvantageous to the Conservative Party. Such processes were inherently rigged to the advantage of social unrepresentative elites and to the disadvantage of more meritocratic and socially representative Conservative parliamentarians (Garnett, 2005:196-197). An inherently undemocratic process which produced an anachronistic party leader appeared to be symptomatic of their outdated thinking and circuitously their unfitness to govern (Evans and Taylor, 1996:131).

Although both Powell and Macleod agreed to serve in the newly constituted Douglas-Home Shadow Cabinet after the general election defeat, it was clear that residual hostility surrounding his acquisition of the party leadership was still evident (Garnett, 2005:197). Furthermore, although it was clear that Douglas-Home was ill suited to the role of Leader of the Opposition, he remained determined to continue as party leader[2] (Evans and Taylor, 1996:131). However, he did reluctantly recognise the need for institutional reform and modernisation. He acknowledged that the secretive processes for determining the succession had to be amended, and as Garnett eloquently suggests, that the magic circle would have to be conjured away (Garnett, 2005:197).

Discussion on reforming this antiquated process commenced in November 1964, under the guidance of the Party Chairman, Lord

Blakenham. In considering various options on how to proceed, three key considerations would be regarded as pivotal. On the first consideration, it was decided that Conservative MPs should have the predominant voice in selecting the party leader. Considerable discussion was given to the question of how to incorporate the party membership into the decision-making process. The devisors of the 1965 leadership election rules decided to limit their participation to a consultative (and thereby) token role. This consultative role was based on the assumption that the views of the party membership, constituency chairs, and Conservative peers, could be expressed to Conservative parliamentarians, prior to the holding of the ballot. By feeding their views into the process at the pre-ballot stage, it negated the fear of the wider party being able to override the choice made by Conservative MPs (Bogdanor, 1994:83).

The second consideration was more straightforward but was tied in with the first. It reflected a desire that the process of selecting the party leader should produce an outcome without a significant delay. The third and final consideration was that the process must produce an outcome through which the newly elected party leader could claim to have a mandate: i.e. a mechanism that would enhance their legitimacy as party leader and their authority over the parliamentary Conservative Party. This final consideration was designed to ensure that the outcome of the process was deemed to be definitive.[3] Stark identifies the significance of this final consideration, which

> Meant that the leader could not be elected by a first past the post system, which would award the leadership to whomever won a mere plurality of the votes…[this would lead]…toward what would become one of the unique characteristics of the Conservatives' rules: the first ballot requirement of a majority plus fifteen per cent more than the votes of the second-place candidate. (Stark, 1996:21)

The new rules governing the selection of the leader of the Conservative Party were made public in February 1965. Although unelected Conservative grandees could still nominally make their preference evident, the ultimate decision would rest with the parliamentary Conservative Party, who would be free to ignore the view of the House of Lords.[4] The customary processes of consultation and ritual acclamation were brought to an end and the new rules stipulated that:

> An election could be called every year, within twenty-eight days of the opening of each session of a new parliament, but only if the leadership was vacant. Any MP wishing to stand only needed to secure the support of a proposer and a seconder, who could remain anonymous. A single ballot would be sufficient, provided that the leading candidate

enjoyed an overall majority plus a minimum lead of fifteen per cent over the runner up. If no one jumped these hurdles, the slate would be cleaned for a second ballot. Prospective candidates could hold back from the initial contest,[5] if they calculated that no outright winner would emerge and preferred not to declare themselves at the outset. An overall majority was still required, and the top three candidates would go forward to a final run off if necessary. This third ballot would allow MPs to declare a second preference, ensuring that a clear winner would be found once the least popular candidate had been eliminated.

(Garnett, 2005:197)

Douglas-Home had acquiesced to the drive for internal democratisation due to the inherent weaknesses in authority and legitimacy that he possessed due to first, the means by which he acquired the party leadership; and, second, the fact that he was party leader when they had been evicted from office.[6] It was at this juncture that Douglas-Home made a tactical miscalculation. He had been sensitive to the accusation that his original acquisition of the party leadership had been undemocratic (Fisher, 1977:110). If he used the newly devised rules with immediate effect he could eradicate these accusations of illegitimacy, and the associated concerns surrounding his authority could be eradicated. Had he resigned and stood in the self-created vacancy with immediate effect then he would have received a resounding vote of confidence, thus enhancing his authority and legitimacy. Such an argument is predicated on the view that at this juncture (March 1965) the parliamentary Conservative Party would not have agreed on a likely successor (Ramsden, 1996:234; Gilmour and Garnett, 1998:217-218).

Having rejected this tactical option, the best short-term protection available to Douglas-Home was the prospect of a snap general election being called (Gilmour and Garnett, 1998:218). Given the presumed immediacy of a general election Douglas-Home announced that he would not resign and that no party leadership election would occur in 1965. Shortly thereafter, however, the Prime Minister announced that there would be no general election in 1965 either and that he would not dissolve Parliament until 1966 at the earliest (Shepherd, 1996:291). This had two consequences: first, it removed the protective clothing that Douglas-Home had draped himself in; and, second, it reopened the debate on merits and demerits of his continuance as party leader. Conservative parliamentarians realised that a window of opportunity now existed in which to elect a new and potentially more appealing party leader for a general election in around twelve months time[7] (Blake, 1998:298).

A mobilisation of dissenting forces began to undermine the position of Douglas-Home. It was widely assumed that the discrediting of Douglas-Home was being stimulated by supporters of Heath,[8] with rumours circulating that one hundred Heath supporters were lobbying intensively to ensure that Douglas-Home was replaced with Heath[9] (Gilmour and Garnett, 1998:218). The sands of time were slipping away from Douglas-Home. He knew that on the essential precursors of effective leadership – authority and legitimacy – he was on questionable ground. Questions surrounding his authority and legitimacy were now compounded by three critical aspects of his performance as party leader. First, he was perceived to be a weak performer in the House of Commons. Second, the Conservatives position in the opinion polls was deteriorating and perceptions of his leadership competence trailed that of the Prime Minister. Finally, he was being subjected to increasing levels of criticism from the Conservative press[10] (Gilmour and Garnett, 1998:218). The cumulative effect of these factors undermined his resolve to continue. Once he became aware that his parliamentary colleagues believed that he was standing in the way of more effective alternative leaders, he found the idea of remaining increasingly unpleasant (Ramsden, 1996:235). In mid July 1965, he informed the 1922 Executive Committee that he wished to resign as party leader, having been persuaded by the Chief Whip, William Whitelaw, that this course of action was in the best interests of the party[11] (Watkins, 1998:186). In announcing his resignation, Douglas-Home stated:

> I myself have set up the machinery for this change and I myself have chosen the time to use it. It is up to you to see that it is completed swiftly and efficiently, and with dignity and calm.[12]   (Home, 1976:221)

The first democratic election of the leadership of the Conservative Party would be held on the 27th July 1965. Prospective candidates and their acolytes would have a short period of time in which to engage in campaigning.

3.2   Three Candidates Emerge

The two previous succession battles, in 1957 and 1963, had focused on R.A. Butler and how he had been outmanoeuvred and passed over for the party leadership. The previous chapter concluded by speculating on how the Conservatives may well have retained power had Butler succeeded Macmillan rather than Douglas-Home. Had Butler succeeded it was unlikely that any senior Cabinet colleagues would have refused to serve under him, thus minimizing the perception of disunity that was created by Powell and Macleod, when they refused to serve under Douglas-Home. Had Butler succeeded Macmillan he probably would have been compared more favourably against Wilson than Douglas-Home was, thus reducing the negative party leadership comparisons that impeded the Conservatives electoral strategy. Given the perception that Butler may well have prevented their electoral defeat, and the sense that he had been deprived of the party leadership by disputed means, he should have been a viable contender to replace Douglas-Home in opposition. However, those two failed attempts to acquire the party leadership and the premiership contributed to his departure from frontline politics[13] (Gilmour and Garnett, 1998:217).

Butler was not the only high profile Conservative removed from the succession equation. Prior to the announcement that Douglas-Home would resign as party leader, advocates of Macleod had been taking soundings within the parliamentary Conservative Party in order to assess his strength of support and the viability of a formal candidature. His advisors informed him that the likely strength of support for his candidature was forty to forty-five Conservative parliamentarians. With the knowledge that he was trailing Heath and Maudling by a considerable margin, Macleod was positioned to announce his non-candidature as soon as the resignation of Douglas-Home was tendered[14] (Shepherd, 1996:291).

With Butler and Macleod removed from the succession equation, it was widely assumed that the leading contenders for the succession were Heath and Maudling. Heath and Maudling were joined in the first democratic election for the party leadership by Powell. All three candidates transcended the elitist establishment figure that had been seen as an impediment to modernisation and a significant constraint of the appropriateness of Douglas-Home (Evans and Taylor, 1996:144).

The candidature of Powell was not viewed as serious. It was widely acknowledged by Conservative parliamentarians and himself that he could not and would not succeed (Stark, 1996:89). As such, his candidature amounted to a serious statement rather than a serious challenge. In seeking to advance the political ideology of economic libertarianism based on the advocacy of classical liberal free market policies, Powell was seeking to redefine Conservatism and ultimately remould the Conservative Party (Evans and Taylor, 1996:145). At this juncture his candidature lacked credibility as the mobilisation of economic liberalism that would underpin the Conservative Party leadership of Margaret Thatcher was still in its embryonic stages within the parliamentary Conservative Party. Powell recognised this limitation and rationalised his candidature on the following premise outlined by Stark:

> He used the metaphor of leaving a calling card 'for public inspection' to describe his intention. This combines both the attention and future motives. His calling card was a signal that he had support for his right-wing views; it also had an indication that he planned to return someday to the place where he had left the card, i.e. the leadership election. Powell is regarded here as a 'future' candidate because a main reason he sought attention was that he saw himself, and wished to be seen, as a potential future leader.   (Stark, 1996:101)

Meanwhile, the candidature of Maudling stimulated considerable debate for a variety of reasons. First, Maudling had been viewed as a serious contender for the succession in the months that had preceded the resignation of Harold Macmillan. Second, he offered credibility given his ministerial experience. Having entered the Cabinet in 1957, he had served at the Board of Trade and the Colonial Office, before being promoted to the Treasury in 1962. Third, his Treasury appointment reflected the positive view that Macmillan had of Maudling from an ideological perspective: i.e. Maudling was foursquare in the Macmillanite Conservative tradition and a self proclaimed apostle of consensus (Evans and Taylor, 1996:144).

As an instrument of modernisation and meritocracy, the lower-middle class origins of Heath seemed appealing as a symbol of a modern and socially representative Conservative Party. Attempting to situate Heath within the ideological spectrum of Conservatism is an immensely complicated adventure and can be clouded by historical retrospection (Evans and Taylor, 1996:148). The confusion about his ideological beliefs has been demonstrated by the fact that Blake has questioned the assumption that Heath was of the Conservative left, whilst Gilmour and Garnett have attempted to debunk the assumption that Heath was of the Conservative right (Blake, 1998:299-300; Gilmour and Garnett, 1998:219). What we can suggest is that, at the time of the Conservative Party leadership election of July 1965, Heath was engaging in an incremental departure from his status as a protégé of Macmillan and the rhetoric of progressive paternalism, yet despite this movement he was assumed to be on the left of the spectrum of Conservatism when compared to Powell, and to the right when compared to Maudling.[15]

On 27th July 1965, the parliamentary Conservative Party engaged in their first democratic election for the party leadership. All 304 members of the parliamentary Conservative Party participated under the guidance of the 1922 Executive Committee and the outcome was Heath first with 150 votes, Maudling second with 133 votes and Powell last with 15 votes. Heath had secured an overall majority over all other candidates of two; but he had failed to achieve a lead of forty-five, which was required to prevent the necessity of a second ballot.

Table 3:   **Candidate Support in the Conservative Party Leadership Election of 1965**

	First Ballot	Percentage
Edward Heath	150	49.3
Reginald Maudling	133	43.8
Enoch Powell	15	4.9
Abstentions	6	2.0

Source: Quinn, 2005:812

In the immediate aftermath of the first ballot, attention was focused on Maudling. As Heath had failed to overcome the second hurdle, (his lead was only 5.5 per cent), Maudling was entitled to participate in a second ballot (Punnett, 1992:60). However, Maudling was shattered by his rejection and would later admit:

> I will not deny that it was a bitter blow…I had been looking forward to success and had reasonable grounds for expecting it.
>
> (Maudling, 1978:134)

His campaign team would admit that they could not understand how their candidate had been defeated. They had a list of presumed supporters and their list suggested that there was going to be a comfortable majority for their man: they predicted 154 supporters for Maudling and only 100 for Heath[16] (Campbell, 1993:183; Gilmour and Garnett, 1998:220). Realistically, however, it was unlikely that Maudling would be able to defeat Heath in a second ballot: the momentum of the Heath candidature was unlikely to dissolve and the main focus of campaigning would be on the fifteen Powell supporters, who in all probability would gravitate to Heath in preference to Maudling (Campbell, 1993:183).

Maudling immediately withdrew his candidature and informed Heath of his willingness to serve under him. In return, he was offered the post of Deputy Leader of the Conservative Party. In explaining why he withdrew, Maudling offered a pragmatic view of the way in which the rules should be viewed, which drew a distinction between an arithmetic and a psychological victory. He argued:

> The party had spoken, and although there was provision for a second ballot on such a narrow result, there was not much point in asking people to say the same thing over again. Ted commanded the support over just over half the parliamentary party (excluding abstentions), and

this I considered quite decisive…That, it seemed to me, was that.

(Maudling, 1978:136)

3.3   How and why did Edward Heath win?

How should we interpret the new democracy within the Conservative Party or in other words how do we explain the election of Heath as leader of the Conservative Party? This is a significant dilemma worthy of analytical exploration for the following reasons. First, Maudling was the candidate with the strongest political profile having served as Chancellor of the Exchequer, and he was the best known candidate to the electorate (Blake, 1998:298). Second, Maudling was viewed as the candidate preferred by the electorate. An NOP poll suggested that 44 per cent of the electorate preferred his candidature as compared with Heath at 28 per cent: when restricting the polling to known Conservative supporters that lead remained similar, with Maudling on 48 per cent and Heath on 31 per cent (Roth, 1971:185). Third, Maudling was viewed as a more credible and dangerous political opponent than Heath within the Labour Party (Campbell, 1993:182). Finally, as a consequence of the above factors, political journalists predicted that Maudling was the favourite to emerge as the first democratic leader of the Conservative Party (Clark, 1998:409).

It is possible to argue that Heath triumphed due to a number of explanatory factors. The first explanatory factor relates to their respective roles in opposition (i.e. between October 1964 and July 1965) that would create an image of momentum to the Heath campaign that was evident within the parliamentary Conservative Party if not to the wider electorate. This argument demonstrates the centrality of timing in terms of the vacancy for the leadership of the Conservative Party. At the time of the previous vacancy Maudling was widely mentioned in dispatches as a serious candidate for the party leadership, whereas at that juncture Heath was viewed as a marginal and outside candidate. The trajectory of Heath's political career was to alter dramatically in the interim period that constituted the Douglas-Home era, most notably when in opposition.

A significant influence related to the high profile status of Maudling as Chancellor of the Exchequer between 1962 and 1964. Watkins notes that although Maudling was the favourite going into the leadership election, the esteem in which he was held had fallen back somewhat as a consequence of the general election defeat of 1964 (Watkins, 1998:187). Had the Conservative Party emerged victorious in the general election of 1964, Maudling would have been well positioned for the succession when Douglas-Home eventually departed (Clark, 1998:405). However, his credibility was undermined as he became perceived to be the outgoing Chancellor of the

Exchequer who 'was responsible for not delivering the economic keys to unlock the draw to electoral success' (Campbell, 1993:166).

As well as suffering damage to his political reputation for failing to propel the Conservatives to electoral victory in October 1964, Maudling was also undermined by the allocation of portfolios when in opposition. In early 1965, Maudling was switched from Shadow Chancellor to Shadow Foreign Secretary, with Heath being promoted to Shadow Chancellor. This switch was made by Douglas-Home[17] at the request of Maudling and can be viewed as a serious tactical error in terms of positioning for the succession (Gilmour and Garnett, 1998:217). The reallocation of shadow ministerial portfolios would leave Maudling marginalised from the frontline of political debate, and would provide Heath with a platform to showcase his leadership credentials (Gilmour and Garnett, 1998:217). The biographer of Heath, Campbell views this as central. He argues that the:

> shuffle gave a critical boost to Heath at the expense of Maudling. The economy was the central issue of politics: it was on Labour's Budget and subsequent Finance Bill that the Tories would concentrate their attack in the months to come. Choosing Heath…was a recognition of Heath's greater aggression and an opportunity for him to show his paces. Conversely Maudling would be taken out of the political frontline and subordinated to Home in Home's own area of expertise. Foreign affairs could plausibly be represented as the senior portfolio needed to complete Maudling's all-round qualification for the leadership; but the way it worked out was that Maudling was left in a backwater while Heath led the attack on the Government.
>
> (Campbell, 1993:168)

In addition to his role as Shadow Chancellor, Heath was appointed to replace Butler as Chairman of the Advisory Committee on Policy. Heath was assumed to be utilising the wide ranging remit of the position to advance his own candidature for the party leadership (Evans and Taylor, 1996:147). Moreover, Campbell noted that Heath exploited the position to advance both himself and undermine Maudling. He observed how Heath 'even went so far as to forbid the Research Department to supply the papers coming out of the policy groupings to Maudling' (Campbell, 1993:172).

Moreover, Heath displayed a greater level of political commitment in opposition. Maudling viewed a period in opposition as an opportunity to enhance his earnings after the sacrifices of thirteen years in office (Campbell, 1993:167). An enthusiasm for lucrative City directorships – he accumulated thirteen in comparison to one for Heath – sent out the wrong signals, whilst his justification that 'an independent income insulated him from the Chief Whip and provided him with knowledge of the wealth-creating sector' seemed disingenuous (Evans and Taylor, 1996:145). Such diversionary commitments seemed to be indicative of Maudling's detachment for the politics of opposition. They contrasted sharply with the aplomb with which Heath had adapted to opposition. Heath was aggressively projecting himself as a dynamic force for modernisation and in doing so was intensifying the insecurity of the anarchistic Douglas-Home. In effect, Heath was exploiting the detachment of the presumed favourite (Maudling) to rapidly expand his powerbase and influence. The extent to which this was becoming known within elite circles was evident by the fear amongst non-modernising Heathites in mid-1965 that 'they may wake up one morning to find that Heath has silently taken over everything but the title of party leader' (Campbell, 1993:175).

The second substantive explanation for the success of the Heath candidature relates to the organisational strength of his campaign team vis-à-vis that of the Maudling campaign team. The Heath campaign was characterised by its professional and organised approach (Fisher, 1977:125; Whitelaw, 1989:55; Heath, 1998:268). Their campaigning was orchestrated by Peter Walker[18] and ably supported by a wide range of parliamentarians including Iain Gilmour, Charles Morrison, Peter Emery, James Prior, Edward Boyle and Tony Barber (Fisher, 1977:125). Their approach was energetic and involved systematic canvassing of Conservative parliamentarians (Roth, 1971:183-184). Campbell observes that their methods involved contacting every Conservative parliamentarian

> individually over the next two or three days (of the campaigning period), with each member of the team deputed to speak to those colleagues whom they knew best, going back to them again where necessary and using the arguments best calculated to persuade each individual, ticking or crossing them off until they had an accurate picture of how every member was likely to vote. (Campbell, 1993:179)[19]

In comparison the Maudling campaign team lacked organisational strength and was retrospectively derided for its loose, easy-going and almost amateurish approach to canvassing (Campbell, 1993:178). Philip Goodhart, a Conservative parliamentarian, and part of the Maudling campaign team, would later admit that it was 'the worst organised leadership campaign in Conservative history: a total shambles' (Baston, 2004:256).

Indicative of the poor organisation of the Maudling candidature was the fact that they had failed to properly prepare for the leadership election. The supporters of Heath prepared in advance of the resignation of Douglas-Home. For example, Heath and his acolytes were assiduous in their cultivation of the new parliamentary entrants of October 1964. Politically astute, they had realised that there was likely to be a shift to a formalised democratic process within which the parliamentary Conservative Party would determine the succession. They were therefore planning ahead for the future ballot of the parliamentary Conservative Party, in a way that was lacking amongst Maudling and his supporters. This degree of preparation meant that the Heath campaign was mobilising support prior to the resignation of Douglas-Home. They had pre-electioneering momentum underpinning their effort and they were prepared to activate their election plans once Douglas-Home resigned. Whereas the Heath campaign immediately began gathering endorsers the moment Douglas-Home resigned, Maudling reacted to the resignation by having a disagreement with Douglas-Home about the timing of it. The disagreement was on the basis that they were not expecting it and their candidature was not as well prepared as Heath (Roth, 1971:183; Gilmour and Garnett, 1998:219).

However, it is also possible to argue that the organisational approach of the Maudling campaign was a product of the mentality of Maudling himself to the contest. He decided that he wished to engage in a gentlemanly contest. He calculated that support would gravitate towards him because it was the Heathites who had forced Douglas-Home to resign. As part of this approach, Maudling instructed his campaign team not to pester Conservative parliamentarians or engage in deal making such as assurances of promotions in return for support. Maudling expressed such views because he believed that as front runner he should not engage in such pressurising canvassing. He felt this would irritate rather than convert the minds of intelligent politicians, who he believed were capable of deciding who they wanted to vote for without interference[20] (Roth, 1971:185).

The Heath campaign team exploited this. They recognised that the ineptitude and inertia of the Maudling campaign team was a key resource to them. Peter Walker believed that William Clark and Anthony Lambton, the leading figures in the Maudling campaign were clumsy in their limited discussions with parliamentary colleagues. Their naivety made them over-estimate the extent of the support for their candidate. It did not occur to them that Conservative parliamentarians may be lying to them or that they were just being polite when they stated that they would vote for Maudling. As Philip Goodhart, a member of the Maudling campaign team admits:

> The Heath people got the right individuals to approach and talk to those people who were assumed to be wavering. The Maudling people never got anybody to talk really to anyone at all.   (Stark, 1996:107)

They assumed that they would triumph in the ensuing contest and as such they felt that it was beneath them to engage in discussions that would convert presumed Heath supporters. This image of lethargy fatally damaged Maudling. It allowed the approach of his campaign to create and reinforce doubts about whether he could provide the type of energetic leadership necessary to reclaim power (Stark, 1996:108). Campbell concludes that the adult and civilised manner in which the Maudlingites conducted their campaigning was:

> the wrong approach to a contest in which his whole task was to overcome an image of amiable indolence: the leadership was his if he could just convince his fellow Tory MPs that he wanted it badly enough...this he singularly failed to do. (Campbell, 1993:179)

Moreover, perceptions of the leadership style required in opposition created a gravitational pull towards Heath and away from Maudling. His approach which was initially interpreted as displaying self-confidence became viewed as complacent and was to highlight a significant concern amongst Conservative parliamentarians about Maudling himself (Roth, 1971:185). His very name conjured up images of his own limitations: i.e. that he was dawdling (Campbell, 1993:179). Maudling did too little to remove this negative perception and his campaign team appeared to mirror the image of their candidate (Roth, 1971:185). Although Conservative parliamentarians admired Maudling for his ministerial experience, the above factors created doubts about the political leadership style that he would adopt if he assumed the party leadership. Heath was increasingly viewed as a more dynamic potential leader of the Conservative Party (Campbell, 1993:178). In this context, perceptions of political leadership style were framed by the conduct and behaviour of the Labour Prime Minister, Harold Wilson. As an alternative Prime Ministerial candidate to Wilson, the parliamentary Conservative Party faced a choice between the relaxed and less confrontational political style of Maudling or the more abrasive and aggressive political style of Heath. As the biographer of Maudling, Lewis Baston, observed that

> the worry about Reggie was that he would drift along amiably and allow Wilson to get away with too much, and that his image as a slow, comfortable sort of man would suffer by comparison with Wilson's apparent dynamism. (Baston, 2004:255)

For those Conservative parliamentarians who believed that the Conservative Party needed to respond energetically to the task of undermining and attacking the Wilson Government, the dynamism of Heath had a greater appeal than the lethargy of Maudling (Campbell, 1993:166). Evans and Taylor observe that the 'tougher' element within the parliamentary Conservative Party gravitated to Heath as opposed to Maudling (Evans and Taylor, 1996:148). Whereas the electorate were attracted to the consensual persona of Maudling, a significant proportion within the parliamentary Conservative

Party were more aware of the dynamism of Heath and the complacency of Maudling. Effectively the fact that many Conservatives wanted an abrasive, tough leader, who would offer vigorous and unrelenting opposition to Wilson, was to be critical in such a close election ballot[21] (Butler and King, 1966:53).

Tying together these themes relating to the comparative campaigning strategies and leadership characteristics, we can conclude that Maudling, and his campaign team, made a critical strategic error. They failed to fully understand the 'demands of the new leadership system' (Stark, 1996:107). In this context, it can be argued that Maudling

> failed to give a lead to campaign organisation…organising an internal election like this was new territory for the Conservatives, but most of Maudling's men failed to recognise what had to be done.
>
> (Baston, 2004:256)

They assumed that their status as favourite would translate into votes without the need to overtly campaign for them, but they failed to shore up his initial support, as the idea of:

> Canvassing and recording voting intentions was a new and highly suspect one for some of his [Maudling's] supporters…The campaign intelligence system was woeful…many MPs who did not vote for Maudling when it came to the vote were listed as being for Reggie…in a contest where knowledge of the individual peculiarities of each MP was important in determining how to make an approach, the Heath team had the valuable advantage of professionalism. They knew how to count and deliver votes, and the Maudling forces simply did not.
>
> (Baston, 2004:257)

Moreover, members of the parliamentary Conservative Party themselves demonstrated a certain naivety about an electoral ballot based on such a small constituency as a parliamentary party of 304 members. This is evidenced by Watkins who noted that some Conservative parliamentarians misused their votes, which demonstrated a lack of sophistication and awareness. He notes that

> several Conservatives voted for Heath, not because they wanted, still less expected him to win, but because they wished to administer a shock to the 'old gang' as represented by Maudling. (Watkins, 1998:187)

Such observations about voting behaviour of the parliamentary Conservative Party dovetails neatly into the final explanatory factor relating to the surprise election of Heath – i.e. the non-ideological nature of the contest. The candidate offering the most explicit ideological agenda had been Powell. In seeking to advance the political ideology of economic libertarianism based on the advocacy of classical liberal free market policies, Powell was undermined by his own limitations. Powell was an enigmatic and austere individual and thus was viewed as a 'strange figure as a potential leader' (Baston, 2004:254). Consequently the ideology of Powellism was gaining adherents but that did not translate into votes for Powell (Shepherd, 1996:293). His derisory return of fifteen votes demonstrated that his decision to stand for the leadership had been a strategic misjudgement: his vote share made his views seem less influential within the parliamentary Conservative Party than they really were (Gilmour and Garnett, 1998:219). Evans and Taylor observe that the weak performance of Powell was 'erroneously interpreted as the death of Powellism'[22] (Evans and Taylor, 1996:146).

At the onset of the contest it was widely assumed that it would be a two-way contest between Maudling and Heath; they were viewed as the only two candidates capable of winning. In these circumstances many Conservative parliamentarians did not want the purity of the democratic contest to be polluted by candidates standing who could not conceivably emerge victorious. The Powell candidature was a distraction: an act of 'mischief' that provoked 'irritation' within the Maudling and Heath camps (Shepherd, 1996:293). The central determinant is the impact of the Powell candidature upon the eventual outcome – i.e. did his candidature prevent Maudling from emerging victorious? Baston notes that the Maudlingnites felt that the Powell candidature had been significant as they argued that the 'Powell vote would otherwise have been theirs and resulted in a virtual tie' (Baston, 2004:254). We can postulate that such an assertion is open to question. In assessing the poor performance of the Powell candidature, his biographer, Shepherd observes that given Maudling's adherence to consensus, then economic libertarians who feared that a Powell vote was a wasted vote, were more likely to gravitate to the candidature of Heath than that of Maudling[23] (Shepherd, 1996:293-294). That capacity to appeal to economic libertarians within the parliamentary Conservative Party came more easily to Heath than Maudling, as Roth noted:

Heath was able easily to adapt himself to this rightward swing in the current of Tory opinion, which found Maudling immovable.

(Roth, 1971:181)

As the campaign progressed Maudling would lose support from both the economic right and the Tory left. On the right was the defection of Margaret Thatcher. She was initially inclined to support Maudling due to his experience, intellect and command in Parliament, but was persuaded by

Keith Joseph to endorse Heath after Joseph offered an insight into the
limitations of Maudling; an insight that focused on this lack of intensity and
dynamism (Thatcher, 1995:134,146). On the one-nation left, the influence of
Iain Macleod was evident and detrimental to Maudling; indeed it was the
'most wounding defection' (Baston, 2004:258). As a fellow consensus
advocate there was a rationale for Macleod to endorse Maudling after
calculating that his own candidature was doomed to failure. Rejecting the
premise that a Maudling-Macleod alliance would prevent Heath acquiring the
leadership of the Conservative Party, positioned Macleod as the 'king-maker'
for Heath. The vast majority of the core Macleod grouping of approximately
forty Conservative parliamentarians gravitated towards Heath rather than
Maudling (Fisher, 1977:126; Campbell, 1993:181; Watkins, 1998:186).
Ultimately the defections from the Tory consensual left, whom Maudling had
assumed would endorse him, destroyed his candidature and handed the party
leadership to Heath. Had Macleod embraced Maudling then his acolytes
would probably have likewise and thus Maudling would have defeated Heath.

In assessing how he failed to sustain the favoured status of his
candidature, Maudling would hint at his complacency when admitting that:

> Had I fought for the leadership as a matter of personal ambition, had I
> seized it as a result of some campaign or stratagem, the weight of
> subsequent responsibility would have been ultimately multiplied.
>
> (Maudling, 1978:137)

However, the subsequent degeneration of the political career of Maudling
and his descent into financial scandal and alcoholism can be traced to the
shattering humiliation of being defeated in a popularity contest by Heath
(Baston, 2004:264). Ultimately the complexities inherent within his
personality meant that:

> Rather like Michael Portillo in 2001, Reggie Maudling was unwilling to
> stoop to conquer in 1965. He was ambitious and very much wanted to
> lead, but he wanted the party leadership on his own terms, and was not
> going to cajole and twist arms to engineer a victory. He would have
> been happy enough to have been invited to be leader, but he was not
> going to spoil the prize by striving for it…He wanted the party to
> recognise its true nature in him, and come to him of its own volition. It
> was a very Hegelian approach to running a leadership election
> campaign. There was something reminiscent of the attitude of the
> bridegroom about Maudling and the Tory party, in that true, free
> consent is essential and that to use trickery invalidates the whole
> exercise…While it was honourable of Maudling to seek an unforced

mandate, it also maximised the psychological impact of defeat.

(Baston, 2004:262)

3.4 Conclusion

The new democratic rules through which Heath had been elected as the new leader of the Conservative Party had been designed to avoid the embarrassing fiasco of the leadership crisis following the resignation of Macmillan. Home wanted to avoid a scenario in which any of his successors would acquire the party leadership devoid of the following pre-requisites for effective party leadership: an aura of authority over the parliamentary Conservative Party and a perception of legitimacy as leader of the Conservative Party. In the immediate aftermath of the outcome the new democratic rules were praised. It was widely admired for the decorous manner in which it was conducted. It was conducted without rancour, without recriminations, and without significant ideological conflict. After the tribulations of the post-Macmillan succession, this amounted to a bloodless contest in which the disputation surrounding the succession and the future of the Conservative Party was concluded. It appeared that the debilitating divisions that had undermined the previous three years of Conservatism had ended. This conclusion, through the democratic election of a next generation and socially representative Conservative politician, seemed to validate the new democratic rules.

The positivism surrounding the shift to internal democracy was understandable. However, a hidden problem lay within these new party leadership election procedures. When debating how to configure these new democratic procedures, one factor was implicit. It was assumed that these procedures would be activated when a vacancy for the party leadership existed. A vacancy would only emerge when the incumbent chose to resign. No provision existed to allow an incumbent to be challenged for the party leadership. Trying to ensure that the incumbent party leader was secure had been deliberate. Douglas-Home had been influential in ensuring that there would be no disputing the legitimacy and authority of the incumbent. He argued that 'once the party had elected a leader that was that and it had better stay with him'[24] (Hutchinson, 1970:138). The decision to avoid permitting a challenge to the incumbent had rested on the assumption that a discredited and failing incumbent would voluntarily resign and create a vacancy and an ensuing ballot to determine the succession, but as Fisher observes:

It had not occurred to anyone when the rules were first devised in 1965 that a leader who had lost the confidence of a substantial section of the party would wish to continue in office.   (Fisher, 1977:147-148)

THE PEASANTS REVOLT? THE ELECTION OF MARGARET THATCHER

The previous chapter outlined how Edward Heath became the first democratically elected leader of the Conservative Party in July 1965. His tenure as party leader proved to be a tempestuous period within the history of the Conservative Party. It was characterised by an absence of traditional Conservative statecraft: i.e. the ability to win elections (the politics of support) and the ability to govern competently (the politics of power) (Bulpitt, 1986:19-39). Under his leadership tenure the Conservative Party, the self-proclaimed natural party of government, would lose three general elections out of four (1966, February 1974 and October 1974) and their period in office, between June 1970 and February 1974, became defined by perceptions of governing incompetence and accusations of ideological betrayal (Gamble, 1988:76-78).

Given that the primary requirement of the party leader is to ensure that the Conservative Party is in a position to win the next general election, it was not surprising that doubts were openly expressed by late 1974 about whether Heath could propel the Conservatives to electoral success in 1978 or 1979. The central concern surrounding Heath was the perception that he was an electoral liability; he was derided by his critics as a three-time loser (Wickham-Jones, 1997:74). His position was becoming increasingly untenable, as the rumblings of discontent surrounding his leadership extended beyond the electoral arithmetic (Gilmour and Garnett, 1998:295).

His critics identified concerns about his political acumen. Doubts surrounding his leadership competence and his ideological beliefs were widely articulated from the right of the parliamentary Conservative Party. They believed that the Conservative Party had triumphed in the June 1970 general election with the intention of implementing the 'Selsdon' programme that had been formulated during the period in opposition. The Conservative

Party had entered government in June 1970 with a supposed commitment to a less interventionist approach to the regeneration of the economy. This involved lowering taxation and public expenditure; legal regulation of industrial relations; an end to government assistance for failing industries; and a rejection of incomes policy (Coxall and Robins, 1998:33). However, the pressure of economic failure as evidenced by rising unemployment and inflation, threatened to incur destabilising social costs that could undermine national unity (Evans and Taylor, 1996:186). Besieged by such economic pressures, the Heath Government engaged in a discrete and incremental disassociation with the Selsdon rhetoric and initiated a reverse in policy direction: the so-called U-turn. The Heath government quietly abandoned the Selsdon agenda on the perceived basis of its impracticability and reverted back to the economic interventionism of the one-nation Conservative era (Blake, 1998:314).

The abandonment of the hands off economic philosophy raised two questions to his right wing critics: his leadership competence and his ideological stance. They believed in the economic and political viability of the Selsdon policy agenda and believed that the short term difficulties that were associated with its implementation should have been accepted before it would realise its intentions. Implicit within this interpretation was the accusation that Heath lacked the leadership competence and political resolve to see it through and that his lack of political nerve amounted to an abdication of leadership. Aligned to this interpretation was the ambiguity that was now surrounding the ideological attitudes of Heath: was he a neo-liberal as indicated by the evolution of Conservative policy between 1965 and 1971/72 or was he a traditional one-nation Tory as indicated by his governing approach between 1972 and 1974? To his burgeoning body of critics, his volatile pragmatism, his nebulous political ideology and his legacy made his an inappropriate conduit for their ideological convictions (Evans and Taylor, 1996:147).

Alongside concerns about his leadership competence and ideological direction were reservations about his strategic judgement. Most notable was his handling of the 1973-1974 Miners' Strike. Despite the fact that he held a working parliamentary majority and did not need to face the electorate until June 1975, Heath decided to call a snap general election in February 1974. He had taken a strategic decision that he needed a mandate from the electorate to support the stance of his government with regard to the miners. He asked the electorate to decide: who governs Britain, democratically elected politicians or militant trade unionists? (Dorey, 1995:125) Heath took a calculated gamble that failed and it left him politically humiliated. His expected authority reinforcing mandate translated in a Conservative share of the vote of at 37.9% (down from 46.4% in June 1970), and ultimately Harold Wilson and Labour entered government as a minority administration.

In the interim period between losing office and the second general election of 1974, Heath attempted to strategically reposition himself as a unity figure and proposed the idea of a coalition of national unity. The further erosion of the Conservative share of the vote (down to 35.8 per cent) in the general election of October 1974 provoked a delusional response from Heath according to his successor. Thatcher was scornful of the way Heath reacted. When he informed the shadow Cabinet that the election campaign had been quite a good containment exercise and that the mechanics had worked well, Thatcher realised that Heath:

> could not change and he was too defensive of his own past record to
> see that a fundamental change of policies was needed...everyone except
> Ted knew that the main problem was the fact that he was still leader.
>
> (Thatcher, 1995:261, 263)

The cumulative impact of electoral failure and governing effectiveness, aligned to concerns about his leadership competence, ideological beliefs, political style and strategic judgement would contribute to the political execution of Heath. He was to become the first leader of the Conservative Party to be forcibly evicted by his own parliamentary Conservative Party against his wishes.

4.1 The Refusal of Edward Heath to Resign

In the aftermath of the October 1974 electoral rejection, Heath faced a strategic dilemma given the hostility surrounding his continuance as party leader. In essence he had five choices.

1. He could follow the Douglas-Home precedent and voluntarily resign in the interests of the party
2. He could ask the 1922 Executive Committee to in effect hold an immediate vote of confidence, by seeking a renewed mandate for his party leadership by defeating a challenger in an open contest[1]
3. He could ignore the concerns of the party about his position as party leader and act as though nothing was wrong
4. He could acknowledge the concerns of the party but emphasise that a debate on the party leadership was unsuitable at this juncture as the Labour Government might fall over either the economy or the European referendum. He could ask the party to hold a moratorium on the party leadership issue, which could be reconsidered at a less febrile political time. He could intimate that when politically appropriate (dependent on external factors) a party leadership election could occur.

5.   He could adopt an adaptation of the fourth option, without the details, explanations and commitments. He could temporize and consider the best course of action dependent upon how political events unfolded (Fisher, 1977:152-153).

Heath was simply too politically ambitious, personally stubborn and arrogant to consider the first option: he simply refused to resign. Had he called a snap leadership election (i.e. the second option), and voluntarily sought a renewed mandate, it would have left less time for his critics to coalesce around an alternative to him. The third option carried with it the risk of destroying the unity of the party, thus making it ungovernable and therefore not worth leading as it would be unelectable. The fourth option, of playing for time and aligning that to external circumstances would be unacceptable to his critics who would demand guarantees that Heath would honour the agreements to hold a leadership election at a politically convenient time. Given the unacceptability to him of the other four options, Heath choose to delay, a strategic option that would bring him on a collision course with Edward Du Cann, the Chair of the 1922 Executive Committee.

Du Cann detested Heath. He was obsessed with engineering his removal from the party leadership. Their mutual hostility dated back to fact that Du Cann had backed Maudling instead of Heath in the 1965 party leadership election. Heath had repaid this disloyalty by excluding Du Cann from ministerial office when the Conservatives entered government in June 1970 (Clark, 1998:457). Du Cann had then developed leadership ambitions of his own and had attempted to overcome his ministerial exclusion by cultivating a powerbase amongst the Conservative backbenchers. His election to the chair of the 1922 Executive Committee provided him with access to influence, whilst the role afforded him guardianship of any future contest for the vacant leadership of the Conservative Party (Clark, 1998:457). Whilst this meant that Du Cann had to be perceived to be neutral, it did enable him to craft a strategy based on destabilising Heath on *behalf* of the backbenchers. Then, in the absence of any other credible alternative they would turn to him[2] (Clark, 1998:457).

In October 1974, Du Cann informed Heath that it was the view of the 1922 Executive Committee that he should resign. Heath rejected the notion of resigning. He informed Du Cann that 'there is no method for re-electing or challenging a leader' (Stark, 1996:27). Du Cann then informed Heath that it was the view of the 1922 Executive Committee that the rules governing the election of the leader of the Conservative Party should be revised (Clark, 1998:458-459). Heath initially attempted to avoid the Trojan horse symbolism of the second proposition. He disputed the legitimacy of the message conveyed to him by Du Cann. He argued that they could not represent the views of the parliamentary Conservative Party as convened in the current Parliament (i.e. since the October 1974 general election) as they were elected during the previous Parliament. In arguing that the officers of the 1922 Executive must be re-elected, Heath was attempting to buy himself crucial political time, during which he could mobilise his supporters and ensure a more pro-Heath 1922 Executive (Fisher, 1977:147-149; 151).

The elections for the 1922 Executive and a Shadow Cabinet reshuffle occurred in early November 1974 and brought the era of Heath closer to its end. Any attempt by Heath to argue that an unrepresentative faction was undermining his leadership was exposed as a chimera; the existing membership of the 1922 Executive was returned en masse[3] (Ramsden, 1996:438). This overcoming of the pro-Heath slate of candidates was politically debilitating for Heath, as was the unopposed return of Du Cann as Chair (Blake, 1998: 316). Heath attempted to negate this by reshuffling his shadow cabinet, but the outcome constituted a tilt to the one-nation left rather than an effort to placate the dissident right. Heathite representation was enhanced by the inclusions of Tim Raison and Nicholas Scott but crucially Du Cann rejected Heath's offer to join the Shadow Cabinet[4] (Thatcher, 1995:264). The offer to Du Cann had been intended as a mechanism to forestall the debate surrounding the rules governing the elections for the leader of the Conservative Party. Its failure compelled Heath to adapt his tactical position. In November 1974, Heath accepted that the rules governing the election of the party leader needed to be revised and agreed in principle to an election once those reconfigured rules were complete (Blake, 1998:318).

Under the chairmanship of Alec Douglas-Home, who was now Lord Home again, a committee was convened to examine those leadership election procedures. The committee reported back to Heath in early December 1974. The committee would offer the following three crucial amendments to the procedures for electing the party leader:

1. That there should be provision for annual elections for the party leadership. This solved the dilemma of an unpopular party leader refusing to resign. If there was no challenge to the incumbent leader, then they were re-elected unopposed. To initiate a challenge, the challenger only needed the support of a proposer and a seconder. Challenges were to be held within the first three to six months of a new Parliament, or during the first twenty-eight days of a parliamentary session.[5]

2. That the fifteen percent surcharge should be of the whole electorate of Conservative MPs, rather than of those actually voting. This provision would make it more difficult for an incumbent to retain the party leadership, as abstentions would undermine the leading candidate almost as much as votes for an alternative candidate could. Due

to this provision, it was impossible for anyone to be elected on the first ballot, (even if there was only one candidate), if half of the Conservative MPs abstained.[6]

3.   That although the electorate would remain unchanged (i.e. it would remain the parliamentary Conservative Party), the arrangements for consulting with the extra-parliamentary sections of the party should be formalised[7] (Shepherd, 1991:168; Stark, 1996:28-29; Watkins, 1998: 189).

When considering the saliency of the amendments of the Home Committee, Bogdanor notes that the subsequent removal of Heath was a by-product of the interaction between these new provisions and the existing provisions from 1965, most notably the first ballot requirement for a majority, plus a fifteen percent lead of the second placed candidate. He argues that:

> If an incumbent leader is forced to face a leadership challenge, the first ballot should be seen as a vote of confidence in the leadership, a vote to see whether the leader has sufficient authority to continue. It is natural that more than a simple majority of the parliamentary party should be required as evidence that the leader still enjoys sufficient support to be able to exercise that authority. If the leader cannot secure the special majority, of course, he or she can still choose to enter the second ballot, at which an absolute majority is sufficient. But the first ballot may have shown, that neither of the candidates can command sufficient unity amongst MPs. Therefore, new candidates should be allowed to enter the second ballot so that a unifying figure can be found...in 1975 it was this provision allowing new candidates to enter on the second ballot that stuck the decisive blow for Heath...if on the first ballot in 1975, every MP had thought their vote would be decisive, Heath would have won a majority. But that is not the point. It is the essence of the first ballot that this vote is not a decisive one. It is a vote, not to choose a new leader, but to consider whether the existing leader retains the party's confidence. That confidence, Heath, by 1975, had clearly lost.
>
> (Bogdanor, 1994:87)

Having reconfigured the procedures for determining the party leadership (but providing for both leadership election *and* leadership ejection) it was probable that Heath would be challenged.[8] As the process of reconfiguring those party leadership procedures evolved, attention focused on three Conservatives - William Whitelaw, Keith Joseph and Edward du Cann – all of whom would choose not to formally challenge Heath[9] (Blake, 1998:318).

Whitelaw had served in the Heath Cabinet and was an instinctive party loyalist. As such, Whitelaw could not bring himself to formally challenge

Heath for the leadership directly (Clark, 1998:454-455). The attraction of a Whitelaw candidature was two-fold. First, he had emerged from the debris of the Heath administration with his political reputation unscathed; and, second, he was viewed as a competent administrator and an individual whose background as a former Chief Whip and Party Chairman would assist him in managing the evolving ideological tensions within Conservatism (Clark, 1998:455). The tactical approach for advocates of Whitelaw was to prepare for a second ballot entry after an inconclusive outcome to the first ballot had forced Heath to resign, but had prevented any alternative candidate gathering momentum to their candidature.

However, Whitelaw would not have been the favoured candidate of the evolving neo-liberal right of the parliamentary Conservative Party due to his proximity to Heath. The figure who was now publicly repudiating the Heath era and thus mobilising an ideological motivated critique of Heathite Conservatism was Keith Joseph (Blake, 1998:319). An intellectual but austere individual, he did possess significant limitations as a potential party leader. His excessive intellectually based concern about the meaning of Conservatism aligned to his negative public persona had led to the label of the 'mad monk'[10] (Clark, 1998:456). Moreover, his behaviour since the Conservatives had lost office in February 1974 had inspired and divided with equal measure, thus raising concerns about his capacity to unify a post-Heath Conservative Party (Gilmour and Garnett, 1998:294).

Neo-liberal economic critics of Heath gravitated to Joseph as he denounced both the direction of Conservative policy under Heath and the trajectory of post-war Conservatism (Wickham-Jones, 1997:78). Joseph now claimed that the Heath Government had reneged on the policy platform that had been developed in opposition between 1966 and 1970 and once in government it had embraced 'the false gods of governmental intervention and prices and incomes control' (Blake, 1998:319). In a series of speeches throughout 1974 Joseph reiterated the same mantra. The Conservative Party had been too collectivist in the policy prescriptions. In doing so they had 'consistently overestimated the abilities of governments to tackle problems' (Wickham-Jones, 1997:77-78). Influenced by the thinking of Milton Friedman and Friedrich Hayek, Joseph passionately embraced economic neo-liberalism: he argued for control of the money supply, promoted the case for the moral superiority of the free market economy over state intervention; advocated cuts in public expenditure; and stated the case for the private enterprise economy (Dorey, 1995:135). To underpin his drive to re-educate the Conservative Party and re-define their ideological and policy direction, Joseph launched the Centre for Policy Studies (CPS) as a forum to develop new economically liberal ideas (Wickham-Jones, 1997:79).

However, the prospect of Joseph emerging as the new party leader was destroyed before the new rules for determining the leadership had been agreed. In October 1974 he delivered a speech that raised questions about his political judgement. He had argued that the task for the Conservative Party was to develop a social policy platform that would contribute to the remoralisation of society (Clark, 1998:461). He identified the primary social problems as being crime and juvenile delinquency. He attempted to argue that the cycle of poverty and social deprivation had to be broken, and argued that the cause of this cycle of social deprivation was the increasing proportion of children being born to working class adolescent girls. In doing so he appeared to be arguing that stricter birth control (i.e. promoting contraception) should be applied to girls of lower socio-economic groupings (Blake, 1998:319). This was political dynamite to his detractors. Joseph was denounced by social commentators as a mad eugenicist (Thatcher, 1995:262). The extent of the denunciation and the accompanying media harassment derailed the Joseph bandwagon. He announced in late November 1974 that he would not stand in any hypothetical leadership contest (Denham and Garnett, 2002:275).

The implosion of the Joseph option appeared to suggest that the most viable anti-Heath candidate was Du Cann (Blake, 1998:318). The Heathites feared Du Cann the most. They assumed that Whitelaw would remain loyal, and believed that they could defeat Joseph as he would be too unpalatable to the majority of mainstream Conservatives (Clark, 1998:457). His machiavellian plotting as Chair of the 1922 Executive had ensured that a review of the rules governing the election of the party would occur and that Heath would have to submit himself for re-election. The timing at which he was attempting to execute Heath chimed with his own political ambitions. The absence of any credible senior candidate suggested that anti-Heath Conservative parliamentarians could gravitate towards him, should he stand. Moreover, he was being actively encouraged to challenge Heath by his parliamentary colleagues (Du Cann, 1995:205). However, two simultaneous events served to ensure that Du Cann would not enter the ensuing contest. First, speculative innuendo began to circulate around the financial circumstances of Du Cann: the implication being that this could create potential embarrassment to the Conservative Party in the future should he acquire the leadership (Fisher, 1977:160-163). Second, the surprise candidature of Margaret Thatcher ensured that a Du Cann candidature would be futile; citing personal reasons, Du Cann ultimately decided not to stand (Clark, 1998:464-465).

4.2   The Challenge of Margaret Thatcher

In November 1974, two months before the new procedures for the party leadership election rules were finalised, Thatcher decided to enter the assumed leadership contest after Joseph had decided that he would not

(Thatcher, 1995:266). The following exchange occurred between Heath and Thatcher to confirm her candidature:

> Thatcher: 'I must tell you that I have decided to stand for the leadership'
> Heath: 'If you must...you'll lose'.   (Ramsden, 1996:442)

Few within the parliamentary Conservative Party had anticipated a Thatcher candidature. The general reaction to her attempt to acquire the party leadership was one of incredulity (Fowler, 1991:13). Her candidature was dominated by the perception that her sex was unsettling to traditional Conservatives,[11] and aligned to this assumption was the view that her political profile did not make her a conventional leadership aspirant (Wickham-Jones, 1997:74-75). Although she had served in Cabinet (as Education Secretary 1970 to 1974) she had retained a relatively low public political profile and furthermore, she had not publicly criticised the policy direction that the Conservatives had pursued in the Heath era (Blake, 1998:320). With the Du Cann candidacy failing to materialise, the Thatcher candidacy became seen to be 'indicative of the trouble Heath's critics had found in finding a potential alternative leader' (Wickham-Jones, 1997:75). With constituency chairman indicating their continuing support for Heath over Thatcher, no newspaper supported Thatcher and no newspaper predicated that Thatcher could defeat Heath. The expectation was that Heath would retain the party leadership by default (Campbell, 1993:671).

Thatcher recognised the implications for herself of her candidature. If her first round performance failed to remove Heath and he retained the party leadership, she realised that her political career would face an abrupt end (Thatcher, 1995:267). Her intention in standing was to ensure Heath's removal even if that did not result in her acquiring the leadership. She argued that:

> It seemed to me most unlikely that I *would* win. I did think that by entering the race, I would draw in other stronger candidates who, even if they did not think like Keith and me, would still be open to persuasion about changing the disastrous course on which the Party was set.   (Thatcher, 1995:267)

Despite the limitations outlined below a Thatcher candidature was not without merit. Her peripheral status within the Heath Cabinet was now spun as a political advantage. Her role as Education secretary had ensured that she remained detached from the controversies surrounding economic policy decision-making. She could thus absolve herself of responsibility for the abandonment of the Selsdon agenda or the subsequent U-turn. Such a strategy enhanced her outsider status, thus encouraging Conservatives who wanted a change in style (i.e. not Heath) and/or substance (i.e. a shift in policy and philosophy) to consider endorsing her.

Moreover, the Thatcher candidature received considerable momentum due to the confluence of three factors. The first demonstrates the capacity for history to repeat itself. Ten years earlier Heath had utilised his elevation to the position of Shadow Chancellor to his political advantage: indeed, the previous chapter identified how his strong parliamentary critique on the Finance Bill in early 1965 alerted many Conservative parliamentarians to his leadership capabilities. Although Heath had included Thatcher in his shadow Cabinet and Cabinets since 1967, it had been in what could be perceived as peripheral briefs: fuel and power (1967-1968), transport (1968-1969), education in opposition (1969-1970) and as Education Secretary (1970 to 1974) and then Environment from March 1974. In doing so, Heath had kept her away from the issues that were the central drivers of political debate: economics, finance and industrial relations (Blake, 1998:320). In the post-October 1974 general election reshuffle Heath switched Thatcher to Shadow Chief Secretary to the Treasury. Although it was not the Shadow Chancellorship it did provide Thatcher with an opportunity to oppose the Finance Bill adopted by the Labour Government. Her conduct in opposing the Finance Bill won converts just as Heath had done so a decade earlier[12] (Behrens, 1980:39).

Thatcher had utilised this window of opportunity to showcase her leadership credentials. In doing so, she had contributed to the de-railing of the Du Cann bandwagon, a factor which dovetails neatly into the second factor that aided the Thatcher candidature. Speculation about a Du Cann candidacy had pre-dated Thatcher's entry into the contest. Both Thatcher and Du Cann agreed that the primary objective of the forthcoming ballot was the removal of Heath. Their dilemma was which one of them was best positioned to fatally wound Heath. The early announcement of Thatcher's formal candidacy (late November 1974) aligned to the financial innuendo swirling around Du Cann had persuaded him to formally stand aside (early January 1975) and allow Thatcher to act as the main anti-Heath candidate. This resulted in a considerable advantage being handed to Thatcher.

The mobilisation of Du Cann forces was being co-ordinated by Airey Neave. He immediately transferred his management of the Du Cann campaign to the Thatcher campaign. Fisher has alluded to the centrality of this as a highly organised campaign, with powerful links to the backbench of the parliamentary Conservative Party (i.e. the majority of the electorate) which was simply inherited by Thatcher (Fisher, 1977:163; Wickham-Jones, 1997:81). In addition to simply inheriting the organisational infrastructure of the abortive Du Cann leadership bid, Thatcher inherited the intellectuals who had originally placed their hopes on a Joseph candidature: this amounts to a third piece of good fortune that aided the Thatcher candidature and provided its initial momentum (Gilmour and Garnett, 1998: 298).

4.3   The Ballots: Rejecting Edward Heath and Electing Margaret Thatcher

With Du Cann removed from the equation the date for nominations passed (30th January) with three candidates standing: Heath, Thatcher and Hugh Fraser, a reactionary and marginal right-wing figure whose candidature threatened to split the anti-Heath right-wing vote and was thus welcomed by Heathites (Gilmour and Garnett, 1998:296).

As the first ballot approached the Heath camp publicly predicated a significant victory for their candidate. (Campbell, 1993:671) This optimism within the Heathite camp was to be misplaced and retrospectively viewed as being indicative of the poor quality campaigning that Heathites engaged in. Whereas ten years earlier his positive campaigning approach was crucial in defeating the favoured Maudling, Heath appeared to resent having to participate in the re-election contest. Whilst the Thatcher camp and Thatcher herself were proactively courting Conservative parliamentarians, Heath did little to endear himself to potential supporters (Campbell, 1993:663-669; Shepherd, 1991:168-169). The ineptitude of his campaign team and his complacency as candidate was so pronounced that it succeeded in alienating 'even those who should have ranked amongst his loyal supporters' (Cowley and Bailey, 2000:600). Cowley and Bailey have observed that some one-nation Tories decided to vote negatively – i.e. against Heath and therefore for Thatcher by default – and lived to regret their decision. One one-nation Conservative parliamentarian informed Cowley and Bailey that:

> My vote is a typical example of Edward Heath losing his basic support. There were various reasons for this and almost all of them were personal rather than having to do with his political beliefs and policies, with which I agreed then as now. If he had taken the trouble to address one sympathetic or personal word to me after my election in February 1974 he could have had me…[but]…his whole style and manner continued to irritate me; I was courted by the Thatcher campaigning team and fell for it.   (Cowley and Bailey, 2000:602)

In comparison to the ineptitude and amateurish Heath campaign was a competent and professional Thatcher campaign, which was skilfully mobilised, indeed manipulated, by Neave (Wickham-Jones, 1997:81). Neave used pessimism as a central manipulative weapon (Gilmour and Garnett, 1998:297). Canvassing amongst the Thatcherite campaign led them to believe that Heath had approximately eighty pledged supporters and that they had around 120, yet Neave informed wavering undecided Conservative parliamentarians that there was a danger that Heath might secure a decisive victory in the first ballot (Thatcher, 1995:274; Ramsden, 1996:449). This strategy of stating that every vote counted and that there was no room for abstaining had a duel effect: it mobilised the minority of ideologically motivated economic liberals to vote for Thatcher rather than Fraser, and encouraged some of the majority one-nation Conservatives who were potential Whitelaw supporters[13] to tactically vote for Thatcher to ensure that a second ballot would occur[14] (Wickham-Jones, 1997:81).

This strategising by the Thatcherite campaign team ensured that Thatcher led on the first ballot and created crucial momentum for her as she entered the second ballot. Most significantly, it achieved the objective of removing Heath from the party leadership.[15] Fisher would reveal that as Du Cann announced the results of the first ballot there was:

> A moment of almost awed silence as we absorbed the figures and realized the implications of what we had done...not even the most optimistic of Margaret Thatcher's expected that she would actually achieve a convincing lead on the first ballot...If the result was a triumph for Thatcher, it was a tragedy for Heath...it had all ended in the personal humiliation of rejection by those he had sought to serve. This was the fate that so many of his friends had feared in the immediate aftermath of the October election.   (Fisher, 1977:172-173)

Table 4:   **Candidate Support in the First Ballot of the Conservative Party Leadership Election of 1975**

	First Ballot	Percentage
Margaret Thatcher	130	47.1
Edward Heath	119	43.1
Hugh Fraser	16	5.8
Abstentions/Spoiled Papers	10	4.0

Source: Quinn, 2005:812

Heath accepted defeat and announced his resignation by indicating that he would not put his name forward to the second ballot.[16] With Heath removed Whitelaw could now stand for the party leadership without being perceived as disloyal. However, the capacity of Whitelaw to emerge as the successor to Heath was complicated by the nature of the outcome of the first ballot and the existence of a bloated field of candidates for the second ballot. The latter point is crucial. The best strategy for ensuring that Thatcher was defeated, and unifying the parliamentary Conservative Party under a one-nation leader, was for Whitelaw to be the only alternative to Thatcher. The ability of Whitelaw to garner a sufficient number of anti-Thatcher votes to obtain victory, was undermined by the existence of three new second round candidates: James Prior, Geoffrey Howe and John Peyton.[17]

Table 5: **Candidate Support in the Second Ballot of the Conservative Party Leadership Election of 1975**

	First Ballot	Percentage
Margaret Thatcher	146	52.9
William Whitelaw	79	28.6
James Prior	19	6.9
Geoffrey Howe	19	6.9
John Peyton	11	4.0
Abstentions/Spoiled Papers	2	0.7

Source: Quinn, 2005:812

Whitelaw did attempt to persuade the other candidates to withdraw, but to no avail. Prior justified entering into the second ballot on the basis of putting down a marker for a future leadership contest: he did not expect to emerge victorious (Wickham-Jones, 1997:82; Prior, 1986:99-101). His political attitudes placed him alongside Whitelaw and thus ensured that they were fighting against each other for Heath's votes. Prior could justify this on the basis of the outcome of the first ballot aligned to the rules governing the election of the leader of the Conservative Party. On a second ballot, the leading candidate only needed to secure a simple majority – i.e. 139 votes not the simple majority plus the fifteen per cent threshold. As Thatcher had secured 130 votes she only had to hold onto his existing support and add an additional nine from the Fraser vote and the abstainers. Although Thatcher could lose some of the votes she had obtained for negative reasons in the first ballot, and the Howe candidature threatened to remove support from her, there is an arithmetic argument to suggest that she was in a very strong position entering the second ballot. The essence of this argument was best expressed by Prior, who felt 'that it was simply too late for Whitelaw to make up the lost ground' (Prior, 1986:101). The observations of Prior proved to be prescient. In the ensuing second ballot on 11th February 1975, Thatcher secured a majority of eighteen over the remaining candidates[18] and was thus elected as the new party leader.

4.4   Explaining the Election of Margaret Thatcher

The immediate reaction to Thatcher annexing the leadership of the Conservative Party was one of amazement at how an anti-establishment female candidature had triumphed within a party renowned for its establishment mentality and its adherence to tradition. Her acquisition of the leadership of the Conservative Party had occurred against the instinct of the elites within the parliamentary Conservative Party. Her dramatic rise as an outsider candidate would not have occurred in the era of the magic circle that pre-dated 1965; and she could only challenge Heath due to revisions to the leadership election results that required Heath to resubmit himself. Indeed, shortly after her dramatic acquisition of the leadership of the Conservative Party she confessed that 'even now, I am not quite sure how it all happened' (Cowley and Bailey, 2000:600).

The remainder of this chapter seeks to explain this by considering two interpretations of the Conservative Party leadership elections of 1975. The first interpretation emphasises the impact of personality and the notion that the outcome was negative and accidental – in this context Thatcher was the inadvertent corollary of divesting the Conservative Party from the leadership of Heath (Cowley and Bailey, 2000:600). The second interpretation implies that there was an ideological dimension to her acquisition of the leadership of the Conservative Party as her endorsers were predominantly on the economic right (pre-Thatcherite dries) and her non-supporters were predominantly traditional one-nation Conservatives (pre-Thatcherite wets) (Cowley and Bailey, 2000: 599-629; Wickham-Jones, 1997:74-97).

4.4.1   The Influence of Personality: The Anti-Heath Interpretation

The first explanation of the outcome of the Conservative Party leadership election of 1975 suggests that Thatcher was elected as an unintended consequence of having to remove Heath. The whole process was driven by an anti-Heath agenda and the endgame of this process was the accidental emergence of Thatcher on the back of a negative support base, aligned to a heavy dose of campaign manipulation, fortune and political courage (Cowley and Bailey, 2000:600).

Analysis conducted earlier in the chapter has alluded to the manipulation inherent within the Thatcher campaigning strategy to inflate her first round vote and create that crucial momentum to her candidature. It also benefited from good fortune: the removal of Powell as a home for ideologically motivated anti-Heath votes; the implosion of the embryonic Joseph candidature; the external factors that prevented Du Cann for entering; the instinctive loyalty of Whitelaw that prevented him from challenging Heath; the mobilisation of factors that caused the alteration to the rules governing leadership elections that compelled Heath to resubmit himself; and the ineptitude of the Heath campaign. The consequence of those factors was that Thatcher emerged as the only possible alternative to a deeply unpopular leader: nearly all of the anti-Heath votes would gravitate to her in the first ballot (Cowley and Bailey, 2000:600). Alongside astute manipulation of the process and political kismet, was the perception that Thatcher was ultimately rewarded for her political courage. In the aftermath of the first ballot, Thatcher actually derived credit amongst some Conservative parliamentarians for having the political courage to challenge Heath. This was spun wisely by her campaign team to imply cowardice on behalf of the second round entrants (Whitelaw, Howe, Prior and Peyton), thus implying that her political courage deserved to be rewarded with a second ballot triumph[19] (Wickham-Jones, 1997:76-81, 82).

Over and beyond the emphasis on manipulation, fortune and courage, has been the view that her acquisition of the party leadership can be attributed to an accident. The accident theory places the issue of personality as a central determinant: it revolves around the argument that the process was shaped by an anti-Heath agenda. This interpretation has been expressed by numerous political historians and Conservative parliamentarians of the era. Brock and Wapshott, Keegan, and Shepherd all highlight the accidents theory as a partial explanation for her ascent (Brock and Wapshott, 1983:106; Keegan, 1984:65; Shepherd, 1991:170). Implicit within the accident theory is the recognition that the parliamentary Conservative Party did not intend to propel Thatcher to the leadership of their party. Her strong showing in the first ballot was a by-product of negative votes – i.e. a protest against Heath to ensure his removal. This interpretation is endorsed by Conservative parliamentarians who endorsed her and opposed her. Nigel Lawson noted that it was 'more a rejection of Ted – on personal and political grounds alike – than a positive endorsement' of Thatcher (Gilmour and Garnett, 1998:298).

The cumulative impact of the above factors provides a partial explanation. It forms the basis of the personality based account (i.e. the anti-Heath account) which emphasises

Thatcher's luck and the strategic campaign her supporters ran. It suggests that two types of MPs had supported her. First, there were a small number of right-wingers, those who positively and publicly endorsed the re-think on which Keith Joseph had embarked. Second, and numerically much greater, there were those anti-Heath MPs who were determined to replace Heath regardless of who the alternative might be. Margaret Thatcher received their support because she was the only serious challenger. If a more plausible candidate had stood, many of the anti-Heath MPs might have gone elsewhere.

(Wickham-Jones, 1997:80)

This interpretation assumes that the outcome of the Conservative Party leadership election was shaped by personality rather than ideologically based factors. The personality driven explanation, with its associated assumptions regarding the saliency of manipulation, fortune and courage suggests that 1975 did not constitute the birthplace of Thatcherite ideology by design.[20] This personality accident negative theory suggests that in their over-enthusiasm to evict Heath, the parliamentary Conservative Party handed the leadership of the Conservative Party to Thatcher in ignorance of her ideological beliefs: i.e. it was a peasants' revolt against a discredited incumbent rather than an ideologically driven takeover of the party by the right (Young and Sloman, 1986:33).

4.4.2   The Influence of Ideas: The Ideological Explanation

The negatively induced accident theory does carry weight in explaining the outcome of the Conservative Party leadership election of 1975. However, it is worth noting that such arguments may have considerable utility in explaining the outcome of the first ballot, but they offer less of an explanation for the outcome of the second ballot.

The whole premise of the negative / accident theory downplays ideological factors and emphasises personality factors – i.e. the desire to evict Heath. This provides Thatcher with a base of negatively induced protest votes of sufficient number to remove Heath and ensure a second ballot. At this juncture the personality negative accident theory implies that momentum now propelled her to victory in the second ballot. Such an argument is intellectually limiting and an over-simplification. For example, the negative accident theory suggests that protests votes gravitated to Thatcher in the first ballot as they were voting against Heath to ensure his removal and an open second ballot with more candidates. However, as the campaigning for the second ballot commenced the fear for the Thatcher camp was that there was nothing to protest against anymore and that her negative induced votes might switch to other candidates in a wider field (Wickham-Jones, 1997:83). That such fears proved to be mostly unfounded lends credence to the argument that the influence of ideas – an ideological explanation – did contribute significantly to the outcome of the second ballot.

As implied above, an element of the orthodox interpretation is the notion that Thatcher acquired the leadership from a parliamentary Conservative Party that did not truly appreciate the ideological implications of her candidature. Critchley argues that in their ignorance, the parliamentary Conservative Party had handed the leadership of the Conservative Party to an ideological zealot, whose fundamentalist beliefs were not, at the time of her election as widely known as they are today (Critchley, 1994:122).

However, the assumption that the ideological beliefs of Thatcher were unknown to the parliamentary Conservative Party should be questioned in the view of Wickham-Jones. He argues that her 'ideological position was recognised by critics and supporters during the 1975 contest' (Wickham-Jones, 1997:86). He notes that her public denunciations of the Heath government and her close association with Joseph should have provided Conservative parliamentarians with sufficient evidence to locate her on the right of the parliamentary Conservative Party (Wickham-Jones, 1997:85-86). For example, one anonymous backbencher informed Cowley and Bailey that Thatcher would abandon one-nation Conservatism, as her stance was 'too far to the right and her opinions often narrow-minded and over-ideological' (Cowley and Bailey, 2000:619).

Moreover, of those who voted for her in both ballots, there was evidence to suggest that the vast majority did know the consequences of what they were doing. In this sense the views of two leading Thatcherites of the 1980s are informative. Both Norman Tebbit and Nicholas Ridley observed that the process was more than simply the removal of Heath. It was the removal of Heath for a reason, and that reason was the insertion of a new leader who would change that philosophical direction of the Conservative Party and challenge the Keynesian social democratic consensus of the post-war era (Tebbit, 1988:142; Ridley, 1991:95; Wickham-Jones, 1997:89).

The extensive research undertaken by Cowley and Bailey endorses the idea that there was a pro-ideological explanation that has to be recognised alongside the traditional or orthodox anti-Heathite explanation. (Cowley and Bailey, 2000: 599-629). They attempted to examine the voting behaviour of all 276 Conservative parliamentarians in both ballots of the 1975 Conservative Party leadership election. Three sources were utilised in an attempt to determine voting behaviour: first, the listings kept by the Thatcher election campaign team; second, through correspondence with Conservative parliamentarians of that parliament; and, third, by extensively researching newspapers and magazines from the campaigning period. Taken together, Cowley and Bailey argue that the information derived from these methods provide 'an excellent (if not perfect) guide to the voting of MPs in the 1975 contest' (Cowley and Bailey, 2000:604). This assertion appears to be appropriate given that they secured information on the voting behaviour of all but six Conservatives on the first ballot and all but twelve on the second ballot (Cowley and Bailey, 2000:604).

They also defined all Conservative parliamentarians on a typology of Conservative thought devised by Norton, in which a split between the economic right (i.e. critics of one-nation Conservatism) and the economic left (advocates of one-nation Conservatism) of Conservative thought was seen as the central ideological determinant (Norton, 1990a:41-58). Through this methodological process, Cowley and Bailey observed that:

ideology was a key determinant of voting in both rounds of the contest... The right – however defined – strongly supported Thatcher; the left – however defined – Heath and then Whitelaw.

(Cowley and Bailey, 2000:628-629)

The validity of this assertion is evidenced from the second ballot result and the flow of the vote from first to the second ballot. Some first ballot Thatcher protest votes now gravitated to Whitelaw in the second ballot. However although Thatcher lost some of these votes she did increase her vote. When her return of 146 is added to the Howe return of 19 and the Peyton return of 11 (both of whom broadly adhered with the critique of Heathite policies), this demonstrates that a majority of Conservatives wanted a change of substance and direction as well as style and leader (Ramsden, 1996:453). It was as much an ideologically motivated religious war (especially the second ballot) as it was a peasants' revolt.

4.5   Conclusion

Having been forcibly evicted from the leadership of the Conservative Party, Heath would become a bitter and resentful critic of the policies and rhetoric of the Thatcher Governments between 1979 and 1990. This chapter suggests that his own political execution could have been avoided had he displayed greater tactical and strategic acumen. His political antennae should have informed him that successive electoral defeats had left him politically vulnerable and that it would erode his leadership credibility. He should have recognised in either March or October 1974 that he needed to either voluntary resubmit or resign. Had he voluntarily submitted himself for re-election in March or October 1974 (even though he was not required to do so) it is likely that he would have triumphed over his critics, who would not have coalesced around an agreed alternative. By delaying and then being compelled against his wishes to re-submit under reconfigured procedures, he succeeded in creating an image of political weakness. Moreover, he provided his critics with crucial time in which to develop the infrastructure of anti-Heathite sentiment in preparation for a leadership election when the opportunity arose. He did not consider the voluntary submission option nor did he consider the resignation option. Had he resigned in either March or October then the likelihood is that Whitelaw would have been elected as leader of the Conservative Party, thus preserving one-nation influence and blunting the excesses of economic liberal thought (Ramsden, 1996:436).

The previous chapter concluded by noting how the Conservative Party leadership election of 1965 had been conducted with decorum and without significant ideological influence in its outcome. The Conservative Party leadership election of 1975 was characterised by internal bitterness and infighting and *was* influenced by ideological factors. The contrived nature of the changes to the leadership election procedures reflected badly on the way in which the Conservative Party conducted itself. Stark encapsulated that cynicism when he observed that the rule changes constituted a 'political exercise', in which the overriding objective was to provide the opportunity to remove Heath (Stark, 1996:30).

The Conservative Party leadership election of 1975 can retrospectively be viewed as a referendum on the Selsdon agenda that was agreed in opposition in 1970 and that the Heath and his acolytes abandoned once in government. Those who supported the abandonment of Selsdon and defended the Heathite u-turn tended to be one-nation conservatives who were inclined towards Heath or Whitelaw. Those who were supporters of economic liberalism and critics of one-nation conservative approaches tended towards Thatcher. The critics of one-nation Conservatism and consensus politics had prevailed under a new and unexpected champion. The new party leader greeted the assembled media and announced:

> With my predecessors, Edward Heath, Alec Douglas-Home, Harold Macmillan, Anthony Eden, and of course the great Winston, it is like a dream. Wouldn't you think so? I also wept when they told me. I did weep'. (Ramsden, 1996:456)

Thatcher then politely posed for the photographers. When responding to one particularly request that would improve the angle of one photographer's shot, she informed the remaining photographers:

> And now I am going to take a turn to the right, which is very appropriate. (Ramsden, 1996:456)

TREACHERY WITH A SMILE ON ITS FACE: THE DOWNFALL OF MARGARET THATCHER

A pervasive sense of crisis had engulfed the Conservative Party during the party leadership tenure of Edward Heath. When he was forcibly evicted from the party leadership, it was clear that the party required a new statecraft strategy and an alternative narration of Conservatism, in order to regain its electoral hegemony and governing credibility. His successor, Margaret Thatcher, exploited the political vacuum that existed. Aided by her ideologically motivated acolytes, she took a directionless and demoralised Conservative Party on a rightwards ideological trajectory. The discrediting of social democracy and Keynesian economic approaches[1] provided a window of opportunity for Thatcher to advance a new ideologically motivated governing philosophy. This revisionist approach, which was designed to restore the electoral, ideological, economic and political dominance of the Conservative Party, would repudiate the pillars of the post-war consensus, and post-war Conservatism. It became defined as Thatcherism[2] (Gamble, 1996:23).

That Thatcher became the first British Prime Minister to have an –ism attached to her name was indicative of her dominance over British politics from 1979 onwards. Under her party leadership the Conservative Party reclaimed their mantle as the natural party of government. Prior to her accession to the party leadership, the Conservatives had suffered four electoral defeats in five attempts over a ten year period. Having entered government with a comfortable majority in 1979, Thatcher then led the Conservatives to two further electoral landslide victories, in 1983 and 1987. Her dominance was absolute and she indicated that it was her intention to seek a fourth term of office by leading the Conservative Party to the next general election (Thatcher, 1993:755).

Thatcher was to be denied this opportunity. Despite her impressive electoral record, a commanding parliamentary majority, no significant parliamentary defeats and an overwhelmingly desire to continue, Thatcher was
forcibly evicted from Downing Street, not at the behest of the electorate but
due to her own parliamentary and ministerial colleagues. This occurred after
a protracted struggle that involved two challenges to her party leadership:
one lightweight challenge by Anthony Meyer; and one heavy-weight
challenge by Michael Heseltine.

5.1   The Lightweight Challenge of Anthony Meyer

Having assumed the party leadership in February 1975, the annual
unopposed re-election of Thatcher occurred through the era of opposition
(between 1975[3] and 1979) and then in government from 1979 onwards. The
explanation for her unopposed annual re-election was simple: she had
demonstrated that she was an electoral asset to the Conservative Party, and
by doing so, critics of her leadership style or ideological approach could easily
be marginalised and discredited. It was only when periods of unpopularity
happened to coincide with the annual re-election timetable that speculation
that she may face a challenge would emerge. This had occurred twice since
entering office: once in the autumn of 1981 when it was rumoured that
disaffected economic wets might mount a challenge, and once again in the
autumn of 1985 from the same group of critics. However, despite the
speculation, no formal challenge had been forthcoming (Norton, 1990b:249;
Alderman and Smith, 1990:270).

By 1989 Thatcher had been party leader for nearly a decade and a half and
had been Prime Minister for exactly a decade. Many Conservatives were now
considering the direction of the party in the post-Thatcherite era; the
question of the party leadership was beginning to dominate their thoughts.
However, Thatcher remained committed to the notion of serving a fourth
term. She claimed that her desire to remain for the duration of her third term
and beyond stemmed from her concern about the succession. She admitted
that she did not think that any of her own political generation, Norman
Tebbit, Nicholas Ridley, Cecil Parkinson, Nigel Lawson and Geoffrey Howe,
amounted to suitable successors (Thatcher, 1993:755).

In her memoirs, Thatcher would outline the reservations or limitations of
these candidates. Norman Tebbit, who had served as Employment Secretary,
Trade and Industry Secretary and Conservative Party Chairman, was ideologically acceptable given that he was an economic liberal and a Eurosceptic,
but he had retired from front-line politics to care for his paralysed wife,
Margaret. Nicholas Ridley, a fellow economic liberal Eurosceptic, who had
served as Transport and Environment Secretary and was her Trade and
Industry Secretary by 1989, lacked the necessary presentational skills and

would be unacceptable to a sufficient number of Conservative parliamentarians. Cecil Parkinson had been forced to resign as Trade and Industry Secretary in 1983 due to an extra-marital affair, and although Thatcher had brought him back into Cabinet as Energy Secretary and then Transport Secretary, she recognised that his private life was an impediment to the succession. Her long standing Chancellor, Nigel Lawson, shared her economic philosophy but his increasing Europhilia and desire to join the Exchange Rate Mechanism, made him unacceptable to Thatcher. Her incumbent Foreign Secretary and former Chancellor, Geoffrey Howe, was unacceptable to her as he shared the same European views as Lawson (Thatcher, 1993:755).

This left one outstanding claimant to the succession, Michael Heseltine. Heseltine was economically on the left of the Conservative Party and was pro-European. Ideologically he was an anathema to Thatcher and she could not countenance the idea of him succeeding her. Heseltine was no longer a member of the Cabinet having dramatically resigned as Defence Secretary in January 1986 in the Westland Affair.[4] His status outside of the Cabinet, his differing ideological stance, his known critique of the leadership style of Thatcher, and his charisma and known ambition, made him a likely candidate to challenge Thatcher.[5] What was potentially threatening to Thatcher was the electoral appeal that Heseltine possessed. Opinion polling on alternative leaders to Thatcher repeatedly demonstrated that Heseltine would be the best candidate for bringing back wavering Conservative voters and eradicating the lead that the Labour Party possessed (Crick, 1997:316).

The fiercely ambitions Heseltine faced a tactical conundrum. He believed that he was well positioned to succeed Thatcher, but he feared the consequences of directly challenging her for the party leadership. A direct challenge to an incumbent Conservative Party Prime Minister would lead to accusations of disloyalty and may impede his chances of defeating her. Given this, Heseltine choose to address all questions about his leadership ambitions with the carefully worded statement that he could not foresee any circumstances in which he would challenge Thatcher. This was deliberately phrased to avoid any accusation of disloyalty but had an inbuilt caveat: circumstances have a habit of being unforeseen (Shepherd, 1991:4).

A direct challenge could lead to one of three hypothetical outcomes. First, there could be an overwhelming rejection of Thatcher on the first ballot, with Heseltine securing the party leadership in one ballot. This scenario was highly unlikely and Heseltine and his acolytes recognised this (Stark, 1996:193). Second, the instinctive loyalty of many Conservatives could ensure a strong Thatcher performance. This could contribute to her securing her re-election and ensuring political oblivion for Heseltine. This seemed a distinct possibility, especially if Heseltine wielded the dagger too early. The third scenario was particularly problematic for Heseltine. He could challenge and secure enough support to force Thatcher to stand down after the first ballot. Heseltine would then have to face other candidates in an open second contest, in which alternatives to Heseltine could argue that they were unity candidates, whereas Heseltine was a divisive and disloyal figure. The second and third scenarios outlined here demonstrated the political risks for Heseltine in initiating a direct challenge to Thatcher. Given these risks, Heseltine hoped that his ambitions would be aided by one of two hypothetical events. First, that Thatcher would resign as the degeneration of her government made her position untenable. Heseltine could then enter a vacant contest without accusations of disloyalty and without being tainted by the failings of the late-Thatcherite era of decline. Second, that Thatcher would face a challenge from someone other than Heseltine and that this would precipitate her removal, but would not involve the hypothetical challenger emerging victorious. Heseltine could then enter at the second ballot stage once Thatcher had been removed, at which point the protest votes that had gone to the challenger would gravitate to him (Crick, 1997:343).

By the autumn of 1989 it became increasingly likely that the second of those hypothetical events would occur – i.e. a formal challenge to the annual re-election of Thatcher by someone other than Heseltine (Howe, 1994:609). Anthony Meyer, an obscure backbencher with no ministerial experience, decided he would dispute her re-election.[6] He no longer believed that it was appropriate for her to be re-elected automatically. Meyer knew that his candidature was for a specific purpose. It was about enhancing the feasibility of a more serious challenge from the economically damp, Europhile wing of the parliamentary Conservative Party. Put crudely, Meyer was interested in enhancing the probability of Heseltine succeeding Thatcher (Punnett, 1992:61; Stark, 1996:92, 208).

Table 6:   Candidate Support in the Conservative Party Leadership Election of 1989

	First Ballot	Percentage
Margaret Thatcher	314	84.0
Anthony Meyer	33	8.8
Abstentions	27	7.2

Source: Quinn, 2005:812

Given his peripheral status, it was unconceivable that Meyer could garner enough protest votes to prevent Thatcher from securing a first ballot triumph and thus securing her re-election[7] (Norton, 1990b:254). However, the politically astute realised the implications of the Meyer candidature and the hidden implications of the resulting ballot. Meyer had begun the destabilising of Thatcher which culminated in her removal twelve months later (Cole, 1995:354). The fact that sixty Conservative parliamentarians were unwilling to endorse her needed to be interpreted as a warning about policy direction and her leadership style: i.e. faith in her leadership was eroding irrespective of the outcome of the ballot[8] (Howe, 1994:611). It was rumoured that beyond the sixty non endorsers there were approximately one hundred Conservative parliamentarians who had reluctantly endorsed Thatcher and that their endorsement was conditional. Their support was on a probationary period and, unless significant changes were made, they may withdraw their support in any future leadership election (Howe, 1994:670; Cole, 1995:354). The evidence that faith in her leadership was eroding despite her re-election was put to her by her Deputy Chief Whip, Tristan Garel-Jones, as recalled by her eventual successor, John Major:

> he told the Prime Minister that pro-European members were deeply unhappy with the 'tone' of her policy, and that dissatisfaction with the Poll Tax was everywhere. 'Unless you're careful,' he warned her, 'they'll be back. Hezzie [Michael Heseltine] will run, and they'll kill you…It will be daylight assassination of the Prime Minister'. (Major, 1999:168)

With the benefit of hindsight, we can argue that the candidature of Meyer was significant and should constitute more than a mere footnote in the history of Conservative Party politics. The most obvious consequence of his candidature related to precedent.[9] By disputing her annual re-election, Meyer was establishing a unique precedent in which Conservative parliamentarians were being asked for the first time to determine whether the incumbent Prime Minister should retain their position as Conservative Party leader. Meyer had broken down the psychological barrier that existed against challenging an incumbent party leader who was also the incumbent Prime Minister. His stalking horse candidature amounted to a necessary pre-requisite for a challenge that would cause the eviction of Thatcher (Norton, 1990b:252; Carter and Alderman, 1991:139).

5.2   The Heavyweight Challenge of Michael Heseltine

Those who remained loyal to Thatcher were dismissive of the Meyer challenge and the limited support that his candidature garnered. They failed to detect the political symbolism that a challenge had been mounted and thus failed to grasp the increasing vulnerability of her position. The political landscape did not improve for the Conservative Party over the ensuing months and thus speculation on her continuance remained omnipresent. This culminated in an intriguing proposition being put to Thatcher by her former Foreign Secretary, Lord Carrington. In April 1990, Carrington advised Thatcher that 'the party wanted [her] to leave office both with dignity and at a time of [her] own choosing' (Thatcher, 1993:832). There were two logical consequences of the idea of leaving office 'with dignity'. First, it suggests that removal 'would occur before a general election'; and, second, that removal 'would be in advance of, rather than consequent to, a challenge under the leadership rules' (Clark, 1998:487). Thatcher reacted negatively to the advice given by Carrington, given that she suspected that it he was speaking on behalf of the Tory establishment. She argued that:

> I took this to be a coded message: dignity might suggest a rather earlier departure than I would otherwise choose...I reflected that if the great and the good of the Tory party had had their way, I would never have become party leader, let alone Prime Minister...I would fight – and, if necessary, go down fighting – for my beliefs as long as I could. 'Dignity' did not come into it.   (Thatcher, 1993:832)

However, the primary reason why she had been able to retain the party leadership without a challenge (prior to that of Meyer) had been due to the fact that she had been perceived as an electoral asset to the party. As the new decade began, Thatcher had morphed into an electoral liability to the party, with her disapproval ratings demonstrating that she was the least popular Prime Minister since polling began. The proximity of the next general election meant that many Conservative parliamentarians feared defeat for the party, and possibly the loss of their own constituencies, if she was retained as their party leader (Carter and Alderman, 1991:127, 137).

Perceptions of her electoral liability stemmed from three factors. The first factor was the extent of the escalating economic recession. Inflation rates had increased whilst manufacturing output and consumer spending levels were falling (Blake, 1998:380). The second factor was the poll tax, which provoked widespread opposition. Opinion polling evidence suggested that 70 per cent of the electorate disapproved of the poll tax, and more worryingly for Conservative parliamentarians, approximately half of those polled regarded it as the most likely determinant of their future voting behaviour (Jeffreys, 2002:240). However, Thatcher remained implacably committed to the poll tax and would not consider the idea of abandoning it. It became an issue of personal authority for her. The fact that one of the central attractions of a potential Heseltine challenge was his willingness to reform the poll tax did not induce a more pragmatic mentality from her. Conservative parliamentarians fearing a ballot box backlash from the poll tax would have to remove her if they wanted to get rid of the poll tax (Gilmour and Garnett, 1998:344).

The third factor was more complex. It involved the ideological disputation at elite level within the Conservative Party surrounding the vexed question of

European integration and aligned to this the leadership style of Thatcher. A visceral dispute between the Eurosceptic Thatcher and her pro-European Chancellor Lawson and Howe as Foreign Secretary, was damaging the operational effectiveness of the Thatcher government.[10] The degeneration of the working relationship between Thatcher, Lawson and Howe was at its most evident at a meeting of the European Council in Madrid in June 1989. Thatcher did not want to commit Britain to membership of the Exchange Rate Mechanism. Howe and Lawson informed Thatcher that unless she made a commitment in principle to join the Exchange Rate Mechanism, then they would both resign. Faced with the potentially cataclysmic implications of a joint resignation, Thatcher was forced to relent.

Thatcher secured her revenge for the Madrid ambush by Howe and Lawson in her Cabinet reshuffle weeks later. She removed Howe from the Foreign Office and offered him the Home Office (without consulting the incumbent Douglas Hurd) knowing that Howe would reject this. Howe was offered the position of Leader of the House of Commons at which point he drafted his resignation speech. He reluctantly accepted this post on the proviso that he was given the title of Deputy Prime Minister in recognition of his seniority. The humiliation for Howe was complete when he was replaced at the Foreign Office by the relatively unknown and inexperienced John Major (Gilmour and Garnett, 1998:341).

By October 1989, the working relationship between Thatcher and her Chancellor Lawson had all but broken down completely. The Thatcher government was beset by economic difficulties with resurgent inflation and increased interest rates. Alan Walters, who advised Thatcher on economic policy, disputed the shadowing of sterling to the Deutschmark as a prelude to early entry into the Exchange Rate Mechanism. When Thatcher appeared to publicly endorse the view of her advisor, which was opposite to that of Lawson, it made the position of her Chancellor untenable. Unless Walters was removed Lawson would resign. When Thatcher sided with Walters, Lawson resigned and Major was promoted to the position of Chancellor of the Exchequer with Hurd switching to the Foreign Office (Gilmour and Garnett, 1998:345-346).

Her antagonism of Lawson had provoked his resignation and led within six weeks to the lightweight challenge of Meyer. Despite considerable provocation Howe had remained in Cabinet for the remaining twelve months. Ultimately, however, the removal of Thatcher would necessitate a trigger and an issue. In late October 1990, the issue was European integration and the trigger was the parliamentary performance of Thatcher. When reporting back on the recent European Summit, her behaviour / language provoked the resignation of Howe (Carter and Alderman, 1991:127).

Howe had prided himself on his pragmatic engagement with European partners during his tenure as Foreign Secretary between 1983 and 1989. This pro-Europeanism had set him upon a collision course with an increasingly Eurosceptic Thatcher. The patience of the Europhilic Howe finally snapped when Thatcher was asked on her thoughts on a federal Europe, upon which Thatcher deviated from the agreed Cabinet position and tone. She argued that:

> The Commission wants to increase its powers. Yes, it is a non-elected body and I do not want the Commission to increase its powers at the expense of the House, so of course we differ. The President of the Commission, Mr Delors, said at a press conference the other day that he wanted the European Parliament to be the democratic body of the Community. He wanted the Commission to be the Executive and he wanted the Council of Ministers to be the Senate….No, No, No.
>
> (Watkins, 1998:215)

Howe was appalled by the reaction of Thatcher. He decided that he could no longer tolerate being part of her Cabinet any longer. He resigned but then refused to conduct a press conference to explain his resignation and rejected requests for media interviews. His silence, (from his initial resignation on November 1st), appeared to be beneficial to Thatcher, especially as the deadline for nominations for a formal challenge to her party leadership was now only fifteen days away. The longer Howe remained silent, the more commentators assumed that Thatcher would overcome the impact of his resignation.

At this juncture it is worth noting the fact that Thatcher was aware that the resignation of Howe may have led to a challenge to her annual re-election as party leader. The procedures governing the election of the party leader stipulated that a challenge could be initiated within twenty-eight days of the beginning of new parliamentary session. Through consultation with Cranley Onslow, the Chair of the 1922 Executive Committee, Thatcher managed, (as was her entitlement) to bring forward the closing date for nominations forward (to November 15th) and then hold the first (and Thatcher assumed definitive) ballot on November 20th. The motivation for Thatcher of doing so was two-fold. First, she felt that if a leadership election was to be conducted it was in the best interests of the party (and/or herself) to proceed as quickly as possible. Second, and perhaps of greater relevance, bringing the deadline forward limited the time in which further difficulties could emerge and the time in which her critics could mobilise the efforts to evict her. The consequence for Thatcher of these timetabling alterations was that she was scheduled to attend a European Summit in Paris on the day of the first ballot[11] (Watkins, 1998:217).

In the aftermath of his resignation, Thatcher would be publicly dismissive of the significance of her losing the only Cabinet member who remained from when she had entered government. With only three days remaining before the deadline for nominations for a hypothetical leadership challenge she observed that:

> I am still at the crease, although the bowling has been pretty hostile of late. *(applause)* And, in case anyone doubted it, can I assure you there will be no ducking bouncers, no stonewalling, no playing for time. The bowling's going to get hit all around the ground.   (Watkins, 1998:219)

Howe would utilise this cricketing metaphor to devastating effect when he eventually explained the reasons for his resignation to Parliament. He outlined the policy disagreements that had existed between himself and Thatcher and the problems that he had experienced flowing from her leadership style. He then proceeded to ensure that the cricketing metaphor that Thatcher had deployed would boomerang on her. To demonstrate how ministers were often undermined by Thatcher, he observed that:

> It is rather like sending your opening batsmen to the crease only for them to find, the moment the first balls are bowled, that their bats have been broken before the game by the team captain. *(laughter)*
> (Watkins, 1998:220)

He concluded his denunciation of Thatcher with a non- too subtle coded message:

> The time has come for others to consider their own response to the tragic conflict of loyalties with which I myself have wrestled with for perhaps too long.[12]   (Shepherd, 1991:1)

His closing comments were widely seen as an open invitation to Heseltine to challenge Thatcher.[13] How would Heseltine respond to this call for insurrection? If Heseltine challenged now, he risked being cast as divisive, splitting the party, and could fail to win, and perhaps destroy his chances of ever securing the party leadership and the premiership. If he did not challenge now, at a time when the political stock of Thatcher had crashed dramatically, he risked losing all credibility as an alternative to Thatcher, as acolytes and perhaps even critics of the Prime Minister, would argue that he was politically cowardly: willing to stalk but too meek to strike.

The strategy that Heseltine had carefully crafted, which was predicated on avoiding a direct challenge to Thatcher, was fundamentally altered by the Howe speech (Stark, 1996:93; Crick, 1997:344). In the immediate aftermath of the resignation at the beginning of November, Heseltine informed Howe that he did not think that 'his undoubtedly courageous decision had materially altered my own position.' (Heseltine, 2000:355) Heseltine would later admit in his memoirs that the dual impact of the Howe speech and the timing of it in relation to any hypothetical leadership election limited his room for manoeuvre and caused him to rethink his strategic position (Heseltine, 2000:355-356).

However, it is interesting to note that before Heseltine went public with his decision he liaised with Cecil Parkinson, the Transport Secretary, and a political confidante of Thatcher. Parkinson advised Heseltine not to challenge. He suggested that Heseltine issue a press statement, in which he noted that although many parliamentary colleagues had encouraged him to stand, he had decided not to so in the interests of party unity (Parkinson, 1992:24-25). Heseltine rejected this advice because he felt that politically Thatcher was 'finished' due to the severity of the Howe critique.[14] In the end it was the Howe speech that was the unforeseen circumstance that would justify Heseltine challenging Thatcher directly. He admits that the pressure to do so was irresistible (Heseltine, 2000:362).

5.3   The Margaret Thatcher versus Michael Heseltine Ballot

The morning after the Howe speech and only one day before the deadline for nominations for the party leadership election, Heseltine called a press conference and announced his candidature for the leadership of the Conservative Party. He argued that he had decided to contest her annual re-election on the following grounds: first, that over one hundred Conservative parliamentary colleagues had persuaded him to stand; second, that the position of the Conservative Party in the opinion polls would be enhanced if he assumed the party leadership in place of Thatcher; third, that flowing from this he was better placed to lead the Conservatives to election victory in eighteen months time; and finally, that he would remove the electoral impediment of the poll tax (Shepherd, 1991:18-19; Crick, 1997:345).

Despite his extensive Cabinet and ministerial experience, Heseltine crafted his campaign around his status as a political outsider, removed from the collective guilt that Cabinet colleagues had for the current predicament of the Conservatives (Foley, 1993:187). In effect, his outsider status was guaranteed.[15] It was politically impractical for any incumbent ministers, especially Cabinet ministers, not to endorse Thatcher, and do so publicly. The Heseltine campaign was thus managed by two career backbenchers and Heseltine loyalists, Michael Mates and Keith Hampson, whilst his nomination papers were proposed and seconded by one long-time backbencher, Peter Tapsell, and former junior minister, Neil Macfarlane (Crick, 1997:346-347). This contrasted starkly with the insider status of the Thatcher campaign. To demonstrate the united resolve of her cabinet and ministerial colleagues, she was proposed and seconded by Major, her Chancellor, and

Hurd, her Foreign Secretary. Her campaign would be co-ordinated by another Cabinet figure, George Younger, who had successfully managed her re-election campaign the previous autumn, and her Parliamentary Private Secretary, Peter Morrison (Thatcher, 1993:840).

The charisma and electoral appeal of Heseltine made the challenge a serious one. It was a challenge based on a change of style and of substance: the contours of economic and European policy would be reconfigured should Heseltine prevail. Despite the ramifications for her political legacy if Heseltine won and the attractiveness of his candidature to her critics and to MPs defending marginal constituencies, Thatcher engaged in a complacent re-election campaign. Mirroring the campaign strategy adopted against Meyer, Thatcher deliberately remained detached from the re-election campaign. This would justify her decision to attend a European Summit in Paris (which would coincide with the first electoral ballot), rather than remain in London and persuade wavering backbenchers to endorse her. She justified this approach by arguing that it would have been absurd for her behave as if she was campaigning as if she had never been their party leader and Prime Minister before. In effect she was arguing that everyone knew her political, ideological and stylistic approach.[16]

As a dramatic week of political theatre reached its endgame, leading Thatcherites spent the morning of the electoral ballot, debating how Thatcher should set about unifying the party after her re-election. Her campaign team expected a comfortable victory. Peter Morrison, a leading figure in her re-election campaign, predicted that Thatcher would poll between 230 and 250, and emphasised that 230 was a pessimistic figure. His canvassing indicated that Heseltine would poll around 100 votes, with approximately 50 to 60 Conservative parliamentarians indicating their intention to abstain. Thatcher seemed destined for a comfortable technical victory but would it be a sufficiently large enough victory to be proclaimed as psychologically accept-able – i.e. how big would the margin of victory be, and how big would the scale of discontent with her amount to?[17] (Shepherd, 1991:24).

Table 7:   Candidate Support in the First Ballot of the Conservative Party Leadership Election of 1990

	First Ballot	Percentage
Margaret Thatcher	204	54.8
Michael Heseltine	152	40.9
Abstentions	16	4.3

Source: Quinn, 2005:812

The Thatcher campaign team had been grossly inaccurate in their forecasts. Thatcher had garnered twenty-six fewer votes than the pessimistic end of the Morrison prediction of between 230 and 250. Morrison had also been widely inaccurate in assessing the level of abstentions and circuitously the level of support for Heseltine. Michael Mates, who counted for Heseltine, predicted that Heseltine would score 154 and he scored 152, whilst he accurately predicted that Thatcher would score 204. Shepherd speculates that the 'fib factor' is far greater when communicating to the incumbent campaign team than the challengers. Many parliamentarians who voted against Thatcher could not bring themselves to admit to Thatcher's canvassers that they did not intend to endorse the incumbent. The potential for reprisals for lying to the challenger were less (Shepherd, 1991:27-28; Stark, 1996:214).

Crucially, although Thatcher had secured a parliamentary majority, and she had a lead over Heseltine that was three times the size of the lead that Heath had secured over Maudling twenty-five years earlier, she had failed to pass the majority and fifteen percent threshold (by only four votes) (Watkins, 1991:2). Therefore a second ballot was inevitable, as Heseltine was not going to follow the Maudling precedent and withdraw.

The Maudling precedent was an easy one for Heseltine to discount. There was a difference between a vacant contest between two candidates seeking to acquire the party leadership, and a challenge to an incumbent and long-standing party leader. In a vacant contest between two equal aspirants, the performance of Thatcher would have been widely interpreted as an impressive showing.[18] That the result was so damaging flowed from the fact that approximately forty-five per cent of Conservative parliamentarians did not want the incumbent Conservative Prime Minister to remain as Prime Minister. If nearly half of Conservative parliamentarians no longer supported her continuance as Prime Minister, was it credible to expect the electorate to endorse her continuance as Prime Minister in the forthcoming general election? If she did prevail in the second ballot, her continuance would hand a crucial electoral resource to the Labour Party. In the forthcoming general election, Labour would be able to gain considerable political mileage out of arguing that if nearly half the parliamentary Conservative Party could not endorse Thatcher, then neither should the electorate (Shepherd, 1991:35). The damage to her authority was irreversible; she was now fatally wounded and discredited, and even if she did prevail in the second ballot, it would be a pyrrhic victory. Moreover, the question of the succession would remain unresolved. The best interests of the party now required Thatcher to resign, a decision that she would reluctantly come to realise (Jeffreys, 2002:248).

5.4   The Resignation of Margaret Thatcher

The immediate response of Thatcher to the declaration of the result of the first ballot would produce one of the iconographic images of post-war British politics. Emerging from the British Embassy, she happened to be being broadcast live on the BBC. The electorate then witnessed her press secretary, Bernard Ingham, manhandling the BBC political correspondent, John Sargeant, out of the way, to enable Thatcher to comment on the outcome. She announced that

> I am naturally very pleased that I got more than half the parliamentary party and disappointed that it is not quite enough to win on the first ballot, so I confirm that it is my *intention* to let my name go forward to the second ballot.[19]   (Watkins, 1991:3)

If the immediate reaction of Thatcher and the Thatcherites was one of disbelief and confusion, then Heseltine and his acolytes were ecstatic. They assumed that if Thatcher and Heseltine remained the only two participants in the second ballot, then a Heseltine victory was a distinct possibility. To secure a second ballot victory, they required only a parliamentary majority, as the fifteen per cent threshold was removed after the first ballot. Heseltine needed to add a further twenty-seven and his acolytes believed that this was a surmountable hurdle. Their confidence stemmed from a belief that the dynamics of a second ballot between Thatcher and Heseltine would be different. They believed that many Conservative parliamentarians, and especially ministers, had endorsed Thatcher due to their instinctive loyalty to the party and the incumbent leader. Heseltine advocates believed that such individuals had now fulfilled their loyalty obligation, and sensing the way in which the political wind was blowing, a sufficient amount would switch their allegiances to Heseltine. It was somewhat ironic that at this stage, Heseltine needed Thatcher to remain in the second ballot. By remaining in the contest, she would (presumably) prevent Major and Hurd, from entering. The probability of Heseltine emerging victorious was now greater in a Thatcher versus Heseltine rematch, than if Heseltine contested the party leadership against both Hurd and Major. After spending nearly five years waiting for Thatcher to resign, Heseltine now needed her not to (Crick, 1997:349). The Heseltine campaign team were euphoric when Thatcher re-affirmed her intention to continue the following day.[20] She informed the assembled media, in unambiguous language that: 'I fight on, I fight to win' (Thatcher, 1993:849).

Despite her public confidence, Thatcher was increasingly aware of the obstacles that existed to her survival. Tim Renton,[21] the Chief Whip, informed her that his intelligence suggested that she was losing support already. He informed her that twenty-five of her first ballot supporters were now indicating that they would not endorse her in the second ballot. Given that Heseltine was the only positive option available to them, and assuming they all endorsed him, that placed the weight of support at Thatcher 179 and Heseltine 177, with the sixteen abstainers from the first ballot the key determinants of the succession. Renton suggested that Thatcher would lose narrowly and that her best case scenario was a narrow victory, although this would be immensely damaging to the electoral prospects of the party.[22] He advised Thatcher to resign for two reasons: first, she could not defeat Heseltine; and, second, his intelligence suggested that the parliamentary party wanted new candidates to be freed to enter the second ballot (Shepherd, 1991:37).

Having consulted with Renton, Thatcher also took soundings with various senior figures within the Conservative Party, such as the Party Chairman, Kenneth Baker, John MacGregor, her newly appointed Leader of the House of Commons, and John Wakeham, who she drafted in to replace Younger as her campaign manager for the second ballot.[23] Despite the encouragement of Wakeham and Baker, Thatcher would admit in her memoirs that:

> The message of the meeting (on the afternoon after the first ballot), even from those urging me to fight on, was implicitly demoralising. Though I had never been defeated in a general election, retained the support of the party in the country, and had just won the support of the party in parliament, the best thing that could be said of me, apparently, was that I was better placed than other candidates to beat Michael Heseltine. But even this was uncertain since my strongest supporters doubted I could win, and others believed that even if I succeeded in that, I would be unable to unite the party afterwards for the general election. And hanging over all of this was the dread much invoked spectre of humiliation if I were to fight and lose.   (Thatcher, 1993:849)

It was her consultations with Renton that began the process that would drain her of her resolve to remain in the leadership election. That evening she met individually with the majority of her Cabinet. Through these consultations it became clear to Thatcher that her Cabinet colleagues believed that she would not emerge victorious, and that the best interests of the party would be served by allowing a non-Thatcher, non-Heseltine, compromise candidate to emerge.

The collapse of support within the Cabinet was matched elsewhere. Her newly appointed campaign manager for the second ballot, Wakeham, informed Thatcher that he was struggling to form a viable campaign team. Richard Ryder and Tristan Garel-Jones, both of whom had been involved in her re-election the previous autumn, had refused invitations to mobilise support for her as they believed her position was futile. Wakeham also reported that she was haemorrhaging support amongst those who had endorsed her in the first ballot; over and beyond the levels that Renton had indicated to her earlier in the day.

Even a redoubtable political fighter such as Thatcher realised that the laws of parliamentary arithmetic were beyond reversal. On the morning of November 22nd 1990, just two days after the first ballot, she informed that Cabinet

> Having consulted widely among my colleagues, I have concluded that the unity of the party and the prospects of victory in a general election would be better served if I stood down to enable Cabinet colleagues to enter the ballot for the leadership.   (Thatcher, 1993:857)

5.5   The Default Victory of John Major

For Thatcher, the rationale for resigning revolved around protecting her political legacy. By resigning she enabled Major and Hurd to oppose Heseltine. This fundamentally altered the dynamics of the party leadership election in a manner that was detrimental to Heseltine. If his best case scenario had been Thatcher remaining in the contest in a two way contest, then his next best scenario was contesting the succession against either Major or Hurd, preferably Hurd. His worst case scenario was that both entered. That both of them entered was deliberate and was designed to impede the chances of Heseltine being successful.

A three way succession battle, given the configuration of the candidates, undermined Heseltine as ideology, and specifically attitudes towards the European ideological divide, would influence voting intentions. In this context, it was assumed that the Thatcherite Eurosceptic voting block would gravitate towards Major, as the most Eurosceptic of the three candidates, leaving the pro-European Tory left to choose between Hurd and Heseltine. Those who opposed Heseltine ideologically and opposed his disloyalty now had a natural candidate (Major), whilst those who ideologically sympathised with Heseltine had the option of Hurd, if they were repelled by the disloyalty of Heseltine. Major and Hurd could both present themselves as loyalists and unifiers whilst Heseltine would have to fend off accusations of disloyalty and disunity (Shepherd, 1991:68-69).

The Major campaign gathered momentum quickly. Supported by an able team of mid-ranking ministers and rising Cabinet ministers such as Norman Lamont, Michael Howard, Ian Lang and Gillian Shepherd, Major ran an astute campaign (Seldon, 1997:124). His endorsement from Thatcher and her dedication to canvassing support for him (somewhat ironic given her disinterest in canvassing for herself) helped to ensure that her natural Thatcherite allies gravitated to him.[24] In an attempt to demonstrate the breadth of his appeal, Major crafted his appeal around the notion of a classless society which had the potential to appeal to the Tory left. He attempted to erode the bases of the Heseltine first ballot vote, by offering a review of the poll tax, thus critically nullifying one of the rationales for embracing Heseltine. What really galvanised the Major campaign, however, was the reaction of the electorate to a relatively unknown politician. Opinion polling evidence suggested that Major was just as, if not more, capable of leading the Conservatives to electoral victory as Heseltine. This fatally undermined Heseltine. His biggest asset was his supposed electoral popularity. This was now matched by Major, yet Major had fewer enemies, and was not known for his disloyalty. It was assumed that Major was a unifier and healer, whilst Heseltine would cause further disunity. Conservative parliamentarians began to gravitate to Major, under the belief that he was the best positioned candidate to unite the party after the disunity and brutality of removing Thatcher (Norton, 1992:59).

Despite their assumed gentlemanly relationship, much of the Major campaign strategy seemed designed to undermine Hurd, as well as Heseltine. Major attempted to configure the campaigning period around issues to do with economic management. Whilst his rationale for doing so was because it dominated electoral politics, it was also tactically astute as this was where his ministerial experience lay. Whilst this attempted to undermine Heseltine, who was distrusted by Thatcherite dries for his interventionist inclinations, it also served to highlight how the ministerial career of Hurd had been detached from the issues of economic management (Shepherd, 1991:71). Perhaps of greater subliminal impact was the appeal for a classless society that Major embraced. By constructing a class based strategy that emphasised social mobility, he narrated his candidature around his own humble upbringing. The indirect consequence of doing so highlighted the social background of Hurd. Some Conservative parliamentarians admitted that they could not endorse Hurd, due to his Etonian background. This was then compared to the last Etonian compromise candidate to assume the party leadership: Douglas-Home. This image of a discredited compromise and socially elitist figure, and the fact that the Conservatives then lost the forthcoming general election, undermined the candidature of Hurd (Shepherd, 1991:69; Stark, 1996:112).

Hurd's social background became a pivotal issue in destroying the viability of his candidature (Watkins, 1991:198). Despite constructing an impressive campaigning team, including Kenneth Clarke, Chris and John Patten, Malcolm Rifkind and William Waldegrave, his campaign never gathered any momentum (Seldon, 1997:124). His main impediment was his lack of electoral appeal and the fact that he failed to offer a distinctive policy platform or narrate a vision of a Hurd led Conservative Party. The cumulative effect of these limitations and the fact that Major appeared to outdo his biggest appeal – i.e. as a unifying presence – meant that Hurd was unable to mobilise support (Shepherd, 1991:70).

The rapid mobilisation of support around Major had undermined the viability of both Hurd and Heseltine. As the ballot approached it was widely assumed that Major would come first, the key questions were: would he secure a majority; how big would his lead be over Heseltine, and how big would be the gap between Heseltine and Hurd? Although they were pessimistic about their chances, Heseltine supporters still clung to the possibility that Major could be prevented from winning on the second ballot and that Heseltine would be sufficiently close to be competitive in a two-way third ballot. If Major secured around 160, Heseltine could score around 150 votes by squeezing the Hurd share down to around 50, then Heseltine might have a chance of winning a third ballot by sweeping up second preference Hurd votes. Such optimism was misplaced (Shepherd, 1991:77).

Table 8:   Candidate Support in the Second Ballot of the Conservative Party Leadership Election of 1990

	First Ballot	Percentage
John Major	185	49.7
Michael Heseltine	131	35.2
Douglas Hurd	56	15.1

Source: Quinn, 2005:812

When the result was announced, Hurd immediately withdrew and instructed his supporters to embrace Major. Heseltine knew the gap between himself and Major was too large to have any realistic chance of prevailing in the third ballot, and therefore he also withdrew and like Hurd instructed his supporters to endorse Major (Shepherd, 1991:78). Technically the rules demanded that a third ballot be conducted as Major had not secured a majority of Conservative parliamentarians. Given that Major was the only candidate for the third ballot it was decided to cancel it and acclaim Major as the new leader of the Conservative Party and the new Prime Minister. The decision not to hold a third ballot, whilst procedurally incorrect seemed a pragmatic course of action. But Major would have benefited from a third ballot and a unanimous vote as this would have stopped Thatcherites from bleating on about how Thatcher won 204 votes (a majority) and was forced to resign and Major won 185 votes (a minority) and was endorsed as leader[25] (Shepherd, 1991:79).

5.6   Why Margaret Thatcher and Michael Heseltine Lost and John Major Triumphed

To offer a fully contextualised explanation of the cataclysmic events of November 1990 requires us to address three questions: first, why did the challenge by Heseltine result in the resignation of Thatcher; second, why did the wielder of the dagger, Heseltine, fail to inherit the throne; and how did an inexperienced political light-heavyweight (relative to both Thatcher and Heseltine) emerge victorious?

Explaining the political assassination of Thatcher requires an appreciation of the interaction of the tactical and strategic errors of Thatcher and her acolytes with political circumstance. Had Howe offered his resignation at a time that did not coincide with the deadline for nominations for the party leadership election (i.e. any other time than early in the new parliamentary session) then it would not have been so politically significant. The timing of his resignation speech then coincided with the presence of a credible alternative party leader, whose opposition to Thatcher was both ideologically and stylistically based. Without the presence of Heseltine then the reference that Howe made that 'the time had come for others to consider their own response' would have been less politically explosive (Jeffreys, 2002:254, 258).

Although circumstance contributed to the downfall of Thatcher, what is remarkable about her denouement was her own complete failure to protect her position as party leader. She made the strategic error in the second part of her tenure as party leader and Prime Minister of accumulating too many high profile political enemies. Her mismanagement of Conservative elites created a dangerous triumvirate of enemies in the shape of Heseltine, Lawson and Howe (Jeffreys, 2002:254). Despite her contemptuous view of Heseltine, her political antennae should have indicated that his threat to her needed to be negated. She could have negated the threat that he offered as a potential alternative party leader, by identifying an heir apparent and grooming them for the succession. As indicated earlier, she had regarded Tebbit, Ridley, Parkinson, Lawson, Howe and of course Heseltine, as inappropriate for differing reasons. Despite their career advancements she doubted the resolve of Hurd and questioned the experience of Major (Thatcher, 1993:758, 831). The dual impact of her implacable desire to remain as party leader and her failure to advance a non-Heseltine successor, ensured that the viability of Heseltine as the leading alternative was enhanced.

This long term strategic failing was then compounded by a multitude of tactical mistakes made during the course of November 1990. Her campaign for re-election was derided for its ineptitude; indeed the Heseltine campaign team themselves were staggered at the amateurish approach of the Thatcher campaign (Shepherd, 1991:20; Stark, 1996:110). The two pivotal players in her re-election campaign were George Younger and Peter Morrison.[26] Younger nominally headed the Thatcher campaign but his business commitments would make him a detached and ineffective participant (Watkins, 1991:178).[27] His detachment placed increased responsibility on her parliamentary Private Secretary, Morrison, whose contribution to her campaign has been widely criticised.

Conservative parliamentarian, Steven Norris, identified two fundamental faults with the conduct of the Thatcher campaign. First, Morrison did not take any precaution to ensure that pledges of support were real. A passing conversation between Morrison and Norris led Morrison to assume that Norris would endorse Thatcher, when in effect he endorsed Heseltine (Norris, 1996:155). This lack of thoroughness in the approach to canvassing was a contributing factor to the inaccuracy of the predictions that Morrison had of how well Thatcher would perform[28] (Stark, 1996:214). Second, Norris believes that Thatcher misused the advantages of incumbency that were at her disposal. She chose not to engage in any personal canvassing of support.[29] Her rationale for doing so was clear, even if her argument that she should not have to go around begging for their votes appeared somewhat arrogant (Brunson, 2000:173). Her refusal to do so would mean that she failed to exploit two potential advantages: first, persuasive arguments based on loyalty; and second, persuasive arguments based on personal inducements (e.g. ministerial office, knighthoods) (Norris, 1996:155).

Beyond her failure to assemble a credible campaigning team and her refusal to engage in personal canvassing, Thatcher made two key errors of judgement. First, she allowed her personal hostility towards Heseltine to infect the few public pronouncements that she chose to make regarding his challenge to her party leadership. Her denunciation of Heseltine, which involved accusing him of advocating policies akin to those of the Labour Party, was counter-productive. They served to make her look extremist and Heseltine was able to deftly ensure that they rebounded on her. He countered by arguing that if his governing philosophy and political views were so unacceptable to her, then why had she retained him in the Cabinet between 1979 and 1986 (Crick, 1997:348). The second and even more damaging error of judgement was the decision to attend the European Summit in Paris, which coincided with the day of the party leadership ballot. Her desire to play the role of world leader, rather than shore up her position as party leader, suggested that she was indifferent to the concerns of her parliamentary colleagues and that she was underestimating the level of discontent (Stark, 1996:110-111). Given the marginal numerical failure of Thatcher to prevail in the first ballot, it has been suggested that this was the critical misjudgement of the Thatcher campaign. Had she remained and canvassed vigorously she may well have prevailed in the first ballot (Fowler, 1991: 350-351).

Whilst acknowledging that mistakes were made in the implementation of her re-election campaign, Thatcher was clear on who was responsible for her political downfall. Rather than attribute blame to Heseltine or even to Howe, she has attributed responsibility to the Cabinet (Parkinson, 1992:4). She came to believe that the fatal procession of Cabinet ministers, adhering to the same mantra that they would support her but did not believe she could prevail, was the cause of her eventual decision not to fight on. The desertion of her Cabinet colleagues devastated her, on a personal as well as a political level. She would later, somewhat melodramatically, accuse them of 'treachery with a smile on its face' (Thatcher, 1993:855).[30] Such an assertion is understandable, but somewhat misplaced. The Cabinet coalesced to persuade Thatcher to resign for a specific reason: to prevent Heseltine winning. Therefore, the Cabinet critically undermined the party leadership chances of Heseltine. Understanding why provides part of the explanation to the second dilemma: why did the wielder of the dagger, Heseltine, fail to inherent the throne?

The candidature of Heseltine was based on his outsider status (Foley, 1993:187). The loyalty imperative had ensured that virtually all ministers within the Thatcher government were obliged to endorse Thatcher, meaning that the Heseltine vote bloc was a backbench vote bloc. Senior figures who would endorse him (e.g. Lawson, Howe, Walker, Gilmour and Prior) were no longer Cabinet ministers, and therein lay a difficulty for Heseltine (Crick, 1997:353). Heseltine lacked ministerial support and especially Cabinet support. This lack of Cabinet support was crucial when we consider the nature of the resignation speech that Thatcher presented to Cabinet. In resignation, Thatcher extracted an agreement from the Cabinet that they unite to prevent Heseltine from prevailing (Crick, 1997:351). This was hardly surprising given that this had been their rationale for her standing aside. Ultimately, with the exception of David Hunt, all of the Cabinet rejected the idea of gravitating to Heseltine. The virtual unification of the Cabinet against Heseltine, was then broadly replicated at junior ministerial level, thus consolidating the bloc of insider elites opposed to Heseltine prevailing (Crick, 1997:353).

This inability to attract Conservative elites to his cause had created perception difficulties to his candidature for the first ballot. The aforementioned loyalty imperative meant that Heseltine had to base his campaign around backbenchers. Consequently, the calibre of his campaign team was remarkable weak and they did not carry sufficient levels of respect within the parliamentary Conservative Party (Crick, 1997:346). The emphasis on the ineptitude of the Thatcher campaign masks the failings that undermined the Heseltine campaign. The most illuminating and intriguing critique of the Heseltine campaign has been articulated by Crick. He argues that in the aftermath of the first ballot, Heseltine needed Thatcher to believe that she should remain in the contest and ensure that Hurd and Major would / could not enter. As such, everything that they did and said should have been designed to ensure that she did not resign. They chose at this moment to talk of the candidate's momentum and in the process appeared triumphant. Crick believes that this was tactically inept. They needed to downplay their prospects and only talk of momentum once the deadline for nominations for the second ballot has passed (Crick, 1997:350). Crick argues that with greater tactical dexterity they could have engineered it to ensure that the only option to Thatcher was Heseltine. He states that:

> The intriguing and paradoxical question is whether Michael Heseltine could have done anything to persuade Thatcher to stay in the fight. Perhaps his campaign should have arranged for some supporters to announce that, while they had backed him in the first round, the interests of party unity dictated that they support the leader next time. It would have been difficult to pull off, and highly Machiavellian, but deviousness is what leadership elections are all about. A more realistic course might have been to remind people of the precarious nature of Heseltine's first round support. Many people in the first ballot had voted tactically – not so much *for* Heseltine, as *against* Thatcher – knowing that other candidates might join the contest in round two. These tactical voters might easily have returned to Thatcher once it was clear she refused to quit and there would be no alternatives on offer. Had the drift of opinion looked at all ambiguous – or been presented as such – then Thatcher might have been persuaded to battle on.
>
> (Crick, 1997:350)

Tactical ineptitude and campaigning failings undermined both the Thatcher and Heseltine candidatures and provide explanations as to why both of the political heavyweights lost. What we still require is an explanation on how Major, an inexperienced political light-heavyweight (relative to both Thatcher and Heseltine), was able to emerge victorious. Once he entered the succession battle, the Major candidature benefited from three factors. First, he ran an effective campaign. His background in the Whips' Office had helped him to understand the parliamentary Conservative Party and had enabled him to cultivate a network of allies. His campaign was able to mobilise latent support quickly and thus gather momentum in a manner that ensured that the Hurd candidature (as the alternative non-Heseltine candidate) was marginalised (Seldon, 1997:127). Second, momentum was acquired as Conservative parliamentarians were affected by opinion poll findings that suggested that Major was just as capable of winning an election as Heseltine. Major could therefore offer all of the advantages of Heseltine (revisionist thinking on the poll tax and electoral appeal) without the disadvantage of disunity and disloyalty. Third, Major benefited from the fact that he was now the chosen successor of Thatcher. Her vigorous campaigning on his behalf ensured that the Thatcherite right were guided towards the candidature of Major (Seldon, 1997:127-128).

Ultimately, Major acquired the party leadership on the back of an ideologically motivated bloc vote. Utilising the extensive research of Cowley and Garry on how and why Major won, reveals the centrality of ideology as a voting determinant for Conservative parliamentarians.[31] From this they deduce that on the economic policy ideological divide, economic wets were inclined towards Heseltine or Hurd, whilst economic dries tended to endorse Major. On the European ideological policy divide, they concluded that Europhiles were inclined towards either Heseltine or Hurd; whilst Eurosceptics were predominantly Major supporters. On social, sexual and moral policy, social liberals were inclined towards either Heseltine or Hurd, whilst social conservatives gravitated towards Major. Therefore, Major secured the party leadership through the support of the Thatcherite right. His candidature was rejected by the Tory left who voted predominantly for Heseltine with a minority gravitating towards Hurd (Cowley and Garry, 1998:479-480). We can argue, however, that many of the problems that Major was to have in securing his authority over the parliamentary Conservative Party stemmed from doubts surrounding his legitimacy as party leader:

> His acquisition of the leadership of the Conservative Party was not the by-product of a groundswell of pro-Major Conservative parliamentarians proactively seeking his advancement to propel him into power. The vast majority of his support came from Conservative parliamentarians whose preference was still Thatcher and had voted for her continuance only days earlier. Major may have been the choice of the Thatcherite right but he was not their first choice. Moreover, that fact that those Thatcherites gravitated towards him was due to their desire to prevent her nemesis, Heseltine, from acquiring the leadership of the Conservative Party. Collectively, we can argue that he was the second choice of the Thatcherites (after Thatcher) and that his support was not the product of a pro-Major vote, but rather an anti-Heseltine vote. It amounted to a default victory.   (Heppell, 2006:241-242)

5.7   Conclusion

The Conservatives appetite for power explained the brutal removal of Thatcher from the party leadership. They were willing to offer their support to her, and accept her ideological excursions and her confrontational style, when she was able to demonstrate governing effectiveness and electoral appeal. Once her third term administration presided which over economic recession became internally divided, and Thatcher herself became perceived to be an electoral liability, her critics mobilised to remove her from the party leadership.

Her removal and replacement with Major seemed to be a brilliant piece of political renewal. Many of the primary obstacles to retaining power (e.g. the poll tax, electoral hostility towards Thatcher) had been removed. Major then proceeded to achieve what many Conservatives feared Thatcher would not be able to achieve: he won a fourth successive term. Thereafter, the view that it amounted to a brilliant short-term strategy of political renewal was exposed. The subsequent implosion of the Major era was a by product of the fact that the Conservative body politic had been infected with ideologically and personally motivated poison. That poison flowed from the process through which Thatcher was forcibly evicted from office.

The recriminations that surrounded her eviction completely immobilised the party leadership of Major. Once he had retained power for the Conservatives, his capacity to govern effectively and demonstrate his merits as party leader, were constantly undermined by the disputation between Thatcher and the Eurosceptic right (the majority of whom had voted for Thatcher to remain as party leader) and Heseltine and the pro-European left (the majority of whom had voted for Heseltine to become party leader). Therefore, post-1992 Major was thus haunted by two ghosts. On the Thatcherite right and out of government was the ghost of the vanquished Thatcher, bitter and resentful at her eviction. Increasingly critical of Major, her continued high public profile served to undermine her successor and indirectly encourage the Thatcherite right, especially Eurosceptics, to destabilise his party leadership. On the Tory left and now in Cabinet again was the defeated Heseltine, bemused by his failure to triumph but still evaluating his chances to succeed should Major fail.

The two factions became obsessed with revisiting the process that brought Thatcher down. Acolytes of Thatcher bridled at a process that involved her securing a parliamentary majority and losing power, whilst Major secured a minority and was ritually acclaimed. Heseltine and his acolytes had to deal with the ramifications of being accused of disloyalty and disuniting the party. They also had cause to regret their own tactical and strategic miscalculations. Heseltine had wanted to avoid a direct challenge to Thatcher himself, hoping that another backbencher would act as a stalking horse challenge who fatally wounded Thatcher causing her withdrawal, thus enabling the electorally appealing Heseltine to emerge through the second ballot stage. One political heavyweight, Heseltine, knocked out another political heavyweight, Thatcher. In the process he succeeded in knocking himself out, leaving the political light-heavyweight, Major as the victor. Heseltine had been the stalking horse for Major.

PUT UP OR SHUT UP: JOHN REDWOOD CHALLENGES JOHN MAJOR

The Conservatives had deposed Thatcher in an act of self-preservation. To secure an unprecedented fourth successive electoral success necessitated a change in the party leadership. Major had been elected to secure that objective. If he succeeded it would vindicate the decision of the parliamentary Conservative Party in evicting Thatcher. Of greater significance it would provide Major with his *own* mandate to govern. Securing his own mandate would enhance his authority and legitimacy as party leader, and in doing so it would enhance his security of tenure. Major was desperate to win and enhance his position. He knew the implications should he fail. He knew that until he secured his own general election success, he would be compared to Alec Douglas-Home. Both had assumed the party leadership in controversial circumstances; both had acquired the party leadership against expectations, and both were perceived to be affable but limited political operators, devoid of a clear agenda for the future of Conservatism. Furthermore, both had acquired the party leadership towards the end of a third Conservative term. Douglas-Home had then lost the ensuing general election and had ceased to be party leader within a year of leaving Downing Street. Major wanted to avoid the Douglas-Home precedent of a short tenure as Prime Minister, a general election reversal, and an end to his party leadership tenure. It was assumed that the Conservatives would still lose under Major; it was therefore assumed that leading Conservatives were positioning themselves for a hypothetical party leadership election in opposition (Seldon, 1997:219).

Major confounded expectations, both those of fellow Conservatives and the opinion pollsters. In the general election that the Conservatives were expected to lose, Major had saved them. It is somewhat ironic, however, that having secured his own personal mandate to govern, by winning the general election, his authority over the parliamentary Conservative Party and his legitimacy as party leader, was to become widely questioned. The insecurity of tenure that he was to suffer post-1992 manifested itself in a near permanent state of speculation that a formal challenge to his party leadership was imminent.[1] Although no formal challenge was initiated in the autumns of 1992, 1993 or 1994, the speculation surrounding the possibility of a challenge, if not the actuality of one, contributed to the ongoing erosion of his authority over the parliamentary Conservative Party and legitimacy as party leader (Alderman, 1996:317, 329). In June 1995, Major mounted a desperate attempt to reclaim his rapidly diminishing authority and legitimacy and ensure his security of tenure until the general election. He challenged his critics to put up or shut up, by resigning as party leader, but not as Prime Minister, and standing as a candidate for the self-created vacancy. Through this process he emerged victorious having overcome a challenge from the Thatcherite Cabinet Minister, John Redwood. However, the futility of the put up or shut up strategy was evident as the Conservatives suffered a cataclysmic electoral meltdown in the general election of 1997.

6.1   The Multiple Crises of the Major Government

The Major era evolved against the back drop of a ghost from the past and the spectres of the present (McAnulla, 1999:193-194). The ghost was Thatcher herself. As the Conservatives experienced political turbulence under Major, many Conservatives, who had begun mythologizing the Thatcher era, compared him unfavourably to his predecessor. She was radical, ideological and colourful, whereas Major was consensual, pragmatic and dull. Where she offered conviction, Major appeared to be dithering (Smith and Ludlam, 1996:5). Her influence from beyond the grave served to constrain Major. Many of her acolytes believed that the treacherous manner in which she had been forcibly evicted from the party leadership had severed the legitimate order through which authority and legitimacy should be passed from incumbent party leader to the next. A vocal minority would not transfer their loyalty, deference, obedience and allegiance to her successor.

The spectre of the present was the existence of an ideologically fractious parliamentary Conservative Party *and* a narrow parliamentary majority post-1992. This necessitated compromise and contributed to the evolution of a betrayal thesis within the Thatcherite right of the parliamentary Conservative Party. The betrayal thesis was predicated on the assumption that it was the Thatcherite right that had secured Major the party leadership in November 1990, whereupon Major abandoned them (Gorman, 1993:16). The betrayal thesis, which revolved around the contours of economic and especially European policy, would act as the catalyst for the resentment that would destabilize his party leadership from the autumn of 1992 onwards.

In addition to the ghosts of the past and the spectres of the present, Major suffered from the circumstances through which he acquired the party leadership. The calamitous events of November 1990 had destroyed the assumption that an incumbent Conservative Prime Minister should not be challenged. This ensured that successive Conservative Prime Ministers would be vulnerable to the threat of removal. Major would be the victim of the establishment of this destabilizing precedent. He also stood vulnerable to the accusation that the renewal of a degenerating long serving government, (which his was), could be circumvented by changing the leader of the governing party. During their third term, the Conservatives had removed Thatcher. This had created a misplaced assumption within a section of the electorate that a new government had been formed and was thus absolved of responsibility for past misdeeds. The consequence of this misplaced assumption was a sharp increase in support for the Conservatives, an increase which helped to propel them to a fourth successive electoral triumph. Applying the logic that of this regeneration strategy suggested that the removal of Major (mid-term) would have potential benefits. Major stood vulnerable to the renewal precedent that had been established so successfully against his predecessor (Gilmour and Garnett, 1998:373).

These embedded themes within post-Thatcherite Conservative Party politics – the de-stabilizing precedents established through the political execution of Margaret Thatcher and the evolving betrayal thesis of the Thatcherite ideologues on the right of the parliamentary Conservative Party – amounted to a significant constraint upon the party leadership tenure of Major. To overcome these constraints demanded that the Major Government was politically popular and governmentally competent. The Major Government was neither. A symbiotic relationship existed between perceptions of governmental incompetence and the erosion of the authority that Major had over the parliamentary Conservative Party, his legitimacy as party leader, and his insecurity of tenure.

Within eighteen months of securing their re-election in April 1992, the Major Government was irreparably damaged by two catastrophic policy failures – the expulsion from the Exchange Rate Mechanism (September 1992) and the economic mismanagement associated with this that would necessitate increases in taxation (March 1993).[2] The humiliating ejection from the Exchange Rate Mechanism was the defining moment of the Major Government. It carried with it five destabilizing precedents. First, it destroyed the economic and European policy strategies of the Major Government. Second, it destroyed the reputation that the Conservatives had for governing competence in the sphere of economic management. Third, it unleashed latent Euroscepticism within the parliamentary Conservative Party and rapidly increased the complexities of intra-party management with regard to the intended ratification of the Treaty of European Union.[3] Fourth, the post-

Black Wednesday economic policy strategy would contradict an article of faith that the Conservatives were the party of low taxation.[4] Fifth, it destroyed the credibility of Major as party leader. Major was immediately aware of the damage that had been inflicted upon his leadership credibility. He would later admit that:

> My own instinct was clear. I should resign. I was not sure I could ever recover politically from the devaluation of the currency. The collapse of sterling was a catastrophic defeat, and one which I felt profoundly. It had been a traumatic day that would change the perception of the government: we were never able to enjoy the same confidence as before Black Wednesday.   (Major, 1999:334-335)

Ultimately, Major decided to not to resign,[5] having rationalised that he preferred that to the condemnation that he would receive for abandoning the party, and plunging it into a leadership vacuum, at a time when decisions needed to be taken immediately (Major, 1999:334).

The cumulative effect was that criticism of his party leadership entered the recognized protocols of Conservative Party political conduct. The residual gratitude that the parliamentary Conservative Party had for him for retaining their status in government evaporated: the erosion of authority and legitimacy within the parliamentary Conservative Party intensified and his continuance as party leader became a subject of omnipresent debate. Speculation over whether he should be subject to a leadership challenge first surfaced in the immediate aftermath of Black Wednesday (Seldon, 1997:319). As the rumblings of discontent intensified throughout 1993 and 1994, a state of leadership paralysis engulfed the Conservatives.

The critical question is why no formal challenge was initiated in 1993 or 1994, either a stalking horse candidate to aid the chances of an ideological bedfellow, or a serious challenge from a candidate who could realistically defeat Major themselves. On the first dilemma, it is possible to argue that initiating a stalking horse candidature had been complicated by the leadership election rules amendments of 1991. Quinn argues that the amendment, which stated that an annual contest could only be activated if ten per cent of Conservative parliamentarians agreed, made the initiation of a challenge harder than when Thatcher had been disposed. This meant that Major was the subject of endless ideologically motivated plots suggesting that a leadership election was imminent, but his critics could not mobilise the necessary number of dissenters to initiate a challenge (Quinn, 2005:802).

To address the second dilemma, of why a political heavyweight did not challenge Major, requires an examination of the leadership strategies of the leading alternatives to Major: i.e. Clarke, Heseltine, Portillo and Howard. In the 1993 to 1994 period, the leading Thatcherite Eurosceptics, Howard and

Portillo had not acquired sufficient levels of political credibility to be confident that the balance of risk (and the likelihood of victory) would justify resignation and launching a leadership challenge. On the Europhile Tory left, both Clarke and especially Heseltine[6] realised that initiating the challenge would limit their likelihood of emerging victorious. Therefore, Major's critics could not mobilise a stalking horse candidature,[7] as the entry threshold had been raised, and the leading alternative heavyweight candidates could not risk initiating a challenge.

With each year, however, the credibility of the threat to his party leadership was ratcheted up to such an extent that the threat of a challenge was enough to diminish his authority and therefore his legitimacy (Alderman, 1996:17). Moreover, it seemed inevitable that a formal challenge to his party leadership would occur in November 1995 (Gilmour and Garnett, 1998:371; Clark, 1998:512). Given such frenzied speculation Major had three options available to him. First, he could resign in the interests of party unity. Second, he could ignore the speculation, on the basis that the speculation of 1992, 1993 and 1994 had not resulted in a formal challenge. Or third, he could force an immediate Conservative Party leadership election by resigning and standing for the self-created vacancy.

Two destabilizing events occurred in June 1995, which would contribute to a beleaguered Prime Minister selecting the final option. First, the ghost of Thatcher resurfaced. Promoting the second volume of her memoirs, she accused Major of 'dodging key issues, splitting the party over Europe, causing a needlessly long recession (by trying to maintain Britain in the Exchange Rate Mechanism for so long) and for pursuing misguided social and taxation policies' (Seldon, 1997:561). Alongside praise for the leadership capability of Tony Blair, she sent an outline of how the Conservatives could recover, but chillingly noting that it was 'for others to take the action required'. The politically astute realised that this was code for her view that Major needed to be removed from the party leadership (Seldon, 1997:561). Second, given the Eurosceptic tone to Thatcher's interventions, Major attempted to shore up his position by meeting the Fresh Start grouping of Eurosceptic Conservative backbenchers – his most visceral critics. A bruising and disrespectful encounter ensued. Major now realised that the Fresh Start grouping had two campaigning objectives: first, to alter the direction of European policy; and, second, to remove him from the party leadership as a pre-requisite for the attainment of the first objective. Major knew that he was deposable: internal party intelligence presented to him suggested that at least seventy Conservative parliamentarians were now committed to the notion of a leadership election (Seldon, 1997:561, 568; Major, 1999:614).

Major thus opted for the high risk and unprecedented third option, primarily because of his belief that the current position was untenable. The tactic was employed because all other alternative tactics utilized between autumn 1992 and June 1995 to dampen down the frenzy over European policy, (whether confidence votes, dissolution threats, withdrawal of the whip) had failed. The failure of those aforementioned tactics had eroded the authority that Major needed to possess over the parliamentary Conservative Party to ensure his legitimacy as party leader.

In June 1995, in the picturesque surroundings of the Downing Street rose garden, Major stunned the assembled media, arguing that:

> I've now been Prime Minister for nearly five years. In that time we've achieved a great deal, but for the last three years, I have been opposed by a small minority in our party. During those three years there have been repeated threats of a leadership election. In each year they turned out to be phoney threats. Now the same thing is happening in 1995. I believe it is no-one's interest that this continues right through to November. It undermines the government and it damages the Conservative party....To remove this uncertainty I have this afternoon tendered my resignation as leader of the Conservative party and requested that the machinery for the election of a successor is set in motion. I shall be a candidate in that election. If I win, I shall continue as Prime Minister[8] and will lead the party into and through the next election. Should I be defeated, which I do not expect, I shall resign as Prime Minister and offer my successor my full support...*The Conservative Party must make its choice. Every leader is leader only with the support of his party.* That is true of me as well. That is why I am not prepared to tolerate the present situation. In short, it is time to put up or shut up. (Seldon, 1997:571)

6.2   The Critics of John Major: Bastards or Cowards?

The nuclear tactic that Major deployed amounted to a desperate act of expedience into which he had been propelled due to the lack of authority that he possessed within the parliamentary Conservative Party. He had been unable to suppress the dissension of his Eurosceptic critics, who he had derided as bastards,[9] so he manufactured a face off between himself and them. He had calculated that the bastards would be cowards. By initiating the put and shut up strategy, Major had envisaged a scenario within which his authority and legitimacy would be reclaimed after an unopposed contest. From this he assumed that his critics would be silenced and their silence would remain for the duration of the Parliament thus ensuring his security of tenure as party leader (Alderman, 1996:318-319; Denver, 1998:25; Williams, 1998:83).

The rationale for activating the leadership election was that a small and unrepresentative minority of critics, the bastards within the parliamentary Conservative Party, were undermining his capacity to lead. The validity of this assertion rested on one of two scenarios: first, no candidature being put forward (besides Major) to contest the vacancy; or, second, the candidature being put forward being known for their membership of that small and unrepresentative minority. Any candidature from within the ministerial ranks, and especially from within Cabinet, would undermine the apparent motivational basis upon which the Major had activated the election.

As the Conservative Party recovered from the shock of the announcement, it soon became clear that scenario one (no other candidate than Major) was unlikely. Scenario two seemed the most likely outcome (a challenge from the unrepresentative minority). Speculation suggested that the candidate to fulfil that role would be Norman Lamont (Lamont, 2000:435-439). The former Chancellor, who had been the campaign manager that helped Major secure the party leadership, had seen his working relationship with the Prime Minister collapse in the aftermath of Black Wednesday. Lamont was deeply wounded by his subsequent dismissal from the Treasury eight months later. A challenge would be one based on principle (their divergent views on Europe) but it would also be personal (a resentful Lamont could gain revenge on Major). Major had assumed that if a challenge were to emerge, it would be from Lamont. Given the criticism that Lamont had heaped upon him, Major was reported to be welcoming the opportunity to silence his former Cabinet colleague[10] (Seldon, 1997:574).

The expectation that it would be Lamont stemmed from an assumption that the Cabinet had been bound into the decision. The leading Europhile candidates for the succession, Clarke and Heseltine, had been informed of the strategy that Major had in mind, although they were, just like the leading Eurosceptic right candidates, Howard and Portillo, wrong footed by it. At this initial juncture, both of the Europhiles, Clarke and Heseltine, remained publicly loyal. Tactically it made no sense for them to resign and challenge Major directly. Their best case scenario was a stalking horse candidate who wounded Major enough to cause his resignation. They could then enter into a vacant contest without the accusations of disloyalty.

The endorsement of Howard was crucial, but intriguing. It was ideologically significant. Major had implied that he was being undermined by a particular grouping within the party. Given that his three closet Cabinet colleagues, Hurd, Clarke and Heseltine, were all Europhiles, and that Major had imposed an inherently integrationist Maastricht Treaty upon the Conservative Party, it was clear that the supposedly unrepresentative body of critics were Eurosceptics. Major had previously indicated his frustration with Eurosceptic thinking in his bastard outburst. Howard, as Home Secretary, was the most senior Eurosceptic within the Cabinet. He was inclined towards the thinking of the bastard tendency. He endorsed Major but made an assumption. Endorsing Major carried with it two objectives: one policy based, and one personal. Within the confines of supporting his re-election campaign strategy, Howard sought to use this as an opportunity to persuade Major to rule out entry into the single European currency, for the life time of this and the next Parliament. From a personal perspective, Howard hoped that by demonstrating loyalty to Major, alongside the need for Major to placate the Eurosceptics, would result in him being appointed Foreign Secretary[11] (Seldon, 1997:569, 588).

Therefore, with Clarke, Heseltine and Howard all tied into the put up or shut up strategy, and the implication that the instability to Major was induced by the Eurosceptic faction alone (i.e. their fault), attention switched to the assumed bastards within the Cabinet: Michael Portillo, Peter Lilley and John Redwood. Portillo became gripped by indecision. He knew that it was widely assumed that he was the only candidate who could have defeated Major outright in the first ballot, thus negating the need for a second contest (Clark, 1998:521). He was being actively encouraged to stand by Lamont, Leigh and George Gardiner, Chair of the 92 Group, an eighty strong group of Thatcherite Conservative parliamentarians (Clark, 1998:518). Portillo made a delayed endorsement of the Major put up or shut up strategy. Portillo was concerned that should he stand against Major in a first ballot, he might not win outright, but might immobilise Major, causing his resignation. In what would be then an open field, Portillo might not win. His fear was that the elite Euroscepticism could be tarred (further) with the brush of disloyalty and this would impede their chances of annexing the party leadership. A more pragmatic cause of action was to publicly declare for Major, but hope that another candidate could immobilise Major, thus enabling a loyalist Portillo candidature to emerge in an open contest[12] (Seldon, 1997:576).

Portillo, and the Eurosceptic cause, was to be undermined by the lack of agreement amongst the elite bastards. Fellow Thatcherite Eurosceptic, Lilley, failed to offer an endorsement of Major at the same time as Portillo. Lilley was contemplating resigning and disputing the party leadership against Major. However, the possibility of being appointed Chancellor in a post-party leadership reshuffle appealed to Lilley. After liaising with the Major campaign team, he overcame his initial concerns and endorsed the put up or shut up strategy. Any remote chance he had of securing an elevation to the Treasury was probably undermined by his delayed endorsement (Williams, 1998:89).

As Portillo and Lilley reluctantly came on board, Redwood remained silent. His refusal to accept any in calls from the Major campaign team and the absence of any public declaration of support indicated his likely intentions. As speculation of a potential Redwood candidature gathered momentum, Lamont indicated that should Redwood stand he would step aside and support him. How would Portillo react to a Redwood candidature? Portillo attempted to persuade Redwood not to stand, but Redwood had already made his decision. He intended to resign. In standing, he did not expect win, but he hoped that he could be the catalyst to change (Williams,

1998:102). Redwood then met Portillo. Their meeting would see the beginning of the deterioration of the relationship between the two.

> Redwood told him that he had now resigned, but had not yet declared his candidature for the leadership. If Portillo wished to take the lead it was still open for him to do so. Redwood was amendable to an accommodation. Years previously, he had offered to support Portillo when the time came for him to stand for the leadership...For a few more moments the possibility of a Portillo challenge remained...Portillo replied that he would not resign now but that he would be a candidate in the second ballot, on the implicit understanding that Redwood would withdraw at that stage. Redwood might not think he was going to win outright, but he was certainly not going to allow Portillo to be the beneficiary of *his* resignation. 'You do realise', he said 'that if I do well in the first ballot I'm not going to withdraw so you can take over after I've done all the hard work?' It was the start of the collision course between Redwood's moral pride and Portillo's resentment.[13]   (Williams, 1998:103)

So why did Redwood stand? Some assumed that Redwood wanted to usurp Portillo as the standard bearer of the Thatcherite Eurosceptic right, and that this presented him with his opportunity. Others speculated that it was an emotionally motivated act of pique at having not been informed by Major personally of his leadership election plans (Seldon, 1997:575). Redwood chose to justify the challenge on the following grounds:

> What made me stand was his friends [Major's] briefing the press, saying that no one on the right had the guts to stand, and that the right wing case was merely a straw man. I couldn't take that. Once he did that, I had to take him on.   (Seldon, 1997: 575)

Redwood would campaign on a distinctive Thatcherite, Eurosceptic and social conservative agenda. In policy terms he made clear his support for immediate tax cuts, his opposition to Economic and Monetary Union, and his advocacy of tougher policies on law and order (Seldon, 1997:578). In political terms he campaigned on the slogan of 'no change, no chance', seeking to exploit the fears amongst Conservatives that Major was bound to lose the general election (Norton, 1998a:101).

The Redwood campaign was constrained by the following three factors. First, the Major campaign team engaged in dirty tactics designed to undermine the potential appeal of Redwood. They released footage of Redwood miming the Welsh National Anthem; they dubbed him the 'vulcan' (i.e. 'the man from another planet'); and they derided his acolytes as the 'barmy army'[14] (Seldon, 1997:589). Second, Redwood was undermined by a lack of preparation time. His hastily constructed manifesto was viewed as limited and as a disappointment given his reputation as an intellectual (Seldon, 1997:578). Finally, as a result of the aforementioned constraints, the Redwood campaign found it immensely difficult to secure the public endorsement of credible figures within the parliamentary Conservative Party. Whereas the Major campaign was orchestrated by senior Cabinet figures and endorsed by the Cabinet, the Redwood campaign was managed by backbenchers with minimal ministerial experience. Despite extensive lobbying of former ministers, such as Kenneth Baker and John Patten, Lamont would remain their only credible public endorser (Norton, 1998a:101).

The credibility of the Redwood candidature stimulated considerable debate. Three scenarios emerged. The first scenario was a comfortable majority for Major, which could enhance his authority and legitimacy as he had defeated a credible figure from the Thatcherite right. The second scenario was a small technical victory for Major, which adhered to the rules for success, but failed to overcome the notional 'third' hurdle, i.e. the psychological number required to demonstrate success. In this scenario, the authority and legitimacy of Major would be diminished to such an extent that the debilitating divisions which had crippled his party leadership would be more pronounced post-leadership election contest than they had been pre-leadership election contest. The third scenario implied that the first ballot between Major and Redwood was merely a procedural prelude to the real battle for the future of the Conservative Party, between the economic wet, pro-European, socially liberal, as represented by Heseltine and the economic liberal, Eurosceptic, social conservative, as represented by Portillo. This scenario assumed that Major would not clear the two stipulated hurdles required for victory in the first ballot, due to the fact that a sufficient number of Conservative parliamentarians would vote for Redwood (or abstain) in order to force the second contest to enable Cabinet ministers to enter (Norton, 1998a:101).

Those within the parliamentary Conservative Party who had reservations about the party leadership of Major and wished to initiate change – to secure an economic wet, pro-European, socially liberal party leader or to secure an economic liberal, Eurosceptic, social conservative, as party leader, faced a tactical conundrum. How should they utilize their vote to ensure their desired outcome? The first contest would be determined by tactical voting. The supporters of Heseltine and Portillo had to formulate a calculation of the probability of success of their candidate in an open second contest. Supporters of Portillo could support Redwood in the first contest to deflate the Major vote and ensure that an open second contest would occur. However, if they believed that Heseltine would defeat Portillo in an open second contest then they would prefer to stay with Major than tolerate

Heseltine as party leader. Alternatively, supporters of Heseltine could abstain in the first contest to ensure that an open second contest would occur, provided they were sure that Heseltine would defeat Portillo. If they calculated that Portillo would defeat Heseltine in a hypothetical second contest, they would rather stay with Major than accept Portillo as party leader.

There were moderates within the parliamentary Conservative Party who feared the ideological purity of a hypothetical second contest – i.e. the economic wet, pro-European, socially liberal, Heseltine versus the economic liberal, Eurosceptic, socially conservative, Portillo. For such moderates the primary function of the contest would be the resolution of the internal policy and political differences which had destabilized the party leadership of Major over the preceding three years. They feared that a second contest would result in a prolonged and debilitating advertisement of their internal factions leaving the eventual victor to preside over an ungovernable party (Alderman, 1996:323). The existence of this sentiment, enabled Major to construct a campaign built on the fear of something worse (i.e. other options would intensify factional strife) rather than the hope of something better. The Major campaign team argued that it was likely that Major would clear the two required stipulations and therefore in the interests of party unity, and his authority and legitimacy as party leader, it was best to ensure that the victory was convincing.

There was a febrile atmosphere within the parliamentary Conservative Party as the date of the contest drew closer. On the eve of the contest, it was rumoured that having analyzed the range of desired and undesired outcomes the supporters of Heseltine and Portillo had decided to abstain. By doing so they would deprive Major of outright victory, either by the two officially stipulated hurdles or the notional third hurdle. Furthermore, for supporters of Portillo the attraction of abstention was that such a tactic would deny Redwood from gaining an unstoppable momentum (Gove, 1995:338). Gove suggests that the finely calibrated calculations through which a potential abstention strategy emerged were undermined on the morning of the contest by a meeting between Major and Heseltine (Gove, 1995:338).

On the morning of the contest, a three-hour meeting occurred between Major and Heseltine. Major claims that the meeting was arranged to discuss the role that Heseltine would assume in the post-leadership Cabinet reshuffle. Seldon argues that Heseltine now accepted that a second contest was unlikely and that the meeting represented an opportunity for him personally to maximize his power base. Major implies a Heseltine second contest candidature was still a possibility, but despite this principle prevailed. He dismisses the conspiracy theory in which Heseltine was negotiating a powerful job for himself in return for encouraging his supporters to vote for me. No job, no vote – and I would be out.

(Major, 1999:641-2)

Cynics assumed that the length, date and circumstances of the meeting, meant that Heseltine had done a

secret deal with Major to deliver the votes of his supporters in return for a top job and possibly even – the stories varied (including the suggestion that Heseltine had an influence in ministerial appointments in the subsequent reshuffle) – the pledge of the succession when Major retired.   (Seldon, 1997:585)[15]

To secure his re-election as party leader, it was necessary for Major to secure a simple majority of the 329 Conservative parliamentarians; i.e. 165 votes (the first hurdle), and in order to prevent the necessity of a second round, the winner needed to be fifteen per cent ahead of any rival (the second hurdle) (Seldon, 1997:572). Major also introduced a self-imposed third hurdle of 215 votes as the minimum number acceptable to enable him to remain as party leader (Major, 1999:620). Ultimately, he just overcame the self-imposed third hurdle of 215 votes.[16] However, as the contest approached Major had re-evaluated his position and was demanding a decisive win.[17] Whilst decisive was not defined exactly, it was assumed that he would resign if one third of the parliamentary Conservative Party failed to support him. By the morning of the vote Major informed ministerial colleagues that he would resign if over 100 Conservative parliamentarians failed to support him (Norton, 1998a:102). By both stipulations, Major should have resigned; 111 Conservative parliamentarians or 33.74% failed to endorse his party leadership.

Table 9:   Candidate Support in the Conservative Party Leadership Election of 1995

	First Ballot	Percentage
John Major	218	66.3
John Redwood	89	27.1
Spoilt Ballots	22	6.7

Source: Quinn, 2005:812

6.3   A Vote of Confidence?

There are competing interpretations on whether the outcome served to validate the strategy that Major had adopted. Of the earlier scenarios outlined we can see that the outcome was on the borderline between scenario one (a comfortable victory for Major) and scenario two (a technical victory, adhering to the rules for success, but failing to overcome the notional third hurdle).

There is a positive interpretation or vote of confidence thesis. This is based on the fact that it was immediately defined by elites within the parliamentary Conservative Party as a convincing victory for Major. Their reaction to the outcome contributed an uncritical acceptance that the volatile third hurdle (i.e. 215) had been comfortably overcome and that it amounted to a convincing victory (Seldon, 1997:586; Alderman, 1996:326).

The Major campaign initiated an immediate plan that stipulated that they emphasise the following. First, Major had defeated the minority within the pure Thatcherite faction of economic liberal, Eurosceptic, social conservaives, that had attempted to undermine his party leadership since 1992. Second, Major had defeated a young, ambitious, intellectual political heavyweight from within the Thatcherite right, rather than an aged, marginal, discredited political lightweight from the backbenchers. This added credibility and legitimacy to his victory. Third, Major had enhanced his mandate as party leader as his vote share had increased from 185 votes or 47.7 per cent of the 1990 parliamentary Conservative Party when he had originally acquired the party leadership, to 218 votes or 66.3 per cent of the 1995 parliamentary Conservative Party when he retained the party leadership. Finally, Conservatives claimed that Major had a stronger mandate than Tony Blair. Whereas Major had secured 66.3 per cent of the support of his electorate, Blair had only secured 57 per cent of the Electoral College vote that had secured him the Labour Party leadership in July 1994 (Rentoul, 2001:247).

The success of this organized tactic by the Major campaign was evident when compared to the first ballot inquest in November 1990. Then minister after minister went to Thatcher advising her to resign, whilst the response to the first ballot in July 1995 involved minister after minister pleading with Major that he must stay (Hogg and Hill, 1995:281). Stuart argues that in that crucial missing twenty minutes (5.00 to 5.20) between the announcement of the result and Major's first public appearance, senior ministers simultaneously encouraged Major to stay whilst talking up the result with a series of pre-prepared remarks for the waiting media (Stuart, 1998:426). The dual campaign by loyalist ministers to convince Major on the one hand, and the media on the other, that the result was sufficient succeeded to the extent that if Major had any doubts about whether he wished to continue 'his colleagues

gave him little choice in the matter' (Stuart, 1998:426). Major unenthusiasti-
cally agreed that 218 votes was an adequate enough victory, before informing
the assembled media:

> We have now seen the verdict of the parliamentary party. It is a very
> clear cut decision. I believe that this has put to rest any questions or any
> speculation about the leadership of the Conservative Party up to and
> beyond the next election…the [leadership] election is now over. The
> message that I would give to every Conservative is that the time for
> division is over.   (Seldon, 1997:587)

However, the vote of confidence thesis and the assumptions that underpin it
are largely erroneous. In fact a persuasive critique of the put up or shut up
strategy can be advanced. The first strand to the critique of the implementation and outcome of the put up or shut up strategy argues that given that he
was the incumbent Prime Minister it could not realistically be defined as a
resounding victory. Moreover, the extent of embarrassment to Major was
compounded by the 'unequal nature of the contest' (Alderman, 1996:325).
The argument that the election was manipulated or contrived embraces three
inter-related factors: the timing of the election, the nature of resignations,
and the rules or procedures for voting.

The first distortion of the leadership contest relates to the timing of the
election. Following the May 1995 local election results, critics of Major had
pressurized the 1922 Executive Committee by circulating a round robin letter
demanding an immediate leadership election. Their attempt to circumvent
the stipulation that the leadership election must occur at the commencement
of the parliamentary session was rejected by the 1922 Executive Committee
for being incompatible with the rules (Alderman, 1996:318, 330). Their
subsequent decision one-month later to acquiesce to Major's request for an
immediate leadership contest demonstrated that Major was able to manipu-
late events in a manner advantageous to himself and disadvantageous to his
critics.[18]

The leadership election was also fundamentally distorted by the fact that
whilst Redwood was forced to resign from the Cabinet to contest the party
leadership, Major constructed a distinction between resigning from the party
leadership and resigning as Prime Minister. This presented Major with
distinct tactical advantages. Given the importance of political symbolism and
the need to project an aura of success, Major was able to announce his
candidature in a dignified setting of the Downing Street garden. The now
dispossessed candidate, Redwood, who had lost the privileges of office, was
reduced to a hastily arranged and disorganized press conference to announce
his candidature. Moreover, the fact that he retained his office, combined with
the perceived likelihood that Redwood would not secure the leadership

himself through a first ballot victory, meant that Major could secure pledges of support through the promise of ministerial appointments, whereas Redwood could not.

The final distorting aspect of the party leadership election related to the management of the actual voting procedures. The responsibility for managing this *vacant* party leadership election lay with the 1922 Executive Committee. The pro-Major partisanship of the committee was evident and provoked considerable criticism (Alderman, 1996:332). Given their concerns about the impartiality of the committee overseeing the election procedures, the Redwood camp requested that the Electoral Reform Society should be employed as the invigilators alongside members of the committee. This request was rejected on the premise that only the committee itself could act in this capacity. The Redwood camp reacted to this by proposing a secret ballot enabling members to vote in private, away from the scrutineers, who were 1922 Committee members. This request resulted in the erection of screens in the committee room, but with a conditional stipulation that if members wished to vote behind the screen they could do so, but if they wished to vote publicly in the presence of the scrutineers they could also do so (Williams, 1998:115). The Redwood team remonstrated about this stipulation as:

> those who wished to curry favour would seize the opportunity to vote publicly for Major: those who voted behind the scenes would be assumed to have voted for Redwood. Brave Conservative parliamentarians were not so thick on the ground and effectively every vote for Redwood would be declared. (Williams, 1998: 115)

Therefore, an alternative interpretation can be advanced implying that it was a default victory in a fundamentally unequal contest rather than a vote of confidence. Major employed a high-risk strategy that he believed was decisive in saving his party leadership, but does this assertion provide a justification or validation for the put up or shut up strategy? This rhetorical question dovetails neatly into the second strand of our critique – i.e. that the strategy offered no tangible benefits to the Conservative Party. Externally, it demonstrated to the electorate the size and scale of the conflict that had engulfed the Conservatives in the post-Thatcherite era. Internally, the consequence of this unnecessary contest for the leadership (and the troublesome Governmental reshuffle)[19] was to institutionalize their conflict: as such, we can argue that it constituted a divisive rather than a healing process (Alderman, 1996:329).

That it institutionalised the conflict is evident from the perspective of the Eurosceptic Thatcherite right. Notwithstanding their own tactical miscalculations, many of them were apoplectic at the end of the process. To counter the appeal of Redwood to the Eurosceptic Thatcherite right, the Major campaign had (implausibly) argued that after winning the next election, Major did not intend to serve a full term, and in the intervening period Portillo would gain the necessary experience to enable him to secure the leadership mid-term. The mixed messages that the Major campaign team engaged in contributed to some of the hostility surrounding the subsequent reshuffle. They implied to waverers that if reselected, Major would rule out membership of a single currency; that a Eurosceptic (Michael Howard) would fill the vacancy at the Foreign Office and that Portillo would receive a senior position; such understandings 'were not forgotten by those to whom they were conveyed' (Seldon, 1997:582). The Eurosceptic Thatcherite right had entered the process with the prospect of a Portillo premiership, which would have brought with it the probability of a Eurosceptic hue to European policy being adopted and the capacity to marginalize the influence of the Europhile Tory left within ministerial ranks. They had ended the process and had stuck with Major and his ambivalent stance on European policy, but central positions afforded to key figures from the Europhile Tory left, had positions within the reconstructed government.[20]

The argument that this process served to institutionalize the conflict within the parliamentary Conservative Party, would not secure the unanimous endorsement of Major as the architect of the strategy. He admits that the strategy adopted did not eradicate the existence of the conflict but he argues that it dampened the intensity of the conflict. He concludes that his re-election as party leader, as opposed to the election of a committed Europhile such as Clarke or Heseltine, or a Eurosceptic such as Portillo, Howard or Redwood, saved the party from a split. His self-justification thesis states:

> my re-election as leader postponed – and, I hope, saved the party from – an irrevocable split over European policy. It was very likely it would have haemorrhaged if a leader had been chosen who gave unconditional backing to one side or the other in an argument so fundamental to the protagonists that none was prepared to concede.
>
> (Major, 1999:647)

The argument that Major implies with regard to the longer term future of Conservative Party fits neatly into the evaluation of the primary motivation for him activating the contest: the restoration of his authority within the parliamentary Conservative Party, the restoration of his legitimacy as party leader; and the confirmation of his security of tenure as party leader. This constitutes the basis for the third strand to our critique of the put up or shut up strategy. This strand argues that the rationale for initiating the contest was only partially successful – i.e. it enhanced his security of tenure[21] but it did not contribute to the re-acclamation of his authority over the parliamentary Conservative Party and his legitimacy as party leader.

Validation of the put up or shut up strategy adopted implies that the outcome justified the rationale for the strategy in its entirety. The rationale for activating the contest for the party leadership was that a small and unrepresentative minority of critics were undermining his authority within the parliamentary Conservative Party and his legitimacy as party leader. To demonstrate the validity of this assertion required one of two scenarios to evolve: first, no potential candidate emerging to oppose Major; or, second, that any hypothetical candidate must be a member of that small and unrepresentative minority.

The implication underpinning these assumptions was that the small and unrepresentative minority was comprised of an outer core of fifteen to twenty habitual rebels from the parliamentary passage of the Treaty of European Union, within which there was an inner core of nine who had been deprived of the Conservative whip earlier in the Parliament. The perception that it was a small unrepresentative and extremist rump of habitual European rebels that opposed his party leadership was disproved by the fact that over one hundred Conservative parliamentarians (or nearly one-third of the parliamentary Conservative Party) did not endorse his re-election as party leadership. If we assume that the all Conservative parliamentarians holding ministerial office supported Major then nearly half of those on the Conservative backbenchers failed to endorse his party leadership.

If the rationale for activating the contest was based on an assumption that opposition was from a small and unrepresentative minority then it was imperative to ensure that no candidature from within the ministerial ranks, and especially from within Cabinet, should emerge. Implicit within the rationale that Major was advancing was an assumption on the motivational basis of his critics: they were compromised of the dispossessed and never possessed, for whom revenge and resentment were masquerading for political principle. The decision of Redwood to dispossess himself of ministerial office undermined the argument that Major was seeking to imply. The combined impact of Redwood dispossessing himself and the subsequent non-endorsement of one-third of the parliamentary Conservative Party disproved the rationale upon which Major had activated the contest. Before the contest, political analysts had demonstrative evidence that approximately twenty Conservative parliamentarians were critical of the party leadership of Major. After the contest, political analysts knew that the figure was nearly six times higher than previously assumed.

The previous chapter emphasized how Major acquired the party leadership in November 1990 by default. His acquisition of the party leadership had been at the behest of the Eurosceptic Thatcherite right (Cowley and Garry, 1998:473-499). Although their preference would have been the retention of

Thatcher they gravitated to Major to prevent Heseltine from securing the party leadership. He was the anti-Heseltine, second choice of the Eurosceptic Thatcherite right, and thus a default victor. The default theory can be seen to be equally applicable in his re-election as party leader in July 1995. He retained the party leadership by being the least unacceptable option: for Europhiles Major was less unacceptable than Portillo, Howard or Redwood and for Eurosceptics Major was less unacceptable than Heseltine or Clarke. This lack of enthusiasm from those who actually voted for him in July 1995 demonstrated why the process could not re-establish his authority within the parliamentary Conservative Party or his legitimacy as party leader.

These authority and legitimacy difficulties associated with Major can be emphasised by researching the ideological disposition of the Major vote base and the Redwood vote base. From this research it is clear that the Redwood candidature revolved around his Eurosceptic credentials, with eighty seven of his eighty nine endorsers identified as known Eurosceptics.[22] However, although the Redwood support base and the anti-Major vote can be defined as overwhelmingly of the Eurosceptic Thatcherite right, Redwood did not secure the support of all of the Eurosceptic Thatcherite right[23] (Heppell, 2000:427-428). The failure of the Redwood candidature flowed from his inability to mobilise Eurosceptic and Thatcherite sentiment further: had he maximised Eurosceptic and Thatcherite sentiment he would have prevented Major from winning the first ballot.

Moreover, analysis of the ideological disposition of those who rejected Major and gravitated to Redwood demonstrates how Major lacked a consistent power base within the parliamentary Conservative Party. Whereas in November 1990 Major secured the party leadership due to the support of the Eurosceptic Thatcherite right (and was rejected by the Tory left) he regained the party leadership through the support of the Europhile Tory left and loyalist Eurosceptic Thatcherite right but was rejected by inflexible the Thatcherite Eurosceptic right. It amounted to another default victory as it was an anti-Redwood vote rather than a pro-Major vote (Seldon, 1997:586). Norton eloquently identifies the fact that Major had a tenuous hold upon the party leadership:

> In the 1990 Leadership contest, he had no candidate to the right of him. In the 1995 contest he had no candidate to the left of him. He thus picked up support from different constituencies without consolidating his support in either. There was no strong body of 'Majorites' to bang the drum in the support of his beliefs and leadership.   (Norton, 1998a:102)

Therefore, the survival of Major stemmed from the fact that he was the least unacceptable option for the parliamentary Conservative Party. The fact that the oft-rumoured challenges to his party leadership never materialized during the autumns of 1992, 1993 and 1994 demonstrated that a sufficient section of the parliamentary Conservative Party recognized the following. If an ideologically agnostic unity candidate could not unify the Conservative Party and suppress its endemic divisions than an ideologue on the European policy ideological divide would prize those fissures open further. All alternatives to Major would be more divisive.

Despite this, differing factions within the parliamentary Conservative Party advocated the leadership credentials of their ideologically approved standard bearers. Within this ideological context the European policy ideological variable was the most salient. Europhiles, predominantly located on the Tory left, advanced the cause of Heseltine and to a lesser extent, Clarke. Euro-sceptics, predominantly located on the Thatcherite right, advanced the cause of Portillo, and to a lesser extent, Howard (Redwood became a conduit for their ideological aspirations during the leadership contest, but was not so beforehand). For the respective factions within the parliamentary Conservative Party any process that would result in the change in the party leadership carried with it the risk of a new leader emerging who was more unacceptable to them than Major was. The Thatcherite right feared a process that could lead to an economic wet, Europhile, social liberal emerging as party leader, such as Heseltine or Clarke. The Tory left feared a process in which an economic dry, Eurosceptic, social conservative could emerge as party leader, such as Portillo or Howard. Indeed, the probability of a formal split within Conservatism would have been intensified by the emergence of a committed Europhile or a committed Europhobe.[24]

6.4   Conclusion

The party leadership of Major was undermined by a near permanent insecurity of tenure. That insecurity of tenure was characterized by the gradual erosion of authority and loyalty, which so undermined his position as party leader that he resigned to force a leadership election on his terms, rather than on terrain determined by his critics.

In an unprecedented act Major initiated a dramatic pre-emptive strike. The put up or shut up strategy enabled him to secure his position as party leader until the general election, but served to highlight the absence of authority and legitimacy upon which his party leadership was based. Major secured the (albeit unenthusiastic) endorsement of the parliamentary Conservative Party as the unity candidate, despite the fact he had palpably failed to unify the parliamentary Conservative Party in the preceding three years, and despite the fact that as a candidate for the vacancy he had campaigned without a manifesto and without committing himself to any change in policy direction or leadership style.

The strategy adopted did not restore his authority within the parliamentary Conservative Party and his legitimacy as party leader. The lack of enthusiasm for Major as party leader was significant as authority is dependent upon the enthusiasm of those wishing to confer legitimacy upon their leader. The dilemma for Major was once authority is removed it is immensely difficult to reclaim. Moreover, he was seeking to reclaim an authority which had been subject to sustained and prolonged erosion through one defiant action that was against the wishes of the majority of the parliamentary Conservative party. His authority and thereby his legitimacy as party leader was beyond restoration as the perceptions of vulnerability and weakness had become so pronounced that they were beyond reversal (Alderman, 1996:329).

The continuation of Major as party leader, through a process that highlighted his weaknesses and the endemic divisions within the Conservative Party, worked to the long term electoral advantage of Tony Blair and New Labour (Foley, 2002:197-198). It amounted to a pyrrhic victory for Major. Provoking a party leadership election was a risky escapade as it invited a challenge (Barber, 2003:14). By winning, he achieved the short term goal of removing an imminent challenge to his party leadership that autumn, and he ensured that his position would be secured until the general election, as no further challenge would be permitted. However, the strategy masked the fundamental underlying structural problems. It did not remove the criticism from Eurosceptics (and to a lesser extent from Europhiles) surrounding the contours of European policy. Nor could it remove the corrosive stain of defeatism, factionalism and crisis management that had characterised the Major era. The Conservatives had opted for the status quo option and in doing so prevented themselves from initiating a strategy for renewal whilst in government. It delivered an administration to blame, i.e. the Major administration. Put up or shut up was a strategy for personal victory. It would do nothing to prevent the inevitability of defeat at the next general election.

YOU CANNOT BE SERIOUS: THE ELECTION OF WILLIAM HAGUE

The futility of the put up or shut up strategy that John Major had pursued in order to remain as party leader became apparent in May 1997, when the Conservatives suffered a catastrophic electoral defeat.[1] Their performance in the general election of May 1997 was their worst since 1832; their electoral rejection was more pronounced that the crushing defeats of 1906 and 1945. The Conservatives return of 165 parliamentarians was their lowest number since 1906, whilst the Conservative share of the vote at 30.7 per cent was their lowest since the coming of mass democracy (Butler and Kavanagh, 1997:244).

In the interim period between the Conservative Party leadership election of July 1995 and the general election of May 1997, the vast majority of the parliamentary Conservative Party had come to accept the inevitability of defeat at that imminent general election, irrespective of who their party leader was. Therefore, during this interim period the parliamentary Conservative Party was embroiled in a two-dimensional electioneering process: first, to ensure the maximum parliamentary presence for the Conservative Party on the opposition benches after their electoral defeat; and, second, to position potential candidates for the presumed vacancy for the leadership of the Conservative Party in the wake of their electoral rejection. It would evolve into a divisive and debilitating process. Potential candidates acting through backbench representatives began to mobilize support within the existing parliamentary Conservative Party and liaised with potential entrants into the parliamentary Conservative Party from the likely 1997 cohort of new Conservative parliamentarians. It evolved into a remarkable situation in which Major, the incumbent leader of the Conservative Party, had become an irrelevance to many within the parliamentary Conservative Party (Williams, 1998:157).

7.1 The Resignation of John Major

Within hours of the confirmation of their electoral meltdown, Major announced his resignation as leader of the Conservative Party. Major released his grip on the leadership of the Conservative Party for a variety of reasons. First, after fourteen years as a government minister and six and a half years as Prime Minister a sense of fatigue had set in; he had no desire to continue managing his fractious parliamentary Conservative Party. Second, he recognised that his continuance as party leader was not viable. To prevent the new Labour Government exploiting the baggage of his tenure as Prime Minister, it was essential that the Conservative Party made a fresh start under a new leader. Third, Major felt that potential candidates would be campaigning for an autumn leadership election contest and a resolution inside six weeks was preferable to an elongated campaign period over four to five months (Major, 1999:721).

During his tenure as party leader, Major had utilised tactics of dubious validity to ensure that he retained the party leadership (Clark, 1998:512, 523). A certain irony would now exist that many who had campaigned for his removal whilst in government, were now equally critical of him for the speed of his resignation in opposition (Alderman, 1998:3). The critique of the Major resignation strategy comprised two inter-related arguments. First, in the immediate aftermath of their cataclysmic electoral collapse the Conservative Party was collectively in a state of shock. The fatigue and petulance induced by fighting a futile six week general election campaign left the parliamentary Conservative Party ill prepared for the rigours of another immediate six week campaigning period. By his immediate resignation, Major would plunge the parliamentary Conservative Party into what would develop into a highly personalised, ideologically divisive and traumatic leadership election. Without the opportunity to reflect on the reasons for their electoral defeat or fully consider the merits of their multiple candidates, the parliamentary Conservative Party would continue the vindictive and perfidious modes of political conduct that had disfigured and destroyed the Conservative Party leadership tenure of John Major (Williams, 1998:186).

It can be argued that Major did the Conservatives a considerable disservice by his petulant resignation and in doing so he failed to learn from the Douglas-Home precedent. Alec Douglas-Home had lost the general election of 1964 after a long period of Conservative governance. The tail end of that era of Conservative hegemony had been stained by the controversy and conflict surrounding the manner in which Douglas-Home had acquired the party leadership. After losing the general election in October 1964, Douglas-Home set about establishing the existing (albeit modified in 1975 and 1991) system of internal democracy. In July 1965 he then resigned, thus enabling Edward Heath to emerge as the new democratically determined leader of the

Conservative Party (Blake, 1998:297-298; Gilmour and Garnett, 1998:217-218).

Similarly, Major had lost the general election of 1997 after a long period of Conservative governance. Similarly, the tail end of that era of Conservative hegemony had been blighted by debates surrounding his position as party leader. The divisive put up or shut up strategy that Major had deployed in the summer of 1995 had stimulated sufficient dissatisfaction within the Conservative Party to suggest that the existing leadership election procedures needed to be reconsidered and adapted (Alderman, 1996:332). Major could have utilised the Douglas-Home precedent of remaining as leader of the Conservative Party and overseeing new leadership election procedures.[2] The alacrity with which Major bolted from the party leadership meant that there was no opportunity to re-evaluate the leadership election processes. The 1922 Executive Committee quickly resolved to determine the succession under the existing rules, despite the concerns of the grass roots membership[3] (Norton, 1998b:10).

7.2   Profiling the Multiple Candidates

A certain irony existed now that there was a vacancy for the leadership of the Conservative Party. Many who wished to stand for the leadership of the Conservative Party, some of whom had overtly or covertly campaigned for the position when it was not vacant, were no longer able to stand. As a consequence it was a vacant contest (i.e. the incumbent leader had resigned), which was characterised by a depleted field of candidates (i.e. the leading candidates could not or did not stand); which encouraged more candidates to believe that they could emerge victorious (i.e. its complexity was intensified by a multiplicity of candidates).

The electoral meltdown of May 1997 had not discriminated between backbench and frontbench Conservative parliamentarians. Cabinet ministers such as Ian Lang, Tony Newton, William Waldegrave, Michael Forsyth, Roger Freeman and Malcolm Rifkind all lost their parliamentary constituencies. The most surprising and iconographic electoral casualty was Michael Portillo, the anointed candidate of the Thatcherite right, whose political demise created a window of opportunity for other potential candidates on the Eurosceptic Thatcherite right.

In addition to the enforced non-candidature of Portillo, the dynamics of the leadership election process were fundamentally altered by the enforced withdrawal of Michael Heseltine. He was admitted to hospital as he had suffered an angina attack in the immediate aftermath of the general election defeat. He immediately abandoned any plans that he had to stand for the leadership of the Conservative Party. The enforced absence of the prime candidate for the Eurosceptic Thatcherite right (Portillo) and the standard bearer of the Europhile Tory left (Heseltine), combined with the fact that the incumbent leader had resigned created a large field of candidates. In total six candidates emerged. From the Eurosceptic Thatcherite right candidatures emerged in the shape of John Redwood, Michael Howard, Peter Lilley and William Hague; whilst the pro-European Tory left was represented by Stephen Dorrell and Kenneth Clarke.

The absence of Portillo appeared to work to the advantage of Howard as the most senior figure within the loyalist Eurosceptic Thatcherite right. Howard sought to exploit socially conservative sentiment within the parliamentary Conservative Party by reinforcing the populist stance that he had adopted on law and order whilst he was Home Secretary between 1993 and 1997. This socially conservative appeal aligned to his Eurosceptic credentials formed the ideological foundations of his candidature.

The increasingly overcrowded field of candidates from the Eurosceptic Thatcherite right of the parliamentary Conservative Party was completed by the candidatures of Redwood, Lilley and Hague. The supposed strength of a Redwood candidature turned out to be a weakness. Redwood attempted to argue that his status outside of the Cabinet between 1995 and 1997 absolved him of any responsibility or association with the discredited Major era and the resultant electoral meltdown. However, the association that did resonate was that of disloyalty resulting from the challenge that Redwood had made to Major. By constantly reminding Conservative parliamentarians of the failings of the Major era, an indissoluble connection between the candidature of Redwood and the cause of the implosion of the Major era was established (Williams, 1998:188). Redwood was a symbol of ideological division and disloyalty; to many his advancement would be an impediment to unity and renewal.

The candidature of Lilley mirrored the Thatcherite dry, Eurosceptic appeal of both Howard and Redwood, but doubts were cast about the charisma and electoral appeal of Lilley as well as his capacity to unite and bridge the chasm between the pro-European Tory left and Eurosceptic Thatcherite right. For those of the Thatcherite right wishing to advance the call for unity, the attractions of the candidature of Hague became evident. The appeal of Hague reflected the fact that many Conservative parliamentarians were attracted to the notion of skipping a political generation and making a clean and symbolic break with the Thatcher and Major eras, in which other candidates such as Howard, Lilley and Clarke were clearly associated (Alderman, 1998:5). In an attempt to tap into this mindset, Hague launched his campaign around the slogan of a 'fresh start' (Seldon and Snowden, 2005a:250).

Standing in opposition to an overcrowded field of Eurosceptic Thatcherite dries were two pro-European wets, in the shape of Dorrell and Clarke. Recognising that the centre of gravity within the parliamentary

Conservative Party had been shifting in a Eurosceptic direction during the Major era, Dorrell had engaged in an incremental disassociation with his Europhilic past. This calculated shift was designed to increase his appeal to Eurosceptics whilst he assumed that Europhiles would retain an allegiance to his candidature, thus enabling him to emerge as a unity candidate. However, the viability of his candidature was questioned. Eurosceptics doubted his ideological sincerity, whilst Europhiles feared that he was abandoning his principles for personal advancement (Alderman, 1998:6).

Consequently, with the enforced withdrawal of Heseltine, the pro-European Tory left gravitated to the candidature of Clarke. The Clarke candidature had two inter-related limitations: first, his pronounced and uncompromising Europhilia in a parliamentary Conservative Party that was overwhelmingly Eurosceptic; and, second, the fear that his committed pro-Europeanism would make him a divisive rather than a unifying party leader (Brown, 1997:6). However, Clarke had been widely praised for his handling of the economy during his tenure as Chancellor of the Exchequer between 1993 and 1997. He also had considerable experience of a wide range of Cabinet portfolios having served as Health Secretary (1988 to 1990); Education Secretary (1990 to 1992) and Home Secretary (1992 to 1993). His reputation as a competent and experienced politician contributed to opinion polling evidence,[4] which indicated the fact that he was the most popular of the candidates with the electorate.[5]

7.3   Evaluating the Multiple Ballots

In the absence of the preferred candidates of the Eurosceptic Thatcherite right (i.e. Portillo) and the pro-European Tory left (i.e. Heseltine) the momentum in the initial stage of the campaign period in early May 1997 shifted towards Howard for the Eurosceptic Thatcherite right and Clarke for the pro-European Tory left.

The viability of the Howard candidature was based on establishing a bandwagon effect and establishing himself as the preferred candidate of the Eurosceptic Thatcherite right, and the candidate best placed to prevent Clarke from acquiring the party leadership. The central plank of the bandwagon strategy involved securing the endorsement of Hague. It was rumoured that Hague had agreed to support the candidature of Howard in return for the post of Deputy Leader and Party Chairman (an allegation that he denied). His decision to renege on this deal undermined the momentum of the Howard candidature and served to indicate that a gravitational shift towards a Hague candidature was occuring[6] (Williams, 1998:190; Nadler, 2001:4-14).

However, the credibility of the Howard candidature was critically undermined by a vitriolic attack by Ann Widdecombe, a former ministerial colleague of Howard in the Home Office. Whilst in office, they had disagreed over the decision that Howard had taken to dismiss the Head of the Prisons Service, Derek Lewis. Ann Widdecombe publicly questioned the political integrity of Howard, arguing that when under political pressure he could 'do things that were not always sustainable' (Watkins, 1998:195). Moreover, in a deliberate attempt to maximise the damage to his candidature she announced that there was 'something of the night' to his psychological make up that made him unsuitable as leader of the Conservative Party[7] (White, 1997:8). Widdecombe endorsed Lilley,[8] whose candidature appeared to be gathering momentum when another potential candidate, Gillian Shepherd, announced that she would not be entering the leadership contest, but would instead back Lilley (Alderman, 1998:9).

Within the Thatcherite right, momentum was slipping away from Howard and gravitating towards Hague and to a lesser extent to Lilley. The candidature of Redwood was undermined not only by his dual image problems (i.e. to engender electoral appeal and to secure internal unity) but by organisational difficulties. First, it has long been assumed that Iain Duncan Smith would act as campaign manager for Redwood. Duncan Smith was willing to accept this position, and the offer of Party Chairman, should Redwood prevail. However, he would not publicly confirm his support for Redwood immediately as he was contemplating standing himself. Ultimately, Duncan Smith did not stand and did endorse Redwood but his prevarication undermined the Redwood campaign. Second, many assumed Portillo supporters had gravitated to the candidature of Lilley (e.g. Bernard Jenkin, John Whittingdale and Eric Forth). On the basis of this, the Lilley campaign publicly argued that Redwood could not prevail and that he should withdraw and that his supporters should transfer their allegiance to Lilley (Williams, 1998:192-193).

Evolving simultaneous to these tactical calculations within the Eurosceptic Thatcherite right, were the machinations between the two candidates identifiable with the pro-European Tory left. Dorrell and Clarke eventually determined that only one of them should stand. In a desperate attempt to secure momentum to his candidature, Dorrell suggested that he and Clarke should go forward as a joint-ticket, but with Dorrell as the candidate for party leader. When this was rejected, and the Dorrell campaign realised that their projected vote in the first ballot was lower that any other candidate, he withdrew from the contest (Williams, 1998:195). His subsequent decision to endorse Clarke ensured that the pro-European Tory left was united around one candidate. The Clarke candidature then attempted to claim that it had secured that crucial electoral commodity: momentum (Alderman, 1998:9).

The first ballot for the party leadership occurred on 10th June. The result was inconclusive and no candidate came close to the requirement of a majority of those entitled to vote plus a lead of 15 per cent over the second placed candidate[9] (Alderman, 1998:9-10). The sole candidate from the pro-European Tory left, Clarke, came first in the ballot of 164 Conservative parliamentarians, with Lilley and Howard occupying the bottom two places. Neither Lilley nor Howard had expected to perform as badly. They had both assumed that Redwood would finish last and that he and his acolytes would transfer their allegiance to one of them, thus providing their candidatures with crucial momentum in the second ballot. After their poor performances in the first ballot, both Lilley and Howard withdrew from the contest. Moreover, despite his status as the winner of the first ballot the consensus view was that Clarke needed to have secured a larger initial lead over Hague than the eight votes he had obtained. Was it possible for Clarke to expand his vote base from the Lilley and Howard vote base; a vote base built on the foundations of Euroscepticism? With the majority of the parliamentary Conservative Party wedded to Euroscepticism the psychological winner of the first ballot was Hague, who happened to be the most moderate of the four Eurosceptics on offer[10] (Alderman, 1998:10).

The second ballot for the party leadership occurred on 17th June.[11] The forty-seven votes freed by the elimination of Lilley and Howard worked to the benefit of the candidature of Hague, as his vote increased by twenty-one to sixty-two votes. With Clarke increasing his vote from forty-nine to sixty-four votes, the failure of the Redwood candidature became apparent. With forty-seven presumed Eurosceptic votes potentially available, the support for Redwood was increased by only eleven votes. Redwood was eliminated from the contest, as Clarke and Hague proceeded to the final ballot, scheduled for the 19th June. Both candidates needed to obtain a majority of the thirty-votes that Redwood had secured in the second ballot. Given the Eurosceptic basis of the Redwood candidature it was assumed that this favoured the Eurosceptic candidature of Hague and would resign Clarke to defeat.

In anticipation of the crucial third ballot, Clarke attempted to formulate a tactical alliance with Redwood,[12] which would provide him with the majority of the thirty-eight votes that Redwood had secured. Redwood was positively disposed to constructing an alliance with Clarke.[13] Throughout the campaign he had been openly hostile to Hague and his cohorts. He thought the idea of Hague assuming the party leadership was preposterous (Williams, 1998:216, 218). In ideological and policy terms the Clarke-Redwood alliance seemed implausible: the single European currency, the issue that divided them most, was fudged. They agreed that the direction of European policy was no longer within their sphere of influence as they were in opposition. Anyway, they agreed that British participation within the single European currency was unlikely in the short-term and should it arise then they were offered a free vote on the issue (Williams, 1998:218). Present at the deliberations that confirmed their pact was Heseltine, the arch Europhile and hate figure for the Thatcherite Eurosceptic right. As the meeting closed Heseltine, the leading stimulant to the party leadership instability of the previous eight years, announced:

> This is, I think, a historic moment in the history of the Conservative Party. It is the end of the years of conflict.   (Williams, 1998:219)

The nemesis of Heseltine, Margaret Thatcher, was immediately appalled by what seemed to her to be an instability pact. She would privately brief that it was:

> An incredible alliance of opposites which can only lead to further grief.
>   (Williams, 1998:220)

Major, the leading benefactor of the Thatcher-Heseltine dispute, now abandoned Clarke, in irritation that Clarke had aligned himself with Redwood, whose disloyalty had nearly ended the Major era, two years earlier. As Williams noted:

> In a rare agreement with his predecessor, Major jumped ship. He had voted for Clarke at the first two ballots, but now he told colleagues that 'Ken's gone mad'.[14]   (Williams, 1998:221)

The political necessity of this hastily arranged tactical alliance was obvious from the perspective of Clarke. If the Redwood vote base was relatively cohesive then he had it in his power to be king-maker and hand the leadership of the Conservative Party to the leading exponent of Europhilia. The attractiveness of the tactical alliance to Redwood was open to speculation.[15] It was assumed that should Clarke emerge as the new party leader then Redwood would be rewarded with the position of Shadow Chancellor. A leading supporter of Clarke, Ian Taylor, argued the case for their tactical alliance from the following perspective:

> It was obvious that we could not go on with the divisions over Europe, as they had almost destroyed the party....Both Clarke and Redwood knew all too well how profound their differences over Europe were but they also knew that what united them as Conservatives was greater than that which divided them. They had concluded that for the party to govern again, the two sides had to reach an accommodation with one another.[16] Their deal was an attempt to demonstrate that apparently warring factions could come together in the wider interests of the party.
>   (Taylor, 2003:234)

Table 10:   Candidate Support in the Conservative Party Leadership Election of 1997

	First Ballot	Second Ballot	Third Ballot
William Hague	41 (25.0%)	62 (37.8%)	92 (56.1%)
Kenneth Clarke	49 (29.9%)	64 (39.0%)	70 (42.7%)
John Redwood	27 (16.5%)	38 (23.2%)	-
Peter Lille	24 (14.6%)	-	-
Michael Howard	23 (14.3%)	-	-
Abstentions	-	-	2 (1.2%)

Source: Adapted from Quinn, 2005:813

However, it was not to be. The majority of the Eurosceptic Thatcherite right were contemptuous of the Clarke-Redwood alliance. Redwood was derided as a careerist politician who had abandoned his principles for personal advancement.[17] Eventually it was the public intervention of Thatcher, that would extinguish any possibility that the Clarke-Redwood pact could be the solution to the ideological conflict which had bedevilled post-Thatcherite Conservatism. The prospect of a Europhile figure of the Tory left in the shape of Clarke acquiring the party leadership was sufficient for Thatcher to abandon her stance of neutrality.[18] She instructed the undecided on the Eurosceptic Thatcherite right not to support the Clarke-Redwood alliance. Standing alongside Hague outside of the House of Commons and in front of the assembled press, Thatcher left no scope for ambiguity:

> I am supporting William Hague. Now, have you got the name? William Hague for the same kind of principled government which I led, vote for William Hague on Thursday. Have you got the message?
> (Campbell, 2003:788)

In the ensuing third and final ballot the failure of the Clarke-Redwood was confirmed. Clarke could only secure six votes from the Redwood third ballot vote base of thirty-eight, and Hague secured a comfortable victory as the remaining Redwood supporters switched their allegiance to him rather than Clarke. With ninety-two votes Hague was elected as the new leader of the Conservative Party.[19]

7.4   Identifying the Multiple Legitimacy Problems of William Hague

In the immediate post-Thatcherite period, Major had struggled to impose his authority over the parliamentary Conservative Party and establish his legitimacy as party leader. The preceding chapter implied that these factors were a by-product of the means by which he had acquired the party leadership and the perception that he was a default leader. These crises of leadership – of authority and of legitimacy – that had engulfed Major whilst in government were to be replicated under Hague in opposition. The circumstances surrounding the means by which Hague had acquired the party leadership presented him with a multiplicity of legitimacy problems.

The first legitimacy problem that we associate with the emergence of Hague as the new party leader relates to the perception that his was a default victory due to the fact that the best candidates were not available. On the day before the general election it was rumoured that there were twelve potential candidates preparing for the post-election defeat contest for the party leadership (Williams, 1998:186-187). The electorate removed peripheral candidates such as Ian Lang, Michael Forsyth and Malcolm Rifkind, and the rumoured challenge of Gillian Shepherd did not materialise. The presumed final ballot run off, between the figure head for the Eurosceptic right (Portillo) and the pro-European Tory left prime candidate (Heseltine), failed to materialise due to the electorate in Enfield Southgate in the case of the former, and ill health in the case of the latter. Inside a few days the list of potential candidates was halved from twelve to six, thus fundamentally altering the dynamics of the ensuing contest in a manner advantageous to Hague.

The magnitude of the electoral meltdown of May 1997 created a window of opportunity for Hague. Had the swing from Conservative to Labour been less pronounced and the scale of the defeat less significant then Portillo would have retained his Enfield Southgate constituency. Had Portillo retained his parliamentary constituency, it is plausible to hypothecate the following: first, that Portillo would have put himself forward as a candidate to succeed Major (and probably would have won); second, that had Portillo been able to stand then Hague would not have run for the party leadership and instead would have supported Portillo (Nadler, 2001:5; Cowley and Quayle, 2001: 47). The authority that Hague sought to project over the parliamentary Conservative Party to ensure his legitimacy as party leader was undermined by having emerged through a restricted, if nonetheless, bloated field of candidates. Prevented from considering Heseltine or Portillo, Hague immediately appeared as a second division party leader. The validity of this assertion was given credence once Portillo returned to Parliament in November 1999: thereafter, the security of Hague as party leader was constantly under threat (Walters, 2001:202).

The second legitimacy problem that we can associate with the emergence of Hague as the new party leader relates to the fact that his ascent flowed from his status as the most appropriate conduit for the ABC (i.e. anybody but Clarke) brigade that existed within the parliamentary Conservative Party

(Alderman, 1998:13). This mirrored the ascent of Major in November 1990. Just as Major emerged as the candidate best positioned to prevent Heseltine assuming the party leadership, so Hague emerged as the candidate best placed to prevent Clarke from assuming the party leadership (Williams, 1998:224). The emergence of Hague as the most credible ABC candidate stemmed from the fact that he was the least unpopular and the most inoffensive of the other four candidates: given his low profile he also had the fewest enemies (Williams, 1998:224; Butler and Kavanagh, 2001:38; Cowley and Stuart, 2003:67).

In a distended field of candidates, it was inevitable that it would be a leadership contest characterised by multiple ballots. In this context, the successful candidate would be the one best able to attract second and then third choice votes when preferred first choice candidates had been excluded. Due to his relative inoffensiveness Hague was well positioned to sweep up second and third preference votes. His original support increased from forty-one to sixty-two (an increase of twenty-one) and then from sixty-two to ninety-two (an increase of thirty). The respective increases for Clarke were fifteen at the second ballot and six at the final ballot (Cowley and Stuart, 2003:67). Only through these third preference votes was Hague able to overcome Clarke, who had defeated him in both the first and second ballots. Hague was the ABC candidate propelled to the party leadership on the back of second and third preference votes.

The third legitimacy problem that we can associate with the emergence of Hague as the new party leader relates to the tactical misjudgements of the Eurosceptic Thatcherite right. We can argue that ideology was a determinant of voting behaviour and that the European ideological policy divide[20] was the determining ideological variable. Flowing from this we can argue the following.

The Thatcherite Eurosceptic right had four candidates articulating their views and seeking their endorsement. The Thatcherite Eurosceptic credentials of Redwood, Lilley and Howard were well documented.[21] Hague could be situated within their ideological cause but his identification as a Thatcherite Eurosceptic was less pronounced, more moderate, and therefore less widely recognised. Rather than unifying around one candidate, the Thatcherite Eurosceptic right fractured in three different directions. The candidates identified as of the absolutist Thatcherite Eurosceptic right, i.e. Redwood, Howard and Lilley, obtained support that was of the Thatcherite Eurosceptic right in the first ballot; whereas, the support that Hague obtained was predominantly derived from loyalist centrists, rather than from the committed Thatcherite Eurosceptic right (Cowley and Stuart, 2003:67).

There existed approximately seventy members of the parliamentary Conservative Party who could be identified as Eurosceptic.[22] If the majority of them had mobilised around one of Lilley, Howard or Redwood, or if the three had agreed that only one of them should stand as a candidate, then we can postulate that the main and sole Eurosceptic candidate could have secured approximately fifty plus votes in the first ballot (i.e. the combined Redwood, Lilley and Howard vote).[23] Had only one such identifiable Thatcherite Eurosceptic candidate stood and secured this vote then we can hypothecate that it would have been Hague who would have been eliminated after the first ballot. In such circumstances, the second ballot would have been a run off between the Europhile Clarke and one Eurosceptic who would have been well positioned to sweep up the soft Thatcherite Eurosceptic votes that would have existed flowing from the elimination of Hague. By their tactical misjudgements and failure to mobilise the Thatcherite Eurosceptic vote around one candidate, Redwood, Lilley and Howard, guaranteed that they would finish in the bottom three places in the first ballot (Cowley and Stuart, 2003:67). By the end of these multiple ballots it was apparent to the Thatcherite Eurosceptic right that, although Hague was moderately identifiable with their ideological bent, his accession to the party leadership was a by-product of their own tactical miscalculations. A Thatcherite Eurosceptic of greater repute and more identifiable with their cause would have emerged it they had not 'shot themselves in the foot'[24] (Cowley and Stuart, 2003: 67).

The validity of this assertion dovetails neatly into the fourth problem within the multiple legitimacy problems flowing from how Hague acquired the party leadership. The support that eventually emerged and propelled Hague to the party leadership was begrudging support and thus indicative of the shallowness of his mandate to lead the Conservative Party. This is clearly evident when we compare the vote share for Hague to the vote shares that had propelled his three predecessors to the party leadership. Heath assumed the party leadership in 1965 with 150 votes in the first ballot, which amounted to 49.3 per cent of the parliamentary Conservative Party. Thatcher assumed the party leadership of the Conservative Party having defeated Heath in the first ballot with 130 votes (or 47.1 per cent) and then overcoming four new candidates in the second ballot in which she secured 146 votes (or 52.9 per cent). Major secured the party leadership with 185 votes or 47.7 per cent of the parliamentary Conservative Party and did not require a second ballot for confirmation as his main opponents withdrew their candidatures. If we consider the final ballot then Hague stands comparison with his predecessors – he secured 92 votes or 56.1 per cent of the parliamentary Conservative Party. However, a more appropriate comparison is the first ballot, in which Hague secured 41 votes or just 25 per cent of the parliamentary Conservative Party. Given the crisis of leadership legitimacy that had engulfed Major it amounted to a worrying precedent that the support base for Hague appeared to be even more ambivalent than that secured by Major.

Moreover, as we have already emphasised, that miniscule first ballot support base would not have existed had Portillo been able to stand (Cowley and Stuart, 2003:68). Thus in comparative terms his support was not only shallow but was grudging. No factor indicated this more than the belated endorsement of Thatcher. In the earlier rounds she had avoided expressing a preference but was known to harbour doubts about the Thatcherite credentials of Hague (Alderman, 1998:13). However, when faced with the prospect of the Clarke-Redwood alliance, she was compelled out of political necessity to finally endorse Hague.[25] On the one hand, her refusal to do so earlier indicated doubts about his capacity to oversee the Thatcherite policy legacy; on the other hand, her belated endorsement saddled him with an endorsement which undermined the rationale of his candidature: a fresh start and a break from the discredited past which had been overwhelmingly rejected by the electorate (Garnett, 2003:58).

Therefore, when considering the interwoven nature of these factors, it is clear that Hague assumed the party leadership without a strong mandate. His ascent was devoid of the kind of political enthusiasm which is the essential precursor to obtaining and maintaining authority over the parliamentary Conservative Party and legitimacy as party leader. He emerged as the best candidates were unavailable; he emerged because a sufficient section of the parliamentary Conservative party could not abide the thought of Clarke triumphing; he emerged due to the tactical miscalculations within the Thatcherite Eurosceptic right; and he emerged from a shallow and unenthusiastic base of ambivalent second and third preference supporters. He was like his predecessor, a default leader undermined by a multiplicity of legitimacy problems (Norton, 1998b:13; Seldon and Snowdon, 2005:250). It constituted an inauspicious start to his tenure as party leader and a portent of the difficulties that would lie ahead.

7.5   Conclusion

The Conservatives had exited office and entered opposition in a demoralised state. They then propelled themselves needlessly into their fourth party leadership election inside eight years. Given that in the first twenty-four years of internal democracy, only two were deemed to be necessary, this escalation in debating the party leadership was seen as a symptom of Conservative decline. It proved to be a distinctive party leadership election for a number of reasons. Alderman was to observe of the process that:

It set a precedent by going into a third ballot…it was the longest judged by the time between the announcement of Major's intention to resign and the election of his successor…the electorate was far smaller than on any previous occasion….and the campaign expenditure by the candidates far higher[26]…the way in which the contest was conducted, gave rise to the most fundamental questioning since 1965 of the leadership election procedures and the principles of underpinning them.

(Alderman, 1998:1)

And of the outcome, he argued:

> That a junior member of Major's Cabinet, who had at one stage almost been persuaded not to enter the contest, should have been able to win, over the heads of far more experienced rivals, was a remarkable achievement. His having done so in a predominantly right-wing party in spite of doubts about his right wing credentials made Hague's success even more noteworthy. (Alderman, 1998:13)

The scale of the Conservatives electoral defeat in May 1997 suggested that it was probable that they would lose the next general election as well. Given this, the political judgement of Hague has to be questioned. It was well documented that he possessed a burning ambition to become Prime Minister. To enhance his chances of achieving this objective, Hague should have not stood for the party leadership in the immediate aftermath of their electoral meltdown in May 1997. Given that at that time, he held the primary position as the leading candidate from the next generation, he could have allowed his more senior colleagues to contest the succession under the assumption that they would not emerge as the next Conservative Prime Minister. He could then have assumed that the immediate successor to Major would have done the necessary groundwork to ensure that the next party leader would be better positioned to become the next Conservative Prime Minister – i.e. the best case scenario was an election triumph in the general election of 2005 or 2006. Ultimately, Hague allowed his ambition to cloud his judgement. Moreover, given the failure of his party leadership tenure, his successor, Duncan Smith, was remarkably and unexpectedly no better positioned in 2001 than Hague had been when he had assumed the party leadership in 1997. In retrospect it can be argued that for both Hague and the Conservative Party it was regrettable that he emerged as the new party leader in succession to Major.

It had been an acrimonious and a debilitating contest. During the course of the elongated campaign, Hague had been subject to unsubstantiated innuendo about his sexuality, whilst Howard had been the victim of a whispering campaign that possessed elements of anti-semitism. White feathers, a symbol of cowardice, were anonymously posted to third-ballot defectors from the Redwood camp (Alderman, 1998:14-15). If the process was unpleasant, the outcome was self-defeating. The parliamentary Conservative Party had in their infinite wisdom rejected the following political and electoral indicators: the most experienced candidate was Clarke; the candidate most popular with the electorate was Clarke; the candidate most popular with the membership of the Conservative Party was Clarke; and the candidate who the Labour Party most feared was Clarke. The ideological infestation that had convulsed post-Thatcherite Conservatism ensured that the Europhilia of Clarke outweighed these aforementioned indicators. The successor to Major had to be of the Thatcherite Eurosceptic right, but in the absence of Portillo, the Thatcherite Eurosceptic right were tactically disorganised and inept; by knocking each other out, Redwood, Lilley and Howard, ensured that Hague was the last man standing as the ABC candidate, despite the fact that he possessed the weakest Thatcherite Eurosceptic credentials.

His emergence as the new party leader presented Hague with a myriad of legitimacy problems. He lacked an ideological core to his support; the support that he had acquired was default and had gravitated to him because there was no better alternative available to the Thatcherite Eurosceptic right. As Cowley and Stuart observe, his ultimate level of support (when supplemented by second and third ballot votes), was relatively broad but it was inherently shallow. Hague was not elected as party leader because of who he was and what he could deliver; he emerged because of who he was not (i.e. Clarke) and what he was willing to prevent in order to win (i.e. pro-Europeanism advancing as Conservative Party policy) (Cowley and Stuart, 2003:68). The Conservative Party had entered the leadership election seeking to terminate the ideological insurgency that had engulfed the party leadership tenure of Major. Yet, with tragic symmetry the rationale upon which Major emerged was replicated in the emergence of Hague (Garnett, 2003:52).

Few Conservative parliamentarians from the 1992 to 1997 parliamentary Conservative Party had anticipated that the successor to Major would have been Hague. Indeed he was a reluctant candidate whose candidature emerged due to the elimination of his preferred choice (Portillo) and his sense that his second choice (Howard) would not be able to win. The perversity of the events and outcome of the Conservative Party leadership election of 1997 became even more apparent when the candidate who finished last (Howard) was propelled to the party leadership in 2003 by ritual acclamation after the failure of Hague's successor, Duncan Smith. When considering the default and misplaced emergence of Hague as the new party leader, it may be worth reflecting on the view of an anonymous Conservative parliamentarian. Just three months before the Conservative Party leadership election of 1997 it was suggested to him that Hague might emerge as the next party leader. He responded disdainfully with: 'please, you cannot be serious' (Brandreth, 1999:488).

THE QUIET MAN EMERGES: THE ELECTION OF IAIN DUNCAN SMITH

The reaction of the Conservative Party to losing office in 1964 had been the establishment of new procedures to ensure that future party leaders should be democratically determined. The reaction to losing office in 1974 was to amend the procedures governing the election of the party leader to ensure that an unpopular incumbent could be challenged and removed. The validity of the responses to losing office on each occasion was justified within a five year period. In July 1965 Alec Douglas-Home resigned and the first democratically elected leader of the Conservative Party, Edward Heath, was able to return the Conservatives to government at the general election of June 1970. In February 1975 Heath was forcibly evicted and Margaret Thatcher assumed the party leadership and propelled the Conservatives back into office in May 1979. On both occasions the incumbent party leader who had just ceased to be Prime Minister was removed (voluntarily or forcibly) from the party leadership as a consequence of the procedural adaptation. The circumstances following the electoral meltdown of May 1997 were fundamentally different. The timing of adapting the rules governing the procedures for electing the party leader occurred *after* they had elected a successor for the defeated former Conservative Prime Minister. The issue of the timing of the succession and thereby the method of determination proved to be immensely significant.

As the previous chapter intimated, the failure of Major to learn from the Douglas-Home precedent had done the Conservative Party a considerable disservice. Major could have utilised the example of Douglas-Home and remained as party leader in opposition in order to oversee the shift to new governing procedures for the election of the party leader. His desire for a swift departure from front line politics would ensure that the succession would be determined under the existing party leadership election rules. This was despite that their existed a widely held view that the existing rules needed reappraisal, and that new procedures should be adopted that would incorporate the mass membership (Alderman, 1999:265; Norton, 1998b:10). Indeed, when Hague campaigned for the party leadership in the immediate aftermath of the resignation of Major, he campaigned on a platform that emphasised the need for organisation reform. This included a response to the concerns surrounding the existing party leadership election procedures (Alderman, 1999:260; Collings and Seldon, 2001:626-627).

The rationale for shifting to mass membership involvement in the succession process was three-fold. The first factor related to the acrimonious removal of Thatcher from the party leadership in November 1990. Her removal had been at the behest of a minority of the parliamentary Conservative Party in direct contravention to the wishes of the mass membership. The vast majority of the mass membership had remained loyal to Thatcher and wanted her to remain as party leader. The fact that their opinion was disregarded had created outrage amongst party activists (Alderman, 1999:265). The second factor related to the rapid decision to determine a successor to Major without amending the procedures for electing the party leader first. In the immediate aftermath of his resignation, the 1922 Executive Committee had refused to consider the idea of extending the franchise to the mass membership as a prelude to determining a successor to Major. Their intransigence was immensely provocative to party activists, who repeatedly emphasised how the link between the grassroots party activists and the parliamentary Conservative Party had been significantly damaged by the electoral meltdown of May 1997. The consequence of this was that Hague was elected from a minority of parliamentary constituencies, mostly in the south of England, and with no input at all from Scottish or Welsh conservatives. This was deemed to be unacceptable (Alderman, 1999:260). The third factor related to the outcome of the Conservative Party leadership election of June 1997. In the course of the campaign numerous surveys of mass membership opinion repeatedly demonstrated a preference for Clarke over Hague, as the heavyweight political status and experience of Clarke overcame his profound Europhilia. Had the timing of adapting the rules and thereby the method of determining the succession been different, then Clarke would have probably been leader of the opposition and the era of opposition would have been considerably different (Peele, 1998:147).

8.1   The Resignation of William Hague

As had been identified in the previous chapter, it was clear that Hague had assumed the party leadership on an inherently weak mandate. His emergence was as a consequence of the best candidates being unavailable, and his victory was a default victory as it was a by product of an anti-Clarke support base rather than a pro-Hague endorsement. The weakness of his mandate was reinforced by the perception that he had not secured the legitimate endorsement of the Thatcherite Eurosceptic right which was split between numerous candidates. This tactical miscalculation explained why Hague was to receive the poisoned delayed endorsement of Margaret Thatcher. These weaknesses of legitimacy and authority flowing from his mandate impeded his leadership credibility as did his inheritance. Hague was saddled with a legacy of governing incompetence, ideological division, sleaze and corruption, and perceptions of weak leadership. Hague was unable to overcome these impediments to recovery and would fail to adhere to his campaign promise of a fresh future for the Conservatives. At no stage during the Hague era did the Conservative Party present themselves as a credible alternative party of government (Collings and Seldon, 2001:636).

This was immensely depressing for the Conservatives. They had assumed that the general election of May 1997 would be their electoral rock bottom. They predicted that the realities of governing would present considerable difficulties for New Labour. As this evolved, they assumed that belief and faith in New Labour would gradually dissolve. As the honeymoon between the electorate and New Labour passed, so a disgruntled electorate would decide to reengage with a reformed and renewed Conservative Party. They also assumed that Hague would be sufficiently detached from the wreckage of the Major era to present an image of a new beginning. Such optimism proved to be misplaced. The party leadership tenure of Hague proved to be an unmitigated disaster for the Conservatives. He was unable to articulate a narrative of Conservatism, in the post-Thatcherite era, that was appealing externally to the electorate or sufficiently persuasive to ensure internal unity. Moreover, he was unable to provide a coherent and sustained critique of New Labour. Under Hague, the Conservatives remained deeply unpopular with the electorate, with their opinion poll rating oscillating between twenty-three and thirty three for the duration of the 1997 to 2001 parliamentary term. The New Labour lead in the opinion polls would remain around the twenty percentage points for all but a few months (Collings and Seldon, 2001:636; Kelly, 2004a:399).

Policy incoherence and ideological division blighted the Hague leadership tenure, and as a consequence he became viewed as a poor strategist (Collings and Seldon, 2001:628). Whereas the Conservative Party had utilised previous eras in opposition to engage in substantive appraisals of policy direction, Hague was unable to sustain his commitment to any particular policy direction. He was initially attracted to the concept of compassionate Conservatism with an emphasis on embracing social liberalism. However, this moderate approach, with its associated emphasis on inclusiveness, failed to generate any upsurge in support for the Conservatives in the 1997 to 1999 period (Hayton, 2006:3).

The moderate approach reached a road block when Peter Lilley, the Deputy Leader of the Conservative Party, announced that the Conservatives needed to broaden their electoral appeal by shifting their focus away from solely economic concerns. His emphasis on the importance of education and health, and his desire to reconfigure perceptions of Conservatism around the public services, was seen by many on the right as a repudiation of Thatcherism (Hayton, 2006:9). Rather than constituting a strategic review of the meaning of Conservatism and the policy platform of the Conservatives, it stimulated emotional and elemental passions about the legacy of Thatcherism. The chaos that had been caused by the Lilley speech led to him being dismissed as Deputy Party Leader and removed from the shadow Cabinet. To emphasise the impact of the Lilley speech it is worth noting the observations of Taylor, who described the speech as one of the most incendiary speeches ever delivered in post-war Conservatism (Taylor, 2005:146).

Thereafter, Hague switched to a more right-wing and Eurosceptic direction. The emphasis was now on anti-Europeanism, attacking bogus asylum seekers, law and order, and cutting taxation and bureaucracy. Compassionate Conservatism was replaced by the mantra of the common sense revolution. This switch to a cluster of issues aligned around the notion of national identity was supposedly the new narrative around which Hague believed Conservatism could reclaim its former appeal[1] (Taylor, 2003:240; Taylor, 2005:149).

By abandoning the inclusive notion of compassionate Conservatism and embracing the exclusive rhetoric of what was dubbed the common-sense revolution, Hague was accused of chasing panaceas (Walters, 2001:105, 115). Without a settled and coherent strategy Hague undermined his leadership credibility[2] and intensified the ideological divisions within the parliamentary party. The vexed question of European integration hurt Hague just as it had Major, although Hague abandoned the ambivalent stance of his predecessor. Hague ruled out British membership of the single European currency in the next Parliament should the Conservatives be elected, irrespective of a referendum. By abandoning the option of entry, he lost from his shadow Cabinet two pro-Europeans, David Curry and Ian Taylor (Collings and Seldon, 2001:628-629). The fratricidal ideological struggle for the future of Conservatism extended beyond disputes between Europhilic and Euro-sceptic wings of the parliamentary party. The Lilley intervention and the reaction that it provoked, demonstrated the split between pragmatists (including some revisionist Thatcherites), who wanted to emphasis public service reform and a specifically defined role for the state, and those who were committed to the continuation of the Thatcherite economic agenda. Mapped onto these economic and European based ideological disputes was the increasingly salient divide between inclusive, moderate social liberals (optimised by the revisionist Michael Portillo) and traditional social conservatives (represented by the increasingly vocal Ann Widdecombe) (Collings and Seldon, 2001:629).

This incoherence and division demonstrated the lack of a settled and viable narrative of Conservatism. Hague was unable to construct an electoral winning strategy, or effectively manage the ideological currents within the parliamentary party. Moreover, he was unable to secure dominance of elite political debate, where New Labour were in the ascendant on perceptions of economic management and the delivery of public services such as health and education (Taylor, 2003:240). As they did not display the characteristics of a potential party of government, morale plummeted further. It was a demoralised and dispirited party that faced the electorate in the general election of June 2001. The core vote strategy that Hague had embraced post 1999 had been designed to ensure that the Conservative vote participated rather than abstained, thus limiting the scale of the victory for New Labour. In chasing the core vote Hague succeeded in alienating those voters that the Conservatives most needed to deliver an electoral victory (Norton, 2005:34).

The outcome of the general election of June 2001 was catastrophic for the Conservative Party. The Conservative share of the vote increased by just one percentage point and they made a gain of only one parliamentary seat as their parliamentary representation increased from 165 to 166 seats (Cowley and Quayle, 2001:46). The outcome amounted to the first time that the Conservatives had suffered two successive landslides defeats. Moreover, at 8.3 million, the total number of Conservative votes was the lowest return that they had received since 1929, when there was a far smaller electorate. Their electoral performance was a shocking rebuke to those Conservatives who assumed that their electoral nadir was four years earlier. The Conservatives had seen the vote count crash by a further 1.2 million, leaving them nearly six million short of the number of Conservative votes that they secured the last time they had secured electoral endorsement back in 1992 (Butler and Kavanagh, 2002:254; Kelly, 2004a:399).

Hague accepted full responsibility for the electoral defeat[3] and immediately announced that it was intention to resign.[4] The rationale for an immediate resignation echoed that of his predecessor four years earlier:

> whatever I do, the leadership election is going to start now. I can't stop it, and if I'm not careful the focus will all be on me and I don't want that to happen. The party will tear itself apart if I stay on. It must start talking about what it must do to put things right, not agonise over whether I should remain.   (Walters, 2001:2-3)

8.2   New Leadership Election, New Leadership Election Procedures

By resigning Hague triggered another leadership election. This would be the fifth contest for the party leadership in the past twelve years but the first to be conducted under the new election procedures.

Those new procedures constituted the most pronounced adaptations since the inception of internal democracy in the aftermath of the loss of office in 1964. The provision for annual elections, that had been inserted as a method for removing Heath over twenty years ago, and had resulted in his removal and that of Thatcher fifteen years later, had been removed. This was replaced with a new mechanism for initiating a leadership contest which would follow after an incumbent voluntary resigns, or when the incumbent was defeated in a confidence motion. The confidence motion could be triggered by notification to the 1922 Executive Committee that 15 per cent of the parliamentary Conservative Party wanted a ballot[5] (Collings and Seldon, 2001:627).

By resigning Hague would put to the test the new procedures relating to the extension of the franchise to the mass membership. The participation of the parliamentary Conservative Party was significantly reduced. The new procedures meant that if more than two candidates emerged then the parliamentary Conservative Party would conduct a series of ballots until only two candidates remained. Those two candidates would then be presented to the party membership who, on the basis of one member, one vote, would determine the succession (Norton, 2001:11-12).

The all new and enhanced democratic procedures would be drawn out over a three month period, in comparison to the normal two-three weeks of previous party leadership elections. Hague would announce his resignation on June 8th. The initiation of the party leadership elections was then delayed as the parliamentary Conservative Party had to elect a new chair of the 1922 Executive Committee, whose responsibility it would be to manage the party leadership election. Once Michael Spicer was elected as the new chair of 1922 Executive Committee, he decreed that the deadline for nominations for the parliamentary stage of the succession battle would be July 5th. As more than two candidates would emerge a series of eliminative parliamentary ballots would dominate through mid-July. Once Conservative parliamentarians had whittled the options down to two, they were then presented to the mass membership, who were then able to consider the merits of the two candidates, over a two month campaigning period. Hague would finally stand aside in September. It would be a brutal and discourteous three months for the Conservatives.

8.3 The Candidates: Two Heavyweights and Three Lightweights

Four years earlier one of the defining features of the battle to succeed Major had the depleted field of candidates for the parliamentary Conservative Party to select from. The primary candidate of the Thatcherite Eurosceptic right, Michael Portillo, could not participate following his electoral defeat; a fate that also removed Malcolm Rifkind as a potential compromise unity candidate from the succession battle. The leading figure of the pro-European Tory left, Michael Heseltine was also removed from contention due to ill health. The fact that a vacancy now existed was of no consequence for Rifkind, who had failed to regain his constituency seat and thus could not participate. Heseltine's non-participation four years earlier ended his front line political career. He did not serve in the shadow Cabinet and ended his parliamentary career at the end of the Parliament.

Of those who had contested the succession four years earlier, three had seen their political careers decline to such an extent that participation was no longer viable. The credibility of John Redwood was undermined by the fact that he had now contested and lost two successive leadership contests and the fact that the Eurosceptic right, his natural constituency, no longer viewed him as a plausible candidate. The two other defeated candidates, Peter Lilley and Michael Howard, had both departed the shadow Cabinet in the summer of 1999. Lilley was no longer a credible candidate as his strategic overview for the direction of Conservatism had been divisive and had alienated the base of his natural supporters; i.e. economic Thatcherites. Whereas Lilley had been dismissed from the shadow Cabinet, Howard had voluntarily retired as Shadow Foreign Secretary, which was widely interpreted as signalling the end of his political ambitions.

Although Heseltine, Rifkind, Redwood, Lilley and Howard were non participants, Portillo was now able to contest the succession and Clarke was assumed to be willing to stand again. These two heavyweight political figures with Cabinet experience would dispute the succession with three candidates without Cabinet experience who had seen their political stock rise in the era of opposition: Michael Ancram, David Davis and Iain Duncan Smith. The intended challenge from the socially Conservative Ann Widdecombe did not materialise. Widdecombe had been the first to publicly declare an interest in disputing the party leadership. Within two days of Hague announcing his intention to resign, Widdecombe informed political journalists that she was liaising with her parliamentary colleagues to determine the viability of her mounting a challenge. She would choose not to formally enter the ballots as that process of parliamentary liaison would reveal that she lacked sufficient support amongst her parliamentary colleagues to justify standing[6] (Carter and Alderman, 2002:571).

The candidature of Ancram was the least expected. He had served as a minister in the Thatcher and Major Governments without justifying promotion into the Cabinet. He had served in the shadow Cabinet for the duration of the previous Parliament and had occupied the position of Conservative Party Chairman since 1998. His advocates attempted to emphasise his emollient and consensual style. They argued that his soft affiliation to the Eurosceptic cause, would be sufficiently reassuring to pro-Europeans to ensure unity and end the divisiveness of the past decade. Aligned to the emphasis on unity and consensus was a commitment to take time to reflect on the predicament of contemporary Conservatism before attempting to articulate the strategy for recovery (Carter and Alderman, 2002:573-574).

The main limitation of the Ancram candidature related to the composition of the parliamentary Conservative Party. Ideology was a central determinant of how Conservative parliamentarians identified with the candidates. The parliamentary Conservative Party was increasingly Eurosceptic in its composition (see Hill, 2004; 2007). One candidate, Clarke was identifiable with the pro-European cause and the three other candidates (Davis, Duncan Smith and Portillo) were strongly identified with the Eurosceptic cause. In this context the fact that Ancram tended towards Euroscepticism but was inherently more pragmatic than Davis, Duncan Smith and Portillo, created a danger than he may be squeezed as he had the least identification with a distinct ideologically constructed position.

As a candidate Davis had three potential strengths: first, he had ministerial experience having served just below Cabinet level in the Major Governments; second, he offered credibility as his reputation had been enhanced by his term as Chair of the Public Accounts Committee in the last Parliament; and, third, his council estate up bringing would enable Conservatives to construct a narrative around a Conservative Party which was representative of modern Britain. His limitations were his low public profile, his poor public speaking and his reputation for divisiveness which had contributed to him acquiring, according to Montgomerie, numerous political enemies (Montgomerie, 2005:2).

The candidature of Duncan Smith was widely anticipated. Duncan Smith had supported Redwood in his two previous attempts to secure the party leadership, although he had briefly considered standing himself four years earlier, before eventually campaigning for Redwood (Williams, 1998:192-193). He then ended his alliance with Redwood when the Clarke-Redwood pact was constructed and supported Hague in the final ballot (Williams, 1998:226). His reward for supporting Hague had been membership of the shadow Cabinet, where he had served as shadow Social Security Secretary between 1997 and 1998 and shadow Defence Secretary since 1998. Ideologically, Duncan Smith was a creature of the pure Thatcherite right. Economically dry, strongly Eurosceptic and a social conservative he had gained notoriety during the Major era for having refused ministerial office as he strongly objected to the parameters of European policy. As a consequence, he possessed no ministerial experience whatsoever but had a reputation for being principled, according to his Eurosceptic advocates, or divisive according to his pro-European and party loyalist detractors. His reputation for divisiveness was a by product of his parliamentary reputation for rebellion during the parliamentary passage of the Treaty of European Union (i.e. the Maastricht Treaty) (Carter and Alderman, 2002:573; Walters, 2001:220).

Parliamentarians who were attracted to the candidature of Duncan Smith were assumed to be ideologically motivated Thatcherites, for whom ideological purity (especially on the question of Europe) was paramount. Such ideologues were warned that his candidature had worrying implications for a number of reasons. If one of the objectives to restoring electoral appeal was demonstrating unity, then installing a known rebel would be a foolish move. As party leader it would be problematic for Duncan Smith to legitimately demand loyalty and unity from his parliamentary subordinates without accompanying accusations of hypocrisy. In addition to his inability to unify the parliamentary Conservative Party, there were doubts about his lack of ministerial experience and his media presentational skills. Given the poor public persona of Hague and the assumption that his public relations gaffes had been damaging to the image of the Conservative Party, there was a concern that Duncan Smith was merely an inferior version of Hague.[7]

Of the five candidates who declared by nominations deadline the two who generated the most press interest and intrigue were Portillo and Clarke (Carter and Alderman, 2002:575). As the previous chapter implied Portillo was the 'could have been' candidate had he been able to stand four years earlier, and Clarke was the 'should have been' candidate, if the views of the mass membership had been taken into account. Such assertions demonstrate the importance in politics of timing and method. For Portillo the Conservative Party leadership election of 2001 was four years too late for his candidature as his status as the standard bearer of the Thatcherite right had been eroded in the interim period. For Clarke the Conservative Party leadership election of 2001 was four years too late for him in extending the franchise to the mass membership as his popularity with party activists had waned in the interim period.

The political character of Portillo had been significantly altered by the humbling experience of electoral rejection four years earlier, and led to a personal reappraisal of his political and ideological views and how he projected himself.[8] He came to believe that the Conservative Party had become disagreeable to the electorate. He argued that the Conservatives needed to dispel the assumption that they were uncaring about poverty, disability and single parenthood. Such revisionist rhetoric demonstrated that

Portillo was shedding much of the Thatcherite rhetoric in the social and economic sphere,[9] although he retained his Euroscepticism (Taylor, 2005:147).

The altering of his political strategy and his emphasis on modernising and social liberalism, fractured his appeal amongst the Thatcherites. Those Thatcherites who were primarily motivated by the pursuit of social conservatism (i.e. the defence of traditional values) now found Portillo an anathema. Whilst out of Parliament Portillo revealed that he had had homosexual experiences during his time at University. He was concerned that this could damage his candidature, and overshadow him if he was to become Conservative Party leader, as it would become a focal point of media attention. The fear that an anti-gay agenda would be advanced against him proved to be correct. In endorsing Duncan Smith, former Thatcherite Cabinet minister, Norman Tebbit argued that the Conservative Party needed a leader who was a 'normal family man with children'. This amounted to a crude jibe about the previous homosexuality of Portillo (Carter and Alderman, 2002:572-573).

With Portillo, Davis, Duncan Smith and to a lesser extent Ancram all being aligned to the Eurosceptic wing of the parliamentary Conservative Party, the only pro-European candidate was Clarke, just as had been the case four years earlier. The strengths of a Clarke candidature mirrored that of his previous campaign; i.e. his extensive ministerial experience and his reputation for competence. Similarly the limitations of his previous candidature remained; i.e. the parliamentary Conservative Party was increasingly Eurosceptic in its ideological outlook and Clarke was a committed Europhile; and his Europhilia would impede his capacity to unify the Conservative Party should he emerge as their new leader. The perception that Clarke was a divisive figure had intensified in the Hague era for two reasons. First, his refusal to serve in the shadow Cabinet impeded the capacity of Hague to demonstrate unity within the parliamentary Conservative Party; and, second, his appearance alongside Tony Blair in a Britain in Europe conference had enraged loyalist Conservatives as well as Eurosceptic Conservatives (Walters, 2001:52).

Despite these concerns Clarke believed that his Europhilia would not impede his chances with the mass membership as they had preferred his candidature to that of Hague four years earlier. However, he was concerned as to whether he could garner enough votes to be one of the two candidates presented to the mass membership. A further concern worried Clarke. He realised that he could secure the leadership through the support of the mass membership even though only a minority of the parliamentary Conservative Party had voted for him in the preliminary parliamentary ballots. In this context, the concern for Clarke was whether it was feasible for the Europhile to lead the Conservative Party with such a small base of support within the parliamentary Conservative Party (Carter and Alderman, 2002:574).

8.4   The Parliamentary Ballots

As the first ballot approached, the candidature of Portillo seemed to have secured a number of advantages. First, he had secured the public support of the majority of the shadow Cabinet. Second, with over forty declared supporters he had the largest declared supporters' base, and that list was ideologically broad. Third, he had the support of respectable senior figures with Thatcherite credentials, such as Peter Lilley and Francis Maude. Utilising these advantages, the Portillo camp wanted to create a bandwagon effect based around the diversity of the declared supporters. They emphasised how known economic damp, pro-European, social liberals, such as Stephen Dorrell, Tim Yeo and Damien Green, had all declared for Portillo. The depth and breadth of his list of declared supporters ensured that Portillo entered the first ballot as favourite (Carter and Alderman, 2002:573; Norton, 2001:12-13).

His leading leadership rival and fellow political heavyweight, Clarke, recognised the strength of the Portillo campaign. In announcing his candidature, Clarke had observed that all of the other candidates, with the exception of Portillo (and himself), would be incapable of engineering a recovery that would propel the Conservatives to an electoral triumph in four to five years time. By recognising the merits of a Portillo candidature, Clarke was admitting that his most realistic ambition was to come second to Portillo in the final parliamentary ballot, and then campaign for the party membership vote (Carter and Alderman, 2002:576). Clarke was securing declared support from traditional figures from the Tory left such as John Gummer and Ian Taylor, but his campaign garnered media attention when he secured the support of Ann Widdecombe. A figure of the traditional Tory right, Widdecombe, should have felt inclined to Duncan Smith or Davis. She gravitated to Clarke due to her overwhelming detestation of Portillo and his social liberalism and her belief that only Clarke was capable of preventing Portillo annexing the party leadership for the modernisers (Norton, 2001:13).

The three remaining candidates were hoping to exploit the existence of the 'stop Portillo' and 'stop Clarke' agendas that existed. Duncan Smith and Davis, as ideologically identikits, both hoped to garner votes from Euro-sceptics who feared the pro-European Clarke emerging. They also hoped that their social conservative credentials would attract social conservatives who felt uncomfortable with the recently acquired social liberalism of Portillo. Ancram was actually the most overt in his displeasure of Portillo. His acolytes sought to exaggerate the divisiveness of Portillo on social, sexual and moral matters, and Clarke on European policy. The implicit suggestion was that a vote for Ancram was a vote for unity. That the unity candidature of Ancram, as an ideological moderate, failed to gather momentum seemed to be indicative of the intense ideological insurgency that was still engulfing the parliamentary Conservative Party.

Portillo, as expected, came first in the first parliamentary ballot. However, the size of his parliamentary support proved to be less than his campaign had assumed (Norton, 2001:14). Given his extensive list of declared supporters, from differing strands of Conservatism, forty nine votes was a disappointing return. Just as had been the case with Clarke at the first ballot four years earlier, Portillo had come first but had in the process managed to look vulnerable. The fear for the Portillo campaign was that they had hit the peak of their possible support base already (Carter and Alderman, 2002:579-580). Despite his lower than expected return the assumption remained that Portillo would secure one of the final two places. The fears were mainly within the Clarke camp. Clarke had failed to secure second place missing out by three votes to Duncan Smith. Clarke remained competitive entering the second ballot, but Duncan Smith was moving from an outsider to a viable candidate. As Norton argues, Duncan Smith had now assumed the mantle of the standard bearer of the pure Thatcherite right (Norton, 2005:36).

The returns for the remaining candidates, Ancram and Davis, would produce one of the farcical elements to the three month succession. They finished tied on twenty-one votes. They were fifteen votes behind Clarke and twenty-eight behind Portillo in first place. Their candidatures had secured the endorsement of less then twenty per cent of their parliamentary colleagues. It was clear that they were unlikely to be able to finish in the first two of a forthcoming parliamentary ballot. However, as the leadership election rules made no provision for candidates securing an identical number of votes, they selfishly decided to continue and in doing so brought ignominy upon the Conservative Party.[10] Michael Spicer, as Chair of the 1922 Executive Committee, was thus compelled to arrange a rerun of the five way ballot and this time the tied ballot conundrum was addressed: if Davis and Ancram tied for last place in the rerun they would both be eliminated (Carter and Alderman, 2002:579).

The rerun ballot saw minimal movement in support for the respective candidates. Ancram and Davis both lost support and with Ancram coming last he was automatically eliminated. Having seen his candidature lose three votes from the first to second ballot, Davis decided to voluntarily withdraw. A three way ballot would now take place between Portillo, who had come first twice, Duncan Smith and Clarke. The expectation was now that Portillo and Duncan Smith would be presented to the mass membership. Duncan Smith was assumed to be the chief benefactor of Ancram and Davis departing the contest, as both the defeated candidates stated that they were switching their allegiance to Duncan Smith.

Between the second and third ballots the Portillo campaign would implode. Despite his Cabinet experience, his high public profile and his personal charisma, doubts had existed about his candidature throughout (Norton, 2001:12). Those doubts centred around his ideological revisionism and the methods that he and his campaign team deployed. His ideological revisionism produced converts but seriously angered his former constituency of the pure Thatcherite right of economic liberals, Eurosceptics and social conservatives. Portillo sought to articulate his inclusive agenda around the adoption of a more moderate and tolerant line on the legalisation of cannabis and section 28 (which prevented the promotion of homosexuality in secondary education). He also encouraged the party to adopt a more aggressive approach to securing more female parliamentarians. His whole approach angered traditionalist social conservatives. They derided his emphasis on inclusion by suggesting that Portillo should concentrate on mainstream political issues, rather than his current obsession, with what they claimed was the 3W's – weed, women, and woofters (Carter and Alderman, 2002:576).

His socially conservative critics were determined to derail the Portillo bandwagon and were prepared to engage in vicious personal attacks on Portillo and his private life. Their hostile agenda, which carried with it none too subtle homophobic undertones, formed the basis of a 'stop Portillo' faction. Mapped onto the invective that they subjected Portillo to for his personal background were their accusations of indecisiveness, disloyalty and poor judgement. The indecisiveness accusation was derived from the way in which Portillo had behaved in the party leadership election seven years earlier when Major had defeated Redwood. Portillo had made initial preparations to either challenge Major or be prepared for a hypothetical second ballot. That Portillo dithered then was now used by many of his former advocates to suggest indecision and cowardice, and that such characteristics were inappropriate for a party leader (Carter and Alderman, 2002:570). That aborted challenge to Major also formed the basis of rumours of disloyalty. This view of disloyalty was reinforced by Ann Widdecombe who accused Portillo of being a destabilising influence under Hague and that his supporters had engaged in backbiting which had been immensely damaging to morale and unity[11] (Carter and Alderman, 2002:578; Cowley and Green, 2005:3).

These accusations of indecisiveness and disloyalty were seen to be indicative of the poor judgement and weak political acumen of Portillo. There were two factors that demonstrated this. These became of increasing concern to the former supporters of Ancram and Davis, whose voting intentions were now the key to determining which two candidates would proceed. First, the Portillo campaign had been poorly managed and orchestrated (Walters, 2001:214-215). Although Portillo had a strong initial base of support from amongst the shadow Cabinet, he had weak links with the backbench of the parliamentary Conservative Party. His lack of close associates impeded his capacity to secure more supporters beyond his initial declared list. The weak communication that he and his acolytes engaged in would contrast sharply with the approach of Duncan Smith. His prominent backbench rebel status in the Major Government ensured that he had good links with an overwhelmingly Eurosceptic backbench parliamentary Conservative Party. Whereas Portillo was lethargic in appealing to this core group, Duncan Smith was assiduous.

Second, poor tactical judgement within the Portillo camp compounded their campaign management failings. As the third parliamentary ballot approached, the Portillo camp appeared to be engaging in longer term strategic planning in advancement of the party membership ballot. In this ballot an endorsement by Margaret Thatcher would be beneficial given the reverence in which the former Prime Minister was held amongst the party membership. The Portillo camp briefed that Thatcher was supporting their candidate, despite the fact that at this juncture Thatcher had made no public comment on her preference. When she failed to confirm this it made Portillo and his campaign team seem foolish (Carter and Alderman, 2002:580).

Going into the final ballot, the Portillo camp was confident that Portillo would be one of the final two candidates submitted to the party membership. Their confidence was so pronounced that there was Machiavellian plotting being hatched to ensure that they would face Duncan Smith rather than Clarke in the party membership ballot. This rumour revolved around the assumption that the lightweight and inexperienced Duncan Smith would be easier to defeat than the heavyweight and experienced Clarke. To ensure this desired outcome it was rumoured that some Portillo supporters might tactically vote for Duncan Smith to inflate his vote and defeat Clarke. Given that Portillo failed to secure a place in the final two by one vote then the consequences of this (if it is true) were devastating[12] (Carter and Alderman, 2002:578).

Table 11: **Changes in Support for Candidates in the Parliamentary Stage of the Conservative Party Leadership Election of 2001**

	First Ballot	Second Ballot	Third Ballot
Michael Portillo	49 (29.5%)	50 (30.1%)	53 (31.9%)
Iain Duncan Smith	39 (23.4%)	42 (25.3%)	54 (32.5%)
Kenneth Clarke	36 (21.7%)	39 (23.4%)	59 (35.6%)
David Davis	21 (12.7%)	18 (10.9%)	
Michael Ancram	21 (12.7%)	17 (10.3%)	

Source: Adapted from Quinn, 2005:813

The ineptitude of the Portillo campaign had been a significant factor and his failure to attract second and third preference votes in the final two ballots proved to be fatal. His decline from leading in the first ballot to last place and exclusion in the final ballot was a by product of his failure to attract former Ancram and Davis supporters. Of these thirty five new third ballot votes, Clarke attracted twenty new supporters and catapulted himself from third to first place. Duncan Smith increased his support base by twelve, but Portillo added only three new supporters. The antipathy between Ancram and Portillo explained why Portillo could not attract former Ancram supporters. Ancram switched to Duncan Smith although the majority of his former supporters switched to Clarke. Davis and most of his supporters switched to Duncan Smith (Norton, 2001:14).

The party membership was thus denied a face off between the two heavyweights, Portillo and Clarke. Their view of the direction that Portillo was advocating would be of no consequence; they would be forced to select either Clarke, a popular, well liked, experienced moderate and Duncan Smith, an unknown, inexperienced ideologue. The Conservative peer and political academic, Philip Norton, would eloquently identify how the screening that the Conservative parliamentarians had conducted had produced a lose / lose scenario:

> Had the choice been between Portillo and Clarke, then whichever of the two men won, would have resulted in the election of a charismatic political heavyweight with high public visibility. To some extent, it would have been a 'win / lose' contest, a Portillo victory having the potential to widen popular support for the party, a Clarke victory having similar potential, but with the prospect of a potentially disastrous party split.[13] In the event party members were offered what appeared to be a 'lose / lose' contest'. (Norton, 2005:39)

8.5 The Party Membership Ballot

Clarke and Duncan Smith now began a two month campaign to secure the support of the party membership. Clarke sought to secure momentum and credibility to his candidature by the following tactics. First, he emphasised the raft of opinion polling evidence that suggested that the Conservative Party would benefit from the fact that he was more popular with the wider electorate than Duncan Smith (Norton, 2001:15). Second, he gathered together a significant list of declared endorsers, including seventy-four former Conservative ministers, one hundred Conservative constituency chairs and two-thirds of London council leaders, as well seeking to emphasise the number of leading female Conservatives endorsing his candidature (Carter and Alderman, 2002:582).

Duncan Smith could not boast such an impressive list of declared supporters. However, what was known about the attitudes of Conservative party members was a source of comfort for his campaign. It was assumed that the mass membership tended towards economic liberalism, Euroscepticism and social conservatism, factors which would be potentially beneficial to Duncan Smith and potentially disadvantageous to Clarke (Carter and Alderman, 2002:581). Duncan Smith was appealing to his natural constituency; Clarke needed party members to make ministerial experience and electoral appeal the predominant issues influencing voting in order to transcend his Europhilia.

The difficulty for Clarke was that his Europhilia became the predominant issue as the campaign became increasingly bitter and divisive. The intervention of Thatcher would ensure this. Ending her vow of silence, Thatcher entered the contest in a manner reminiscent of her delayed endorsement of Hague four years earlier. Her reluctant endorsement for Duncan Smith was motivated again by her desire to impede the candidacy of Clarke. She argued that the Europhilia of Clarke would be immensely damaging to the future of Conservatism[14] (Norton, 2001:14). The intervention of Thatcher, however, provoked a reaction from her successor, Major. Arguing that Clarke was clearly more qualified and experienced, Major castigated the candidature of Duncan Smith. Deriding him as a divisive and disloyal figure, Major made it clear that it was not credible, logical or appropriate for Duncan Smith to assume the party leadership (Walters, 2001:221). The Conservative Party was airing its disagreements in public as the electorate were 'treated to a very public squabble between two former Conservative Prime Ministers' (Norton, 2001:14).

As the party membership campaign progressed it became increasingly more acrimonious. The level of personal abuse and smearing that was exchanged, between the two candidates and their campaign teams, intensified and created an unedifying spectacle. Supporters of Duncan Smith sought to make political mileage out of Clarke's age (he was sixty) and his health, which they did by questioning his alleged fondness for beer and cigars. Of greater potential impact were the business dealings of Clarke. His role as Deputy Chair of British American Tobacco was questioned. The insinuation was that Clarke could be implicated in the alleged misconduct of British American Tobacco in the promotion of their products. The implication from the Duncan Smith campaign was that these concerns could resurface in a manner that could be immensely damaging to the Conservatives if Clarke were their party leader (Norton, 2001:14; Carter and Alderman, 2002:578).

In response, Clarke routinely made derogatory comments about Duncan Smith. He dismissed his opponent as unknown and an extremist, whilst his campaign team suggested that the extreme nature of the political agenda that Duncan Smith was advocating could attract racists to the Conservatives

(Carter and Alderman, 2002:578, 584). This issue of race became an increasingly controversial issue between the two campaigning teams. This insinuation would then resonate, when it was revealed that Edgar Griffin, who was a member of the Duncan Smith campaign team, was a supporter of the British National Party. This nearly derailed the Duncan Smith campaign, although he managed to overcome this massively embarrassing revelation by dismissing Griffin, whereupon he was expelled from the party (Norton, 2001:15; Carter and Alderman, 2002:584).

Table 12:   Candidate Support in the Conservative Party Leadership Membership Ballot of 2001

	Membership Votes	Percentage
Iain Duncan Smith	155,933	60.7
Kenneth Clarke	100,864	39.3
Turnout: 79%		

Source: Adapted from Quinn, 2005:813

The party membership ballot came to a conclusion with increasing hostility existing between the two campaigning teams and between the two candidates. In an attempt to sweep up any party members who had yet to vote, the Clarke camp promoted an opinion poll which indicated sixty-three per cent of the wider electorate wanted him in preference to Duncan Smith (Clarke, 2001:1). Despite this it was too late for Clarke. What the electorate wanted and what the Conservative Party membership wanted were different. Duncan Smith had secured victory by sixty-one per cent to thirty-nine per cent and had become the fourth person to lead the Conservative Party in eleven years. Once again, Clarke, who was the Butler of his generation, was rejected for an inferior candidate.

8.6   A Failure of Process and a Flawed Outcome

Evaluations of the previous Conservative Party Leadership elections have demonstrated the predilection of Conservatives to elect unexpected leaders. Maudling was expected to succeed Douglas-Home; Whitelaw was expected to succeed Heath and few expected that Thatcher would succeed; Major emerged contrary to the expectations of many (and certainly the expectations of Heseltine) and numerous Conservatives were assumed to be better positioned to succeed Major then Hague was. However, none of the previous four party leaders could claim that their acquisition of the party leadership was more unexpected than that of Duncan Smith. Just like his two post-

Thatcherite predecessors (Major and Hague), the method of acquisition was disputed and consequently his legitimacy and authority was questioned. He amounted to another default leader. In evaluating the Conservative Party leadership election of 2001 two themes emerge: first, the process was a failure as the new electoral procedures produced a perverse outcome; and, second, that it produced a flawed outcome was indicative of the triumph of the bastards to which Major had referred to a decade earlier.

The fact that Duncan Smith had been elected by the party members having secured sixty-one per cent of the vote should have ensured his legitimacy as leader of the Conservative Party and thus provided him with authority within Westminster. However, the problem was that he had a weak basis of support from within the parliamentary Conservative Party.

The previous four leaders of the Conservative Party could claim to have far greater levels of support from within the parliamentary Conservative Party. Heath secured the leadership from one ballot on the basis of 49.3 per cent of the parliamentary Conservative Party. Thatcher was able to secure 47.1 per cent on the first ballot and 52.9 per cent on the second ballot. Major assumed the Conservative Party leadership with 47.7 per cent support from within the parliamentary Conservative Party. The previous chapter emphasised how Hague was weakened by the fact the in the first ballot secured only 25 per cent of the parliamentary Conservative Party and suggested that, although he ultimately secured 56.1 per cent in the third and decisive ballot, this weak first performance was a constraint upon his legitimacy and thereby his authority. The performance of Duncan Smith was even weaker than that of Hague. His first ballot return of 39 parliamentary colleagues constituted only 23.4 per cent of the parliamentary Conservative Party. However, of greater comparative significance is the percentage return that Duncan Smith secured in the final parliamentary ballot. He secured 54 votes and came second to Clarke which amounted to a support base of less than a third of his parliamentary colleagues. Hague triumphed on the basis of second and third preference votes gravitating to him and thus his vote base more than doubled from the first to final ballots. Duncan Smith could only secure a further fifteen votes from the first to final parliamentary ballots.

This clearly demonstrates profound reservations existed amongst his parliamentary colleagues about the prospect of him assuming the party leadership. Related to this point is the margin of preference that existed in previous Conservative Party leadership elections from within the parliamentary Conservative Party. Maudling did not contest a second ballot with Heath, as the margin of seventeen votes in a three way contest left insufficient scope to suggest that victory was possible. Thatcher had a margin of sixty-seven votes when she defeated William Whitelaw in the second ballot of the 1975 succession contest. Major secured fifty four more votes than Heseltine when he secured the party leadership in 1990. Hague secured twenty-two more votes than Clarke in the final ballot four years earlier.

As table thirteen clearly demonstrates the position of Duncan Smith was clearly not comparable: he was numerically five votes less than the first candidate (Clarke) and was only permitted to put before the mass membership having secured just one more vote than the third candidate (Portillo). The perversity of this was clear when we consider that Thatcher came first in the opening ballot of the 1990 Conservative Party leadership election, yet her lead of fifty-two was insufficient to secure outright victory and resulted in her eventual resignation. In eleven years the rules governing the election of the party leader had produced two incompatible outcomes. How could a political heavyweight (Thatcher) who had come first with a lead of over fifty votes and with a majority of her parliamentary colleagues supporting her, not be declared the victor, but a political lightweight (Duncan Smith) could come second in a final ballot with the support of less the third of his parliamentary colleagues, and thus go onto secure the party leadership?

Table 13:   A Mandate to Lead: Margins of Preference within the Parliamentary Conservative Party 1965-2001

	Leading Candidate	Second Candidate	Margin of Preference
1965	Heath 150 (49.3)	Maudling 133 (43.8)	17 (5.5)
1975	Thatcher 130 (47.1)	Heath 119 (43.1)	11 (4.0)
	Thatcher 146 (52.9)	Whitelaw 79 (28.6)	67 (24.3)
1989	Thatcher 314 (84.0)	Meyer 33 (8.8)	283 (75.2)
1990	Thatcher 204 (54.8)	Heseltine 152 (40.9)	52 (13.9)
	Major 185 (49.7)	Heseltine 131 (35.2)	54 (14.5)
1995	Major 218 (66.3)	Redwood 89 (27.1)	129 (43.2)
1997	Clarke 49 (29.9)	Hague 41 (25.0)	8 (4.9)
	Clarke 64 (39.0)	Hague 62 (37.8)	2 (1.2)
	Hague 92 (56.1)	Clarke 70 (42.7)	22 (13.4)
2001	Portillo 49 (29.5)	Duncan Smith 39 (23.4)	10 (6.1)
	Portillo 50 (30.1)	Duncan Smith 42 (25.3)	8 (4.8)
	Clarke 59 (35.6)	Duncan Smith 54 (32.5)	5 (3.1)

Source: Adapted from Quinn, 2005: 812-813

The perversity of the outcome would lead to considerable discussion about the merits of the new procedures for determining the election of party leader. The rationale for amending the procedures was to extend the franchise to the party membership as part of a wider process of democratisation within the Conservative Party. The decision to allow participation of the party members, once the parliamentary Conservative Party had whittled the candidates down to two for them, had clearly proved to be problematic

(Kelly, 2004b:2). The particular configuration of support for the three candidates entering the final parliamentary ballot, demonstrated that the parliamentary Conservative Party was split in a virtual three way tie between the three candidates. The closeness of this parliamentary ballot angered many of the party activists who felt that they were deprived a full participation within the electoral process. Their anger was intensified by the knowledge that tactical voting rather than principled voting was being deployed to shape the two candidates who would be presented to them. Had one Conservative parliamentarian voted for Portillo rather than Duncan Smith then the run off would have been between two social liberals, Clarke and Portillo, one of whom was a Europhile and one of whom was a Eurosceptic.

That this did not occur ensured that the party membership would be presented with the diametric opposites within contemporary Conservatism. One economic damp, pro-European, social liberal (Clarke) and one economic dry, Eurosceptic, social conservative (Duncan Smith). Their differences extended beyond their ideological standpoints. Clarke was an experienced political heavyweight feared by New Labour, and a figure capable of attracting disaffected former Conservative votes back to the party. The option of a political insider, who was regarded as credible and competent, was rejected in preference for an unproven political outsider and parliamentary rebel, whom New Labour did not fear and could easily deride for his ideological extremism, his record of disloyalty to his own party, and his inexperience. The party membership was to be denied the opportunity to comment upon any candidates located between these two ideological positions. It amounted to an inherently undemocratic process, as the most intriguing candidate who made the most eloquent articulation of a new conservatism was Portillo. His inclusive agenda, with the emphasis on transcending the ideological disputes of the late and post-Thatcherite era, by uniting social and economic liberalism with moderate and intellectually grounded Euroscepticism did, however, provide the essential precursor to the agenda that David Cameron would articulate when winning the leadership of the Conservative Party leadership four years later.

That Duncan Smith emerged as the new party leader after an elongated and divisive process was to demonstrate that a failed process had produced a flawed outcome. The numeric interpretations provided above suggest that Duncan Smith was the fortunate benefactor of an inherently failed set of procedures to determine the succession. Those failed procedures, that allowed *any* leader to emerge on such a weak parliamentary basis of support, ensured that Duncan Smith commenced his tenure as party leader with minimal legitimacy and authority amongst his parliamentary colleagues.

The previous chapters have emphasised how successive Conservative Party leadership elections, (with the exception of when Heath triumphed), have been strongly influenced by ideological factors. Thatcher secured the leadership on the back of a strongly economically liberal support base. Major obtained the leadership through the endorsement of Thatcherite Euro-sceptics, and then retained it through the support of loyalist Eurosceptics and pro-Europeans, after hard-line Eurosceptics abandoned him and supported Redwood. Hague secured the leadership due to the support of the Euro-sceptics with the support of pro-Europeans gravitating to Clarke. What makes Duncan Smith different from these victors is that although they all secured a base of support from ideologically motivated votes, they did still secure endorsements from beyond their core support base. Those who have emerged victorious may have based their candidatures on an ideologically core, but in order to triumph they have had to penetrate into the centre-left of the parliamentary Conservative Party. Duncan Smith defied this tradition. His support base within the parliamentary Conservative Party did not just tend towards his own ideological position but was exclusively derived from it.

We can make this argument by analysing the research of Hill. In an extensive analysis of the ideological disposition of Conservative parliamenta-rians participating in the parliamentary ballots of July 2001, Hill defined each of them on each of the three dominant ideological divides of post-Thatcherite Conservatism: the economic policy ideological divide; the Euro-pean ideological policy divide; and the social, sexual and moral ideological policy divide. After analysing division lists, early day motions, membership of party groupings and public comment, Hill demonstrated the following with respect to the 2001 parliamentary Conservative Party: 80 per cent were economically liberal; 90 per cent were Eurosceptic and 80 per cent were socially conservative.

Hill then determined an accurate guide to voting behaviour in the final ballot of the parliamentary stage of the Conservative Party leadership election of 2001. Hill has demonstrated that the support of Duncan Smith was ideologically defined. All of the fifty-four parliamentarians were economic dries and Eurosceptic and only one was not socially conservative. This re-search produces some illuminating insights. Given the overwhelmingly Thatcherite characteristics of the post-2001 parliamentary Conservative Party, Clarke did remarkably well to secure the level of support that he did. He was able to penetrate the Thatcherite right and secure support from economic dries, Eurosceptics and social conservatives. Most intriguingly was that realisation that the majority of Clarke supporters in the final ballot were actually Eurosceptic, which demonstrated the rapid rate at which the parlia-mentary Conservative Party had embraced Euroscepticism over the previous decade. Moreover, despite his vocal emphasis on social liberalism, Portillo was still able to secure a high support base from social conservatives. The views of Clarke were a minority within the parliamentary Conservative Party, but his candidature transcended ideological categorisation. The views of

Portillo on social, sexual and moral matters were an anathema to the majority of the parliamentary Conservative Party yet he was still able to secure votes from these parliamentarians (Hill, 2004:1-16).

The research of Hill is immensely influential in how we should interpret the support base of Duncan Smith. First, his support was exclusively Thatcherite; he could not appeal to economic wets, pro-Europeans or social liberals. This would be an impediment to his capacity to present himself as a unifying figure within Conservatism. Second, the majority of the parliamentary Conservative Party were economic liberals, Eurosceptics and social conservatives, yet despite campaigning in such overwhelmingly hospitable territory, Duncan Smith could only attract fifty-four votes after three ballots. A sufficient section of his ideological bedfellows repeatedly avoided endorsing him. A combination of an overwhelmingly Thatcherite parliamentary Conservative Party (which impeded Clarke and to a lesser extent Portillo), and bizarre electoral procedures ensured that Duncan Smith was presented to the party membership.

8.7   Conclusion

The Conservative Party leadership election proved to be a debilitating exercise, both for the parliamentary Conservative Party and for the party membership, who were able to formally participate for the first time. The new process for determining the succession was deemed to have failed. It produced an unexpected and, with the benefit of hindsight, a flawed outcome. The length of the campaign, at three months, was seen to be a contributing factor to an extraordinarily bitter and personally abusive contest, during which the Conservative Party demonstrated to their electorate the depth of their internal divisions. Moreover, the new procedures appeared to be unsatisfactory to both the parliamentary Conservative Party and to the party membership. The party membership was only permitted to comment upon two candidates and in doing so this polluted the victory of Duncan Smith. For example, many party members argued that they were compelled to vote for Duncan Smith reluctantly as they opposed Clarke due to his Europhilia (Kelly, 2004b:2). That Duncan Smith could secure the party leadership with such a small base of support from within the parliamentary Conservative Party, would soon prove to be problematic. As he failed to adapt to his new role as party leader, the disputed procedures through which he acquired the leadership became a matter of concern to many Conservative parliamentarians. Many of the limitations that were known to the majority of Conservative parliamentarians who did not endorse him were exposed: his inexperience, his lack of electoral appeal, his weak parliamentary abilities, his poor public speaking; his status as a symbol of divisiveness. The new democratic procedures that enabled Duncan Smith to assume the leadership of the

Conservative Party were now viewed as inherently flawed. The final procedural twist was that Duncan Smith was elected by the party members but the decision on whether he should remain was retained by the Conservative parliamentarians. The self-proclaimed quiet man would be silenced quicker than many anticipated.

BACK TO THE FUTURE: MICHAEL HOWARD BECOMES CONSERVATIVE PARTY LEADER

For the duration of his tenure as leader of the Conservative Party Iain Duncan Smith was in an unenviable position. He had inherited a demoralised Conservative Party which had just suffered a second successive electoral landslide defeat. Conservative parliamentarians seemed incapable of understanding the reasons for their continuing electoral unpopularity. Nor were they capable of engaging in a coherent critical appraisal of their ideological identity and their policy agenda (Hayton, 2006:3). The capacity for renewal and the development of a coherent narrative of Conservatism under Duncan Smith, was continually being impeded by ideological factionalism between Eurosceptics and Europhiles, and increasingly social liberals and social conservatives. Their insularity repelled the electorate (Seldon and Snowden, 2005:726).

The ultimate manifestation of their factional insularity had been the bizarre and disputed election of Duncan Smith as party leader. He acquired this position due to questionable procedures, which had exposed the disharmony that existed between the parliamentary party and the party membership. Nearly seventy per cent of Conservative parliamentarians had identified that Duncan Smith lacked the necessary experience, profile, aptitudes, and potential electoral appeal to be their party leader. His mandate to lead was from the party membership not from parliamentary colleagues, but this mandate was default in nature. Many party members found the thought of electing a pro-European leader in Clarke unpalatable and Duncan Smith was the only option available to them. His participation in the membership ballot was default in nature, as Conservative parliamentarians had mobilised to prevent Portillo going forward, as his social liberalism was unacceptable to them (Kelly, 2004a:400). The method by which Duncan Smith acquired the party leadership was therefore widely disputed. This questioning of his legitimacy undermined his authority over the parliamentary Conservative Party. Given the impediments that existed it was essential that Duncan Smith demonstrated leadership competence. Without leadership competence his credibility would be destroyed and his weak mandate would be vulnerable to being overturned.

This vulnerability was intensified as the responsibility for removing an incumbent party leader who was deemed unfit for the role still remained with Conservative parliamentarians. The new rules governing the leadership of the Conservative Party had changed the mechanism for removal. Instead of a formal challenge which was permitted annually, removal was now initiated via a confidence motion which could be initiated at any time. The means by which a vote of confidence could be activated was as follows. If fifteen per cent of Conservative parliamentarians informed the Chair of the 1922 Executive Committee that they had reservations about the incumbent leader, then a formal vote of confidence would be held. As the parliamentary Conservative Party comprised 166 members after the general election of 2001 then the requisite number of formal dissenters was twenty-five. In a confidence vote the incumbent required a majority to retain their position. Failure to secure this would require their resignation and they would not be permitted to stand in the subsequent leadership election process. For Duncan Smith the key figure would be eighty-three. Given that his known support from the three parliamentary ballots was only fifty-four, it was clear that should Conservative parliamentarians decide to activate the confidence ballot then Duncan Smith would be extremely vulnerable to removal. To avoid such an eventuality Duncan Smith had to offer gravitas: in short, he had needed to close the credibility gap and demonstrate to the Conservative Party, and to the wider electorate, that he was a Prime Minister in waiting (Norton, 2005:39-40).

9.1   The Credibility Gap: The Limitations of Iain Duncan Smith

Before considering why Duncan Smith failed to bridge the credibility gap it is worth recognising that his party leadership tenure has been in some ways misunderstood. Due to his own career profile, he was pigeon-holed as an ideological extremist who was obsessed about the question of European integration. Due to this pigeon-holing of Duncan Smith, it was easy to mis-construe the political strategy that he adopted once he acquired the party leadership.

Surprisingly Duncan Smith did not adhere to his right wing and Eurosceptic credentials. He identified two strategic mistakes about con-temporary Conservatism: first, they were perceived to be obsessed about Europe and divided on the issue; and, second, they were perceived as elitist with a reputation for governing in the interests of the rich, rather than in the interests of ordinary people[1] (Cowley and Green, 2005:5). In a sense his diagnosis did embrace aspects of the modernisation agenda that Portillo had articulated, and it also mirrored aspects of the approach that Hague had advanced in the first two years of his party leadership tenure. On the first dilemma on Europe, the strategy of Duncan Smith was misconstrued, as Cowley and Green observe:

> For sure, one of [his] first acts as leader was to harden the party's European policy. Under Hague, the policy had been to rule out the Euro for two parliaments – effectively eight years. Under IDS, the party ruled out membership for good...but this hardening of policy was not a sign that the party was ever more obsessed about Europe; rather, the shift in policy was designed to ensure that the party did not spend any longer discussing the issue. By 'closing' the issue in this way – and by arguing that it should not be an issue for a general election but for any forthcoming referendum – IDS was determined to escape the criticism levelled at Hague in 2001 for running a single-issue campaign on Europe. IDS was also hoping to avoid the criticisms that had been levelled at Hague of having a policy that ruled out membership of the Euro – but only for the time being.[2]   (Cowley and Green, 2005:4)

The second dilemma, on electoral perceptions of the economic and social policy platform of the Conservatives, required that Duncan Smith construct a narrative that would unite the parliamentary party and the mass membership (an internal dimension) and appeal to the wider electorate, especially floating voters with centrist instincts (an external dimension). The narrative needed to be transmitted in a coherent and digestible package. Initially, Duncan Smith identified public services as the core belief and the basis of a viable narrative. The emphasis on public services, and associated themes such as social justice and inclusiveness, was pursued and culminated in the Fair Deal strategy (Taylor, 2005:149-151).

However, the Fair Deal policy platform with its modernisation foundations failed to mobilise support for the Conservatives. Consequently it generated a Hague like desire to lurch to the right. The attempt to configure the Conservatives around public services and the rhetoric of compassionate Conservatism failed to convince fellow Conservatives. Moderate economic damps and social liberals remained unconvinced about the depth of Duncan Smith's commitment, whilst economic dries and social conservatives had reservations about the rapprochement with the Tory left, having just annexed the leadership of the Conservative Party on behalf of the Thatcherite right. As the inclusive agenda failed to provide the coherent narrative required for electoral recovery, so Duncan Smith reverted to type. By the time of his final conference speech in October 2003, the focus on inclusiveness and social justice was downplayed, and the emphasis on low taxation and anti-Europeanism resurfaced (Taylor, 2005:151). Ultimately, Duncan Smith could not secure the internal or the external dimensions identified above. Internally, the parliamentary Conservative Party remained ideologically divided (although the primary division was now between social conservatives and social liberals). Externally, that sense of division and incoherence ensured that the electorate did not gravitate towards the Conservative Party whilst Duncan Smith was their party leader.

That failure to stimulate a recovery in the opinion polling rating ensured that the disputed method by which he acquired the party leadership would remain a problem. This insecurity surrounding his position was intensified by the following factors: first, his poor political image; second, his inept party management; third, his failure to exploit the vulnerabilities of New Labour; fourth, the perception that he was an electoral liability; and finally, the fear that under him the Conservatives could sink to third party status within British politics. His failure to close the credibility gap meant that he was vulnerable to eviction. In order to fully understand the political downfall of Duncan Smith it is necessary to explore these factors in greater detail.

A significant handicap for the Conservative Party was the image of Duncan Smith. Contemporary political engagement places a high premium on presentational skills as a means by which to connect with the electorate.[3] The photogenic Tony Blair had been an extremely effective presenter of the New Labour brand. Duncan Smith was clearly not as gifted as his New Labour counterpart at such modern political skills, but more worryingly for Conservatives he was clearly inferior to Hague. Hague had been vilified in the mass media and derided as a lightweight figure. If Hague was lightweight, then his successor was featherweight. His public speeches and television interviews were at times inept, but it was his parliamentary performances which embarrassed Conservative parliamentarians the most. Despite numerous public relations gaffes,[4] Hague had been able to perform relatively well at Prime Ministers Questions, and his debating skills and quick witted repartee had been acknowledged by political commentators. In this forum Duncan Smith was completely exposed. The fact that his questioning of the Prime Minister was interrupted by frequent bouts of uncontrollable coughing became a source of amusement to his New Labour opponents. His poor presentational skills on television impeded his capacity to relate to the electorate and his parliamentary performances undermined his attempts to impose his authority over the parliamentary Conservative Party (Garnett and Lynch, 2003:6).

This weak public profile extended beyond his inept presentational skills. New Labour was able to present a particularly negative image of him. He was an ideological extremist, devoid of personal charisma, lacking in electoral appeal, and he was an incompetent figure. New Labour did not need to actively pursue this line too vigorously as his leadership limitations seemed all too evident. One line of sustained attack that New Labour could and would exploit was his record as a parliamentary rebel when the Conservatives were last in government. Many Conservatives agreed with the New Labour argument that Duncan Smith could not demand loyalty and unity from his fellow Conservative parliamentarians, when he himself had been disloyal earlier in his own parliamentary career. The image of Duncan Smith demanding loyalty made him look impotent but also hypocritical (Seldon and Snowden, 2005b:726). Moreover, when Duncan Smith attempted to engage with the electorate and present himself as a figure of political stature he invited ridicule upon himself. During the course of his conference speech in the autumn of 2002, he attempted to demonstrate his leadership credentials by arguing that electors and Conservative colleagues should 'never under-estimate the determination of a quiet man'. The quiet man imagery made no discernable impact upon perceptions of Duncan Smith nor did it improve the opinion of the electorate about the Conservative Party. New Labour parliamentarians appreciated it. When Parliament reconvened they 'amused themselves by calling for hush throughout his interventions' (Garnett and Lynch, 2003:8).

The weaknesses of his public profile were compounded by his inability to effectively manage the Conservative Party. Duncan Smith can be accused of making a number of misjudgements in terms of appointments, both in terms of Central Office and the Shadow Cabinet. In the summer of 2002, he was widely condemned for removing David Davis as Conservative Party Chairman. Despite having been defeated for the party leadership the previous year, Davis retained leadership aspirations. This political ambition intensified the insecurity of an under siege Duncan Smith, who demoted Davis to the position of Local Government spokesperson. The attempt to marginalise a potential rival served to reinforce electoral awareness of the internal personality clashes with Conservative Party politics. That awareness was intensified by the media hysteria surrounding the fact that Duncan Smith had dismissed his rival whilst he was on holiday. The fear surrounding Davis caused the miscalculation in constructing the Shadow Cabinet, but the paranoia surrounding Portillo impacted upon appointments and dismissals within Central Office. In February 2003, Duncan Smith sacked two Central Office officials, Mark MacGregor (Chief Executive) and Rick Nye (Head of Research). He feared that as social liberals, they would be aiming to promote the merits of modernisation and their champion, Portillo (Garnett and Lynch, 2003:6, 10). Duncan Smith then compounded his error by replacing MacGregor with a known sympathiser, Barry Legg. This move antagonised his political enemies further. It also resulted in humiliation for Duncan Smith, when the Legg appointment was not formalised due to the opposition of the lay membership board (Heffernan, 2003:2). The Davis demotion, and the abortive Legg appointment, seemed to be indicative of a political leader with dangerously poor judgement in internal party management. His actions served to antagonise his political rivals (the Davis and Portillo factions) and to isolate himself, at the very moment when his political weakness demanded that he buttress his position by mobilising such factions to his party leadership[5] (Heffernan, 2003:2-3).

In addition to his mishandling of senior Cabinet and Central Office, Duncan Smith was at fault for his management of the parliamentary Conservative Party. His tactical acumen was exposed by a parliamentary division on the adoption of children by homosexual unmarried couples. Such morality based divisions are traditionally viewed as matters of individual conscience. No party instructions on voting behaviour are offered in these circumstances and the division is viewed as a free vote. The incumbent New Labour Government offered a free vote, but Duncan Smith instructed Conservative parliamentarians to vote against. In the ensuring division, eight Conservative parliamentarians defied the instructions given to them by Duncan Smith.[6] These included Kenneth Clarke and Michael Portillo, as well as five former shadow cabinet members (John Bercow, David Curry, Andrew Lansley, Andrew Mackay and Francis Maude).[7] The imposition of the three-line whip was clearly a tactical misjudgement. Duncan Smith had created a self-inflicted problem which would have been avoided by offering a free vote (Cowley and Stuart, 2004:357). Rather than allowing the issue to fade, Duncan Smith then proceeded to intensify his difficulties, as Norton observes:

> IDS read into it a wider agenda, one designed to destabilise his leadership…he called a surprise press conference and announced that 'for a few, last night's vote was not about adoption but an attempt to challenge my mandate to lead the party.' The party, he declared, had to 'unite or die'. It was a melodramatic call that undermined rather than bolstered his position. He was viewed by many MPs as being in a poor position to demand unity when he himself – as a leading Maastricht rebel – had denied it to John Major. It also suggested that he was prone to panic in a crisis, in this particular instance one of his creation.
>
> (Norton, 2005:39)

Such short term tactical miscalculations served to undermine Duncan Smith, whilst long-term strategic thinking was often lacking in his political makeup. The question of the Iraq war served to illustrate this point forcibly. His decision to offer unqualified support for military action against Iraq won approval from the right-wing press in the short-term, but it was a strategically questionable position to adopt. A more ambivalent initial position would have offered options for the Conservatives over the longer-term. A long-drawn out military adventure could impact upon the popularity of the New Labour administration, whereupon ambivalence could have switched to opposition as events unfolded. Unconditional support left the Conservatives without a political outlet. It meant no long-term political (i.e. electoral) gain was derived from this stance, and the Liberal Democrats became the main beneficiaries of anti-war and anti-Government sentiment (Seldon and Snowden, 2005b:727). The main electoral weakness of the New Labour Government could not be translated into a Conservative advantage. This became symptomatic of the problem with Duncan Smith. The honeymoon period that New Labour had experienced when entering government was now ending in their second term. Public dissatisfaction and disenchantment with New Labour was extending beyond the Iraq War. This provided political opportunities for the Conservatives. That Duncan Smith was unable to exploit New Labour discomfiture over foundation hospitals and tuition fees became an issue of increasing concern for Conservative parliamentarians (Seldon and Snowden, 2005b:727).

This failure to exploit potentially favourable political circumstances intensified the view that Duncan Smith was an electoral liability. His image as a principled if quiet political operator, (an antidote to the spin of Blair and New Labour), completely failed to resonate with the electorate. Despite potentially beneficial circumstances, (a second term Government engaging in disputed military action), the Conservatives remained unpopular in public opinion polls, with their support oscillating between twenty-seven and thirty-five per cent. The New Labour advantage in opinion polling data remained, but more worryingly support for the Liberal Democrats had increased from eighteen per cent when Duncan Smith became party leader to twenty-six per cent by September 2003 (Broughton, 2004:351).

Duncan Smith lacked the characteristics or the public persona necessary for success in the media age (Hayton, 2006:12). The consequence of his ongoing leadership of the Conservative Party was clear. A third successive landslide electoral defeat was imminent. The increasing popularity of the Liberal Democrats had the potential to reduce Conservative parliamentarian representation even further. Of the 166 Conservative held constituencies, the Liberal Democrats were in second place in fifty-eight of them. If the opinion polls of mid-2003 were to be reflected in a general election then a further fifteen Liberal Democrats seats would be gained at the expense of the Conservatives (Heffernan, 2003:2). The Conservative fear of being relegated to third party status seemed a possibility (Kelly, 2004a:400).

Duncan Smith was failing to reverse the inexorable decline of the Conservative Party. He became part of the problem rather than the solution. His difficulties stemmed from the disputed method by which he had acquired the leadership of the Conservative Party, which proved to be a significant constraint upon him. Had he been able to construct a coherent narrative of Conservatism that unified them and provided electoral appeal, and then exploited the increasing vulnerability of New Labour and demonstrated that he was an electoral asset, then the complexities of party management would have eased. Had he been able to achieve these objectives and made the Conservative Party appear to be a government in waiting and himself a potential Prime Minister, then the disputation surrounding his acquisition of the leadership would have been overcome.

9.2   The Procedural Dilemma

A recurrent theme throughout this book has been the contingency thesis surrounding successive leaders of the Conservative Party. The primary function of the party leader was electoral success and an incumbent who was an electoral liability would be swiftly removed (Kelly, 2004a:401). Previous incumbents who had been forcibly removed (i.e. Heath and Thatcher) had been evicted by procedures that had since been amended. Both had been removed as an indirect consequence of formal challenges to their party leadership. As Duncan Smith struggled to fulfil his responsibilities as party leader, much ill-informed comment surrounding a possible *challenge* to him was circulating.

The revised procedures may have permitted mass membership participation in a vacant contest, but Conservative parliamentarians retained absolute control over evicting an unpopular or incompetent incumbent. Technically, only they could decide whether to call a vote of confidence, and only they participated in the confidence motion (Cowley and Stuart, 2004:359-360). However, Conservative parliamentarians misinterpreted these rules and the mass media were compliant in this. For example, Cowley and Stuart have observed how:

> there was a great media flurry when David Davis announced on BBC's *Question Time* that he would never run against IDS for the leadership of the party. But the new rules allowed Conservative MPs to vote out their incumbent leader without anyone needing to challenge him: they allowed for a challenge without requiring a challenger. It meant that Davis's pledge was at the same time true and utterly meaningless (as Davis knew full well). He would never challenge Duncan Smith, simply because no one could challenge Duncan Smith.
>
> (Cowley and Stuart, 2004:360)

The procedural dilemma for Conservative parliamentarians was whether (and when) to activate their right to hold a confidence motion. Reservations about Duncan Smith may have been omnipresent, but Conservative parliamentarians had real reservations about initiating a confidence motion. Kelly identified three main reservations. First, a successful confidence motion would *presumably* result in a prolonged and divisive leadership contest. The process could take three months, leaving Duncan Smith as a lame duck party leader for that interim period. Second, it was possible that the party membership could be put in the position of imposing a new party leader, who just like Duncan Smith, did not have a strong base of support amongst Conservative parliamentarians. Finally, Conservative parliamentarians were worried about how the party membership might react if they overthrew Duncan Smith without their consent, especially after 155,000 party members had voted for him relatively recently (Kelly, 2004a:401).

Speculation about utilising a confidence motion to remove Duncan Smith was first muted amongst Conservative parliamentarians before their leader had celebrated his first anniversary (Kelly, 2004a:401). As he entered the second year of his tenure that speculation was ratcheted up significantly. The aforementioned treatment of Davis and the fiasco of the Legg appointment intensified his sense of insecurity. His subsequent handling of the adoption three line whip, and his reaction to it, would demonstrate the paranoia that was engulfing him. As Norton observes:

> his tendency to see conspiracies against him served only to turn the perception into reality. MPs did start to conspire against him.
>
> (Norton, 2005:39)

Widespread and open contempt for Duncan Smith became evident. The question became more of when and how, rather than when[8] (Garnett and Lynch, 2005:10). A series of damaging events occurred in rapid succession in September and October 2003; events of sufficient magnitude to trigger a confidence motion.

The first calamitous event was the Brent East by election. There was no serious expectation of annexing this safe Labour constituency, despite the unpopularity of the incumbent New Labour government. Public hostility with the government contributed, however, to a significant increase in the Liberal Democrat vote share. This enabled them to take a constituency in which they had finished third at the previous general election. That the Liberal Democrats leapfrogged the Conservatives reinforced the fear amongst Conservative parliamentarians that the Liberal Democrats could conceivably usurp them as the main opposition party (Norton, 2005:40).

This outcome intensified the resolve of critics to mobilise a confidence motion. Their willingness to engage in this action was increased by the publication of a YouGov poll on the attitudes of party members to the leadership of Duncan Smith. One of the fears that Conservative parliamenta-rians had about removing Duncan Smith related to how the party member-ship would react. They had elected him relatively recently and removal would be completed without their participation. The findings of the YouGov poll would constitute the second significant event which would make a confidence motion more likely: it revealed that fifty-three per cent of party members believed that they had made a mistake in making him their party leader (Kelly, 2004a:402).

The third contributing factor was personally devastating for Duncan Smith. Despite his numerous failings one of the few benefits that he had enjoyed was that his integrity was widely recognised (Garnett and Lynch, 2003:8). This was to be questioned by the 'Betsygate' scandal; a scandal that Duncan Smith came to believe was manufactured by his critics in order to destabilise his position. It was alleged that Duncan Smith had paid his wife, Betsy, £18,000 from his parliamentary office allowance, even though she had completed no secretarial work to justify the payment. Almost as damaging was the revelation made by Vanessa Grearson, a Deputy Director of Conservative Central Office, that staff were being bullied into signing a rebuttal of the 'Betsygate' allegations.[9]

The attempt that Duncan Smith made to reassert his authority at the subsequent Conservative Party Conference would backfire and amounted to the fourth destabilising event. He needed to deliver his keynote speech competently, and offer a coherent message to mobilise support, but Duncan Smith completely failed to deliver (Norton, 2005:40). The signature phrase from his conference speech was 'the quiet man is here to stay and his turning up the volume'. It managed to create an overwhelmingly negative reaction from Conservative parliamentarians (Wheatcroft, 2005:264). The media reaction mirrored that of the Conservative parliamentarians, as Heffernan observes:

> while his keynote speech read reasonably well, the manner in which it was delivered was shockingly bad, something that starkly symbolised his total lack of leadership skills.   (Heffernan, 2003:3)

The negative reaction to the conference speech contributed to the final damaging event which would ensure that a confidence ballot was an inevitability. The capacity of the Conservative Party to mobilise electoral support was dependent on financial muscle, which was dependent upon significant corporate and individual donations. Such donations remained at low levels so the Conservatives could ill afford to lose existing financial backers (Seldon and Snowden, 2005:727). As a reaction to the weak communication skills that Duncan Smith had displayed during his conference speech, one benefactor, the millionaire spread betting tycoon, Stuart Wheeler, announced that he would be withholding financial support until the Conservatives Party changed to a new party leader. Conservatives now had a financial inducement to remove Duncan Smith from the party leadership.[10]

9.3   The Brutal Execution

Conservative parliamentarians now had two options. They could end the plotting against their incumbent leader and offer him their support, or they could gather the necessary number of critics together and activate a confidence motion. Duncan Smith effectively demanded his Conservative parliamentarians to make that choice. Echoing the put up or shut up rhetoric of a former Conservative Party leader, (that he himself sought to destabilise and evict), Duncan Smith observed that his critics should 'either bring it on or draw the line' (Cowley and Green, 2005:6).

Duncan Smith found out the outcome to his demand by lunchtime the following day. Michael Spicer, Chair of the 1922 Executive Committee, revealed that he had received the necessary number of letters from Conservative parliamentarians for a confidence motion. Duncan Smith had naively assumed, or hoped, that his critics would shut up but they had decided to put up. He immediately declared that he intended to contest the confidence motion, and that he did not intend to resign (or be defeated), as this would inflict a fractious and protracted leadership election upon the Conservative Party. He informed the gathered media outside Conservative Central Office:

> I will absolutely submit my name for a renewed mandate to lead the party to the General Election and to win…I say to my colleagues who will be responsible for making this decision tomorrow, that we have an unrivalled opportunity to take the fight to Labour at a time when they are failing…We should not now let the Government off the hook by giving them this opportunity by plunging ourselves into a fractious leadership election that could last months and give the government the opportunity to escape proper scrutiny.   (ITN News, 28th October 2003)

Duncan Smith attempted to sway the opinion of the parliamentary Conservative Party by identifying, first, the support that existed within the shadow Cabinet and, second, the mandate that he received from the mass membership only two years earlier. From within the shadow Cabinet he was able to garner unambiguous statements of support from five leading figures. Michael Ancram, David Davis, Michael Howard, Oliver Letwin and Theresa May issued a joint statement within which they praised the 'remarkable courage and dignity' that he had demonstrated under considerable pressure. Moreover, Duncan Smith issued a statement warning Conservative parliamentarians that seeking to remove him, when he had a mandate to lead from the mass membership of the Conservative Party, would be viewed with 'despair and contempt' (ITN News, 28th October 2003).

The confidence motion was scheduled for the following day, leaving Duncan Smith with limited time to shore up his fragile support base. In the hours prior to the ballot opening, Duncan Smith gave an impassioned defence of his party leadership to a specially convened gathering of Conservative parliamentarians. He argued that the speculation surrounding his continuance was damaging the electoral prospects of the party. He demanded that this 'vision of hell' had to end and that the parliamentary Conservative Party had to draw to an end the divisions that had plighted post-Thatcherite Conservatism (Sky News, 29th October 2003).

Such pleading was futile. His tenure as party leader had been an unmitigated disaster. The fragility of his support base amongst Conservative parliamentarians was the main impediment to him overcoming the confidence motion. He had only secured fifty-four parliamentarian supporters in the final ballot of the leadership election two years earlier. He needed to retain all of these supporters, and add a further twenty-nine, to ensure that he had a majority of the parliamentary Conservative Party and thus succeed in the confidence motion. In addition, the confidence motion carried with it two forms of success. The first form of success was technical; i.e. the procedural rules stipulated that eighty-three constituted a numerical triumph and would justify continuance. However, the second form of success was psychological. Duncan Smith needed to overcome the technical figure of eighty-three but he also needed the psychological benefit of that victory to be comfortable. Eighty-four votes for Duncan Smith would constitute a technical victory but would completely immobilise his party leadership and would ensure that his continuance became a source of ongoing debate.[11]

Table 14: **Vote of Confidence in the Conservative Party Leadership of Iain Duncan Smith**

	Votes	Percentage
Confidence	75	45.5
No Confidence	90	54.5

Source: Adapted from Quinn, 2005:813

The nature of this imponderable second hurdle of what constituted a decisive victory, intensified the view that Duncan Smith was destined for defeat. In the ensuing confidence motion Duncan Smith was defeated. He secured the endorsement of seventy-five Conservative parliamentarians, but he was short of the requisite number of eighty-three that would have constituted a technical mandate for his continuance. Given the small base of parliamentary support that he was known to possess he did remarkably well (Cowley and

Green, 2005:7). Despite his record as party leader, he was able to add an additional twenty-one votes to the number he had polled in the final ballot of the parliamentary party two years earlier (Norton, 2005:41). A humiliated Duncan Smith was dignified in defeat. Surrounded by the parliamentary colleagues who had just evicted him he informed the assembled media that:

> the parliamentary party has spoken…I will stand down as leader when a successor is chosen… I will not publicly choose between the candidates in the coming election.   (Sky News, 29th October 2003)

It was a humiliating personal rejection for Duncan Smith.[12] He had assumed that he could retain the party leadership as enough Conservative parliamentarians would fear the consequences of a long drawn out and bitter succession contest. This was a misplaced assumption.

9.4   The Unopposed Coronation

The reformed procedures for determining the election (and eviction) of the leader of the Conservative Party were widely misconstrued by political commentators. The dominant aspect of the organisational reform of the Hague era had been the decision to allow party members to participate in the election of the leader of the Conservative Party. This provided an image of increased democratisation within the Conservative Party. However, participation had been offered with particular limitations. They determined which two candidates were to be presented to the party membership. The analysis of the last two chapters demonstrates the inherent flaws in this whittling down process. They alone could decide whether to activate a confidence motion to evict an underperforming incumbent and they alone could participate in the confidence ballot that they initiated. What was not widely noted was that there was no requirement for the parliamentary Conservative Party to put two candidates forward for the party members to decide between (Cowley and Stuart, 2004:360).

If Conservative parliamentarians could agree upon one candidate then they could hypothetically circumnavigate the procedural requirement for party membership participation. There were two overwhelmingly attractions to this: first, it would make the parliamentary Conservative Party appear unified; and, second, it would avoid the damaging effects of a long drawn out process (Norton, 2005:40). The capacity of the Conservative Party to achieve this, was dependant upon the mind set of the leading figures within the parliamentary Conservative Party at the juncture: who still had party leadership ambitions?

Speculation centred on Kenneth Clarke and Michael Portillo. Both had failed in previous tilts for the party leadership, and both had refused to serve in the Duncan Smith shadow Cabinet. The two leading candidates from within the shadow Cabinet were also failed party leadership candidates: David Davis and Michael Howard. Of the four candidates the gravitational pull was towards Howard. It was widely assumed that his frontline political career had ended when he resigned as shadow Foreign Secretary in 1999. It was also assumed that his weak performance in the Conservative Party leadership election of 1997 had brought to end any realistic ambition that he may have had of becoming party leader. The fact that he did not contest the party leadership when Hague resigned appeared to confirm the validity of this assertion.

However, Howard did accept the offer of Duncan Smith to become Shadow Chancellor. He had then seen his political stock rise rapidly as a result of a series of excellent parliamentary exchanges with Chancellor Gordon Brown. His impressive performances were amplified further when compared to what was regarded as a weak and unimpressive shadow Cabinet. Although Howard had political limitations, he was a political heavyweight, an effective parliamentarian, and he was regarded as politically competent[13] (Heffernan, 2003:1; Norton, 2005:41).

Howard had offered unqualified support for Duncan Smith through the confidence motion. Once this had ended in defeat for Duncan Smith, Howard moved quickly to assemble a campaign team. An effective and organised group of Howard supporters were able to ensure a coalescing of support around their candidate. His candidature emerged as a viable one with an alacrity which wrong footed any other potential candidates. By the time Howard formally announced his candidature, just two days after the fall of Duncan Smith, he already had public declarations of support from 130 of the 166 members of the parliamentary Conservative Party (Heffernan, 2003:1). This level of public support placed other potential candidates in an invidious position. Howard could legitimately request the endorsement of the party members on the basis that the majority of the parliamentary party supported his candidature ahead of any other rival. The best case scenario for any alternative candidate was to win the leadership of the Conservative Party by making the party membership vote against the wishes of the parliamentary Conservative Party. Should any alternative candidate succeed in doing so their mandate to lead would be as disputed of that of Duncan Smith. In such circumstances, standing against Howard would be almost futile. Recognising this, Portillo, Clarke and Davis all decided not to stand (Norton, 2005:41).

When Duncan Smith had been evicted on October 29th, the Chair of the 1922 Executive Committee had specified that nominations for the parliamentary ballots would close of November 6th with the formal ballots scheduled for November 11th. If the succession was disputed a realistic timescale for Duncan Smith handing over to his successor would have been mid-January, after a two month party membership campaign. However, the deadline for nominations passed with Howard as the only candidate. No parliamentary ballots were required; no mass membership ballot was required. Howard succeeded Duncan Smith within two weeks of the confidence motion. For Howard it amounted to a remarkable political comeback. He had recovered from finishing fifth and last in the first parliamentary ballot of the Conservative Party leadership election of 1997, to being anointed as leader by ritual acclamation just six years later.

9.5   Conclusion

The parliamentary Conservative Party manufactured a brutal and effective putsch against Duncan Smith in the autumn of 2003. For the duration of his leadership tenure, Duncan Smith had been undermined by two inter-related factors: first, by the disputed nature through which he had acquired the party leadership; and, second, by his own limitations and the perception that he was an electoral liability. Inherently flawed leadership election procedures enabled him to secure the party leadership by default, but they also rendered him increasingly vulnerable to removal. Having acquired the party leadership due to the party membership, the process of evicting him was initiated without their consent, and voted upon without their participation. Their right to participate in the subsequent vacant contest was circumvented by Conservative parliamentarians, who coalesced around an agreed successor. It was a remarkably quick defenestration. The whole process was initiated and concluded within one week, rather than drawn out over three months (Cowley and Green, 2005:7).

By their actions Conservative parliamentarians expressed their disregard for the existing procedures, and the participation of the mass membership in leadership selection. Having finally caught up with Labour and the Liberal Democrats in encouraging mass participation in leadership selection, the parliamentary Conservative Party suddenly acquired a taste for the pre-1965 magic circle. The old system of an emergence following on from consultations amongst elites was revived, as Howard was declared leader by ritual acclamation. It was a remarkable political outcome, as Kelly observes:

the emergence of Michael Howard as the sole candidate, thus negating any formal contest, returned the party to the ballot-free leadership contests it held until 1965…Tory MPs realised by October 2003 that covert deals between the party's senior players, and discreet soundings among its MPs, can be much more conducive to party unity and party efficiency than publicised ballots – especially those involving an unpredictable rank and file.   (Kelly, 2004a:402)

Howard became the first unopposed choice for the leadership of the Conservative Party since Anthony Eden had succeeded Winston Churchill nearly fifty years earlier (Gamble and Wright, 2004:2). As Kelly had implied, the method of his acquisition of the party leadership had suggested that his emergence, and the closing of the ranks to facilitate his unopposed emergence, conjured up memories of the culture and ethos of a bygone age; an age in which the old style Conservative Party was less ideological and more pragmatic, less divided and more united, more electorally appealing and less disliked. Gamble and Wright would expand upon this theme of the Conservatives learning from their past and going back to the future by noting that:

> The embrace of Howard is a sign that the Conservatives may be beginning to realise that they must find a way to unite…and…heal the party's divisions…One of the most remarkable features of the leadership of both Hague and Duncan Smith is that leading Conservatives who stood against them for the party leadership were not included in their shadow Cabinet. Maudling served under Heath, Whitelaw under Thatcher, Heseltine and Hurd under Major…Howard could not persuade Clarke and Portillo to join the shadow Cabinet, but by deliberately including people from all wings of the party he was able to secure their positive endorsement. The long civil war in the party started by Margaret Thatcher when she stood against Heath may at last be coming to an end. If it does, Howard's leadership may come to be seen beginning the Conservative recovery.
>
> (Gamble and Wright, 2004:2-3)

THE TRIUMPH OF THE MODERNIZERS: THE ELECTION OF DAVID CAMERON

The optimism that Conservatives felt when Michael Howard acquired the party leadership reflected the view that two key objectives had been achieved. First, they had removed a party leader who was perceived to be incompetent, inexperienced and an electoral liability. Second, they had removed him via a method that was immensely advantageous to Howard as his successor. The three previous party leaders, John Major, William Hague and Iain Duncan Smith, were all viewed as default leaders due to the method by which they had acquired the party leadership. That default status impeded their legitimacy, which in turn undermined their authority. This was an impediment that did not affect Howard. He had acquired the party leadership unopposed, and by ritual acclamation, thus ensuring that he would possess a level of legitimacy and authority over the parliamentary Conservative Party, which had been denied his three predecessors in opposition[1] (Garnett, 2004:367).

Howard now had the opportunity to address the difficulties that had engulfed post-Thatcherite Conservatism. The complexities of internal party management for Howard would be less pronounced. The strength of his mandate, and the unifying message that it offered, would make Conservative parliamentarians less inclined to be disloyal and rebellious. Howard also had a greater opportunity than Major had in government or Hague or Duncan Smith in opposition, to reconfigure the narrative of Conservatism in the post-Thatcherite era. He was a pure Thatcherite, who was clearly identifiable with the economic liberal, Eurosceptic and social conservative strand of thought within Conservative party politics. Increasingly Conservative parliamentarians were of his ideological ilk, yet electoral imperatives suggested that the Conservatives needed to broaden their electoral appeal by shifting towards the centre-ground of British politics (Hill, 2004:1-16).

Both Hague and Duncan Smith had flirted with that electoral need to reconfigure post-Thatcherite Conservatism, as evident from the briefly utilised rhetoric of modernisation and the briefly noted emphasis on socially inclusive compassionate Conservatism. However, both Hague and Duncan Smith were constrained by the fact that such strategic revisionism appeared to amount to a repudiation of Thatcherite Conservatism. When such revisionist posturing provided no evidence of making an electoral impact, it resulted in sustained criticism of their political and electoral strategies.

The instinctive reaction of both Hague and Duncan Smith was to abandon their flirtations with modernisation and the rhetoric of socially inclusive and compassionate Conservatism. Both abandoned it out of perceived political necessity. Modernisation had provided no electoral dividend, it was causing internal division because it was making no electoral impact, and the by-product of this was that both Hague and Duncan Smith were subjected to continued speculation about their continuance as party leader. It can be argued that neither Hague nor Duncan Smith had the political credibility to engage in such political repositioning. Hague was insufficiently identifiable with the Thatcherites to articulate a new narrative of Conservatism that transcended Thatcherite Conservatism. When he briefly attempted to do so, in the first two years of his party leadership tenure, he succeeded in antagonising the traditional pure Thatcherites.

Duncan Smith was equally unsuccessful in this quest. He was viewed as being located on the extremities of Thatcherite Conservatism. By deviating from this ideological position, as he briefly did in the opening stages of his party leadership tenure, he managed in the same way as Hague had, to antagonise traditional pure Thatcherites. Moreover, moderate Conservatives, who believed in the revisionist merit of modernisation, doubted the authenticity of Duncan Smith. They believed that Duncan Smith was an implausible articulator of the modernisation and inclusive agenda.[2] Furthermore, the modernisation strategy served to divide, as Duncan Smith flip-flopped between social liberalism and social conservatism. He also managed to seem hypocritical when he demanded unity and loyalty, given his disunity and disloyalty towards Major a decade earlier.

It is possible to argue that Howard was better situated than both Hague and Duncan Smith. The strength of his unopposed mandate provided him with scope to transcend Thatcherite Conservatism, and do so successfully. He was a pure Thatcherite himself, who was an experienced political heavyweight (unlike Hague and Duncan Smith) and a career loyalist (unlike Duncan Smith). These factors could have enabled him to convincingly argue the case for defining a narrative of Conservatism that transcended Thatcherite Conservatism, without provoking the levels of dissent and disagreement that overwhelmed Hague and Duncan Smith. That optimism suggested that great things were expected of Howard. In addition to the factors outlined above, the political environment that Howard faced was increasingly advantageous for a party of the opposition. The prolonged honeymoon that New Labour had experienced when entering government had ended. Tony Blair was losing the aura of impregnability that had characterised the first six years of his premiership, as increasing numbers of Labour parliamentarians questioned the New Labour project.[3]

Morale amongst Conservatives was immediately transformed by his acquisition of the party leadership. He made a positive impact in terms of discipline and internal party unity. The venomous ideological factionalism that had characterised Conservative Party politics in the post-Thatcherite era was less evident during his tenure. To emphasise this point, the experienced political analyst, Roth, would observe that Howard had taken command of the habitual back-stabbing parliamentary Conservative Party and had converted them into a credible fighting force (Roth, 2004:362). Moreover, Howard immediately impressed his parliamentary party with a series of devastating parliamentary attacks on Blair, the type of which seemed to be beyond the competency of Duncan Smith[4] (Cowley and Green, 2005:7). His excellent parliamentary performances and the general perception of competence that he offered brought back influential financial donors. The level of donations rose in terms of number and volume. In the third quarter of 2003, which equates to the final three months of the Duncan Smith era, a total of seventy-three declared cash donations were made to the party. In the final quarter of the year, which coincided with the emergence of Howard, there was a dramatic rise in declared donations to one hundred and thirty eight. In financial terms, removing Duncan Smith was a successful act; and that financial upsurge was essential to reinvigorating the grassroots membership (Fisher, 2004:407; Cowley and Green, 2005:7).

However, the fortunes of the Conservative Party in the opinion polls were largely unmoved by the shift from Duncan Smith to Howard. An initial upsurge in the Conservatives poll rating was evident, but thereafter the Conservatives would plateau at around the low 30s in percentage terms; an insufficient figure for a party aspiring to government (Roth, 2004:363). Ultimately, Howard was unable to deliver on the optimism that characterised his emergence as party leader. Just like Hague and Duncan Smith before him, he was unable to construct either a viable narrative of Conservatism, or a raft of credible policy positions, which would offer electoral appeal. Within eighteen months of acquiring the party leadership, Howard would enter the campaign for the May 2005 general election, facing an inevitable defeat (Norton, 2005:41; Seldon and Snowden, 2005b:738-739).

Rather than construct an electoral strategy built around positive reasons to endorse the Conservative Party, Howard engaged in an inherently negative campaign. It amounted to an adaptation of the failed Hague core-vote strategy of four years earlier. The objective was to prevent New Labour from securing a working parliamentary majority, and became defined as a core vote plus strategy. The objective was to maximise the Conservative core vote, but hope that the negative campaigning on the failing aspect of New Labour in government (e.g. school indiscipline) would depress the Labour vote, and provide a small level of additional support for the Conservatives. The dominant themes became tax and immigration. However, the pledge to cut taxation *and* invest in public services seemed disingenuous, and undermined their attempts to appear like a potential party of government. Moreover, the excessive emphasis on immigration amounted to a defensive and negative strategy and conjured up images of the 'bandwagon populism' of the Hague era (Norton, 2005:43; Seldon and Snowden, 2005b:731-732).

A third successive electoral reverse duly followed. New Labour secured a parliamentary majority of sixty-six, despite the fact that their share of the vote slipped as low as 35.2 per cent, which was down from 40.7 per cent in 2001, and 43.2 per cent in 1997. The Conservative share of the vote increased from 31.7 per cent in 2001 to 32.3 per cent, meaning that in eight years they had increased their share by only 1.6 per cent from the 30.7 per cent of 1997. The beneficiaries of hostility towards New Labour were the Liberal Democrats, who increased their vote share from 18.3 per cent to 22.1 per cent (Bartle and Laycock, 2006:78-79).

Despite this, Howard claimed that by increasing their parliamentary representation (from 166 to 198), and by reducing the percentage vote share difference between themselves and Labour from 9 percentage points to 2.9 percentage points, that a Conservative recovery had commenced.[5] However, this interpretation could not hide the fact that the Conservatives had suffered another humiliating reversal. Howard had initiated a limited recovery, but he had failed to provide a springboard for electoral success at the next general election (Seldon and Snowden, 2005b:736-737).

10.1   The Prolonged Resignation of Michael Howard

Debate on the future of Howard began to dominate the thoughts of Conservative parliamentarians, even before the election campaign was completed. Speculation focused around former defeated candidate, David Davis. Days before the general election, his supporters were attempting to secure the swift removal of Howard (Montgomerie, 2005:1-2). They attempted to encourage Howard to resign with immediate effect, and indicated that if he did not then they would attempt to initiate a confidence motion against him. Their objective was clear:

> Presumed to be the darling of the party's grassroots, Davis appeared to be the most likely successor should Howard take the hint and resign in the immediate aftermath of a third successive election defeat. In the

event of an early leadership election, Davis would need only to finish in the first two in the initial series of eliminative ballots among MPs to proceed to the final run off whose outcome would be decided by party members. Assuming he did so, Davis himself, his supporters, and most commentators presumed he would win. Indeed, some of his allies were even entertaining hopes at this stage that he might secure the leadership without the need for a formal ballot of any kind – just as Howard himself had done.   (Denham and Dorey, 2006:35)

The attempt to secure the party leadership for Davis by unanimous acclamation was derailed by the terms by which Howard decided to depart. Rather than offer his immediate resignation, Howard announced that he would resign[6] once a full review of the existing leadership selection procedures had been completed. That Howard decided to engage in such a review was assumed to be indicative of the widespread reservations that existed about the existing procedures (Denham and Dorey, 2005:35-36). However, the more calculating political minds assumed that there was a more cynical explanation, in which Howard:

Was attempting to alter the rules in a way that would stymie those would be leaders of whom he did not approve whilst giving an advantage to candidates he backed. David Davis was the name usually mentioned as an example of the former, with David Cameron being usually mentioned as an example of the latter.[7]
                                       (Cowley and Green, 2005:2)

As discussed in the previous two chapters, the existing leadership selection procedures had been established as part of the wide sweeping organisational reform of the Conservative Party during the Hague era. The process involved two distinct stages. Conservative parliamentarians would conduct a series of parliamentary ballots, eliminating candidates until the leading two were presented to the party membership, who would decide on which one of those candidates should be their leader. Duncan Smith was the only party leader to have been elected through these full procedures, and therein lay an insight into the problem.

As chapters eight and nine have highlighted, both the process and the outcome were deemed to be inherently flawed. The means by which Duncan Smith had acquired the party leadership exposed the disharmony that existed between the parliamentary Conservative Party and the party membership. Duncan Smith was amongst the leading two candidates amongst the Conservative parliamentarians (by only vote) due to some negatively induced voting. At this stage, he was the beneficiary of limited but important anti-Portillo and anti-social liberal sentiment. At the party membership stage, he was the beneficiary of a Eurosceptic sentiment that worked to the disadvantage of the pro-European Clarke (Kelly, 2004a:400).

Both Conservative parliamentarians and party members seemed concerned about these procedures. The party membership was angered by the controlled nature of their participation in the succession process, in that they were asked to comment on only two candidates, thus limiting the extent of their participation. Parliamentarian dissatisfaction was even more pronounced. Questionable procedures had imposed upon them a party leader that over seventy per cent of them disapproved of as a potential leader. In acting to address these concerns it was clear that Howard was eager to ensure that parliamentarians had the ultimate say in who their parliamentary leader should be (Denham and Dorey, 2005:36).

The precedent of Duncan Smith and the fact Conservative parliamentarians had felt the need to deliberately circumnavigate the procedural rules to determine his successor, provided the rationale for change. Proposals for altering the party leadership selection procedures were incorporated within a consultation paper. The suggested procedures seemed somewhat convoluted but can be summarised as thus.

First, if one candidate was able to secure endorsements from over half of the parliamentary Conservative Party then they would be automatically declared the new party leader. Second, should this not be the case then candidatures for the party leadership would only be permitted from individuals who had endorsements from ten per cent of their parliamentary colleagues (i.e. in this parliament that would equate to twenty Conservative parliamentarians). Third, candidates who passed this parliamentary threshold would then be submitted to the National Conservative Convention, which comprised senior figures within the voluntary wing of the party. Members of the National Conservative Convention would then rank the candidates in order of popularity. Fourth, the candidates would then enter a series of eliminative ballots, in which only Conservative parliamentarians were allowed to participate. An important proviso was incorporated at the stage of the eliminative ballot. The candidate who had secured the most votes from the National Conservative Convention would be guaranteed a place in the final ballot of the Conservative parliamentarians; i.e. they would not have to participate in the eliminative ballots. These complex procedures would prevent the party membership from having the final say in the party leadership, but involvement would be retained, albeit in an indirect manner, through the National Conservative Convention (Seldon and Snowden, 2005b:738).

In order for these new procedures to be accepted, it was necessary for them to be approved by a two-thirds majority of a constitutional college, comprising Conservative parliamentarians, voluntary activists, Conservative peers, and Conservative Members of the European Parliament. In the subsequent ballot held in late September, the proposals that Howard advanced were rejected, with only sixty-one per cent endorsing the notion of change.[8] This ensured that the race to succeed Howard would be conducted under the existing, albeit inherently flawed, leadership selection procedures. The fear was a re-enactment of the Duncan Smith scenario.

10.2   Four Candidates Emerge

The period between Howard announcing his intention to resign, which occurred in early May, and his official resignation, which occurred in the aftermath of the annual party conference, was politically ambiguous. His prolonged departure proved to be problematic for the Conservatives, as his time consuming attempt to amend the leadership election procedures, left the party in political limbo (Childs, 2006:64). It would ultimately lead onto an annual party conference, which became a de facto party leadership convention, thus conjuring up images of the annual party conference of forty-two years earlier.

That delay in the leadership election formally beginning created considerable complications for potential candidates, as well as undermining the momentum of the Davis candidature. Ambitious Conservative parliamentarians had to decide whether to formally declare their candidatures for a contest that had not officially commenced, and would be conducted under procedures yet to be determined (Childs, 2006:64). This intensified speculation on who might declare and when and caused many to fear that a divisive and bitter succession battle would develop. The suggestions from early summer made such fears seem justified. Briefly abandoning his cricketing obsession, Major resurfaced for one of his few political pronouncements. He argued that it was essential that the Conservatives elect a new party leader, who could reposition the party in the centre-ground of British politics. The intervention of Major prompted a response from Thatcher. She contradicted his assumptions, and argued that the Conservatives needed to return to first principles. This was interpreted as a coded message for saying that they needed to return to an overtly right-wing Thatcherite agenda (Seldon and Snowden, 2005b:739).

By the time the succession contest formally began in the aftermath of the annual party conference in early October numerous potential candidates had seen their ambitions recede. The intended candidatures of Andrew Lansley, Tim Yeo, Theresa May, Alan Duncan, and Michael Ancram, all failed to gather sufficient momentum to justify entry. The candidature of Malcolm Rifkind was eventually withdrawn after he realised that he would finish last in the first parliamentary ballot. In the end, the four candidates disputing the succession were Kenneth Clarke, Liam Fox, David Davis and David Cameron. As the presumed candidates arrived for the annual party conference in late September, the indications were that Davis and Clarke would proceed, with Fox, Cameron and the then still candidate, Rifkind, all likely to be eliminated. Clarke and Davis were neck and neck amongst party members (both at 30 per cent), but Clarke had clear lead over his rivals amongst the electorate at large, amongst known Conservative voters, and amongst potential Conservative voters. The belated candidature of Clarke now seemed the greatest threat to Davis (King, 2005a:4).

The former Chancellor and two-time defeated candidate, Clarke, entered the contest as the most experienced candidate of the Europhile Tory left. Although a socially liberal, one-nation economic wet, the most identifiable aspect of the ideological make up of Clarke remained his Europhilia. This remained his biggest obstacle amongst his parliamentary colleagues and the party membership, both of which were increasingly Eurosceptic in their outlook.

The former Conservative Party Chairman and recently appointed shadow Foreign Secretary, Liam Fox, stood as a candidate of the Eurosceptic Thatcherite right. A parliamentarian since 1992, he had served as a junior minister in the Major government, before serving in a variety of roles in the shadow Cabinet in the era of opposition. His association with economic liberalism and Euroscepticism was long standing, but his social conservatism was an increasingly important aspect of his political make up. The limitations of his candidature focused on whether he was a credible candidate for party political leadership. If he was to emerge victorious he would need to overcome the accusation that he was a political lightweight lacking in gravitas.[9] He would also need to ensure that his campaign was gaffe free, as he had developed a reputation for political misjudgements.[10]

Although his political lightweight reputation was assumed to be an impediment to his party leadership prospects, the main impediment to Fox was actually the assumption that the Eurosceptic Thatcherite right was likely to coalesce around Davis instead of him. Davis had the disadvantage of being the clear favourite to succeed in what amounted to both a delayed and prolonged contest. The strengths and weaknesses of a Davis candidature replicated those articulated four years earlier. The main problems associated with his candidature remained his relatively poor communication skills and concerns about whether he could engender loyalty from his parliamentary colleagues.

The fourth and final candidate, David Cameron, was potentially the most intriguing. The weaknesses of his candidature were evident: his youth at only thirty-nine years old; the lack of experience having only entered Parliament four years earlier; his low public profile and his lack of a clear ideologically constructed base of support. It seemed implausible that Cameron would emerge victorious, so the assumption was that he was (Powell-like) putting down a marker for a future party leadership bid[11] (Denham and Dorey, 2006:36).

Perceptions of the four candidates would demonstrate the extent of the ideological movement of Conservatism in the last thirty years. When Thatcher defeated Heath in 1975, the central ideological determinant had been economic policy. When Major defeated Redwood in 1995 and when Hague defeated Clarke in 1997, the over-riding ideological concern was the question of European integration. The contest four years earlier, in which Duncan Smith had emerged at the expense of Clarke and Portillo, appeared to straddle two ideological concerns. The questions surrounding European integration remained significant and acted as an impediment to the pro-European Clarke. Questions about social, moral and sexual morality were increasingly salient and the modernising socially liberal message that Portillo advanced impeded his chances, as it mobilised traditional socially conservative hostility. By the time of the 2005 leadership election, the centrality of the European ideological divide had diminished considerably. The leading ideological conflict was between social liberals and social conservatives. The additional conflict between modernizers and traditionalists was also reflective of alternative visions and strategies for electoral recovery. Childs argues that traditional social conservatives tended to be resistant to radical overhaul, believing that 'one more heave', would propel them to victory at the next general election. Reforming social liberals argued the case for a comprehensive modernisation of all aspects of the party (Childs, 2006:64).

This distinction would lead to the following theory of the candidates and the parliamentary ballots. The four candidates were defined as belonging to either the right (Davis and Fox) or the left (Clarke and Cameron). In this context, Denham and Dorey have argued that the parliamentary ballots amounted to a tale of two primaries – the right wing primary between Davis and Fox; and a left wing primary between Clarke and Cameron (Denham and Dorey, 2006:36-39).

The right-wing primary between Davis and Fox is a valid interpretation. The traditionalist social conservative viewpoint became seen as the Thatcherite right viewpoint, thus assuming that it embraced the full range of Thatcherite beliefs: i.e. that this social conservatism was aligned to an economic liberalist and a Eurosceptic mindset. Both Davis and Fox situated themselves here and campaigned to the instincts of likeminded Conservative parliamentarians. The assertion that Clarke and Cameron were engaging in a left-wing primary requires further clarification. Clarke had a long standing reputation as being of the Tory left, and their associated stances of economic dampness, Europhilia, and social liberalism. The assertion that social liberalism was identifiable with modernization, and thus a radical overhaul of all aspects of the Conservative Party, is not fully reflective of the position of Clarke. He was of the Tory left, but the mantra of modernisation and reform did not really appeal to him. Cameron, on the other hand, embraced social liberalism and modernization, and the associated themes that encapsulated the Portillo candidature of four years earlier. However, it would be an over-simplification to define Cameron as of the Tory left. His stance on the economic and European ideological .policy divides could be defined as somewhat nebulous, although they tended (if anything) towards economic dryness and moderate Euroscepticism.

The notion of a left-wing primary is contestable in terms of the ideological and strategic positioning of Clarke and Cameron. However, the tale of two primaries theory does not just embrace the appeal of the candidates, but the attitudes of their presumed supporters. It was assumed that the majority Thatcherite right within the parliamentary Conservative Party, (economic liberal, Eurosceptic, social conservatives) would endorse either Davis or Fox, thus fuelling the right-wing primary theory. It was also assumed that the minority Tory left of economic wet, pro-European, social liberals, would split between Clarke and Cameron, thus fuelling the left-wing primary theory.

10.3   The Parliamentary Ballots

In the interim period between the general election defeat and the formal beginning of the party leadership contest,[12] Conservative parliamentarians and activists had been weighing up the merits of numerous potential candidates. Whereas the over-riding issue in the 1997 and 2001 party leadership contests had been the ideological positions of the respective candidates, there was a broader range of themes informing debate in 2005. This was probably borne out of two factors. First, the experience of three successive electoral defeats had finally encouraged Conservatives to consider re-evaluating the long-term strategy of the party. Second, the experience of Duncan Smith, as a perceived ideologue with poor communication skills, persuaded Conservatives to consider in greater depth the audience that they were addressing (i.e. the mass electorate) rather than themselves and their own prejudices. In 2005, ideology was downgraded as a determinant. Conservatives attempted to evaluate which candidate was the best communicator, the best debater, and thereby the most voter-attractive (Childs, 2006:64). Ultimately, it was not as much a tale of two primaries (a right-wing primary between; Davis and Fox, and a left-wing primary between Clarke and Cameron), but a tale of two speeches, between one badly received speech by Davis and one acclaimed speech by Cameron (Denham and Dorey, 2006:35-42).

This assertion demonstrates the importance of the annual party conference to shaping the direction of the subsequent parliamentary ballots. The conference season actually predated Howard's official resignation, but the candidates knew the importance of it to their chances of ·success.

On the Tory left, Clarke was viewed as having made a positive impression through his party conference speech, but it could not mask the problems that would come to engulf his candidature over the next few weeks (Denham and Dorey, 2006:37-38). Although he still retained considerable respect for his experience and his competence, his candidature was weakened by the passage of political time. He was increasingly perceived as a figure of the political past. His age and the realisation that he would be approaching seventy at the time of the next general election became problematic issues for him. As campaigning for the first parliamentary ballot commenced, the Clarke candidature was suffering from three significant limitations. First, longstanding Conservative parliamentarians, who had supported his bids for the party leadership in 1997 and 2001, abandoned him this time round. Second, he was unable to penetrate into the new cohort of youthful Conservative parliamentarians. Finally, high profile endorsements that added weight to his candidature and provided momentum were not forthcoming (Denham and Dorey, 2006:37).

What ultimately destroyed the candidature of Clarke was the gravitational pull towards Cameron. As the youngest and most inexperienced candidate, Cameron, was able to utilise his conference speech as a means to raise his public profile and enhance the credibility of his candidature.

> The speech was extremely well received by delegates and favourably reported by assembled journalists, with television coverage amplifying its effect....at the end, he received an enthusiastic standing ovation, confirming the speech's immediate and impressive impact.
>
> (Denham and Dorey, 2006:38)

That Cameron performed so impressively was threatening to Clarke in the short term in the so-called left-wing primary. It was also threatening to Davis in the longer term, both for the second parliamentary ballot, but also with the party membership. The acclaimed speech by Cameron now increased the pressure on Davis to demonstrate that he did possess the necessary communication and presentational skills. Whereas Cameron had avoided discussing policy in detail, and offered a positive speech, Davis was more detailed in policy and adopted a negative and defensive stance. To appeal to social conservatives he advocated tougher sentencing and emphasised the sanctity of marriage; and to appeal to Eurosceptics he rejected the notion of further European integration. Rejecting the positivism of the Cameron emphasis on reform, Davis argued that the party should stop apologising for the past and for its values (Denham and Dorey, 2006:38). If the message was negative and defensive, its main limitation was how it was presented. He failed to engage in the necessary preparation and rehearsal for a major conference speech. There was no spontaneous and prolonged applause at the culmination of his speech,[13] as had been the case for Cameron. Instead of that there was a

> moment of real pathos when David Davis had finished his speech flatly and had to gesture to the audience to rise to its feet.
>
> (Montgomerie, 2005:6)

A demoralised Davis campaign team attempted to overcome his poor performance by arguing that there was more to leadership than flamboyant platform oratory. However, their attempt to negate the impact of his soporific conference speech was flawed. They could not escape the fact that it had conjured up images of the communication and presentational difficulties that had characterised the Duncan Smith tenure. Their attempt to make a virtue out of vice, by declaring Davis as the anti-spin candidate, served to reinforce the Duncan Smith comparison, as it replicated the quiet man approach (Jones and Carlin, 2005:1).

The annual party conference fundamentally altered the dynamics of the succession in the run up to the first parliamentary ballot.[14] The tale of two speeches would impact upon the tale of two primaries. Clarke and Cameron were assumed to be competing for the left-wing vote and Davis and Fox for the right wing vote. In the right-wing primary, Fox was winning converts and it was shaping up into a more competitive struggle than Davis and his aco-lytes had anticipated. In the left-wing primary it was assumed that Cameron had overcome Clarke. Davis was thus a victim of a double squeeze. Fox was squeezing him amongst Thatcherite motivated Conservative parliamentar-ians; Cameron was anticipated to squeeze him in the second parliamentary ballot and the subsequent party membership run off. As the first ballot approached (October 18th) the expectation was that Davis and Cameron would come first and second. The conundrum was which of Fox and Clarke would be eliminated.

Table 15:   Changes in Support for Candidates in Parliamentary Ballots of the Conservative Party Leadership Election of 2005

	First Ballot	Percentage	Second Ballot	Percentage
David Davis	62	31.3	57	28.8
David Cameron	56	28.3	90	45.4
Liam Fox	42	21.2	51	25.8
Kenneth Clarke	38	19.2		

Source: Lynch and Garnett, 2007:333

In the event it was Clarke who was eliminated, thus ending forever his ambition to lead the Conservative Party. Despite the aforementioned opinion polling data that indicated the merits of his candidature, his age, his Europhilia, and the meteoric rise of Cameron, ensured that he was defeated in the supposed left-wing primary by a margin sufficient to leave him trailing Fox by four votes. The elimination of Clarke was advantageous to Cameron, as it was assumed that the majority of former Clarke supporters would gravitate to him. It was presumed that former Clarke supporters would be disinclined to support either Davis or Fox. Had Clarke defeated Fox for third place, then the candidature of Davis would have been immeasurably enhanced and the candidature of Cameron disadvantaged. If Fox had been eliminated there would have been around forty predominantly Thatcherite right Conservative parliamentarians, who probably gravitated to Davis. This would have made it more likely that Davis would beat Cameron in the second ballot.

Therefore, despite leading the first parliamentary ballot, Davis was wounded by the result. Political journalists had spent the weeks leading up to the first parliamentary ballot, gathering intelligence on the voting intentions of all Conservative parliamentarians. Having liaised with the campaign teams of each of the four candidates they predicted that Davis had sixty-six publicly declared supporters; Cameron had twenty-seven, Clarke had twenty-six and Fox had twenty-three. Of the remaining fifty-six undecided or would not say, they hypothecated that Cameron would secure a high proportion. Whereas the gap between declared and eventual supporters for the other candidates indicated that they were gaining converts (i.e. Cameron twenty-seven assumed and fifty-six real; Fox twenty-three assumed and forty-two real; and Clarke twenty-six assumed and thirty-eight real), Davis would amazingly poll less than the number of his publicly declared supporters (Jones, 2005:4; Carlin, Isaby and Jones, 2005:8).

The momentum was with Cameron as the second parliamentary ballot approached. He was attracting new supporters from both the Europhile Tory left and the Eurosceptic Thatcherite right. On the left, former first round Clarke supporters such as Andrew Lansley, Stephen Dorrell, George Young and David Curry, all publicly declared for Cameron. On the right, prominent Eurosceptic, David Heathcoat-Amory, indicated that he was abandoning Fox, who he had endorsed in the first ballot, and would now support Cameron. Despite the loss of Heathcoat-Amory, the Fox campaign claimed that the implosion of the Davis candidature demonstrated that their candidate was now the champion of the right.

However, the collapse in the Davis vote did not materialise as the Fox campaign had hoped. In the second parliamentary ballot, Cameron added a further thirty-four votes, ensuring that his support base was ninety, which was just short of half of the parliamentary Conservative Party. The Davis vote fell by only five votes and Fox could only add a further nine, leaving a six vote gap between the two Eurosceptic Thatcherite candidates, Davis and Fox. The party membership had a clear choice, between Cameron and Davis, and a clear steer from the parliamentarians to vote for Cameron.

10.4   The Party Membership Ballot

As the leadership election entered the party membership campaigning stage, it was clear that activists were attracted to the notion of a Cameron led Conservative Party. Even before the final parliamentary ballot, it was clear that Cameron was the overwhelming favoured candidate of the activists. A You Gov poll showed that 59 per cent of them preferred Cameron; 18 per cent wanted Fox, and 15 per cent plumped for Davis, with the remaining 8 per cent undecided (King, 2005a:4). Such figures demonstrated the meteoric rise of Cameron and the modernizers, and indicated the seismic impact of the conference season. Inside two weeks, Cameron had propelled himself from a party membership polling of 16 per cent, before the conference, to 59 per cent, after it. In the same period, Davis had seen his support amongst the party activists collapse from 30 per cent to 15 per cent. Furthermore, once Fox was eliminated, and the party membership contest commenced, polling suggested that Cameron was ahead by 72 to 22 per cent (King, 2005a:4; King, 2005b:4).

The presumed inevitability of a Cameron victory led to speculation that Davis might withdraw his candidature, in the manner in which Maudling had done so forty years earlier. Maudling had been procedurally within his rights to contest a second parliamentary ballot, but withdrew acknowledging the inevitability of defeat. Such speculation surrounding Davis stemmed from deliberations between, the Conservative Party Chairman, Francis Maude and 1922 Executive Committee Chair, Michael Spicer. They were attracted to the notion of Cameron being acclaimed without a postal ballot and intimated to the Davis camp that this would save the party money, and it would save Davis his dignity (Kite and Hennessy, 2005a:21).

The Davis camp decided to proceed, although the ensuing six-week campaign amongst the party membership was a relatively staid affair, in comparison to the widespread hostilities of the Duncan Smith versus Clarke contest of four years earlier. This was bemusing for many Davis supporters, given the ammunition that their candidate had at his disposal, and which he seemed reluctant to deploy. Ultimately, Davis failed to:

> expose and capitalise on Cameron's weaknesses. These included his political innocence and inexperience, his dramatic change in policy tone and substance since the general election (fought on a manifesto of

which he was the principal author) and his refusal to confirm or deny allegations of drug use when at University.

(Denham and Dorey, 2006:40)

That Davis chose not to engage in personal muck raking was to his credit. His reputation as a schemer was disproved by his conduct in what was now a forlorn hope of winning the party membership ballot (Montgomerie, 2005:7). Recognising the inevitability of defeat, it has been speculated that he chose not to poison the atmosphere within the Conservative Party by engaging in a rancorous and negative campaign. He was unable, and probably knew that he would be unable, to break the tumultuous love affair that the Conservatives were beginning with Cameron. His statesmanlike approach did lead to speculation of long-term strategising, as Denham and Dorey have noted:

his conduct perhaps suggests that, while he wanted to lead the party, he realised this was now unlikely…in the short term. If so, he had no alternative but to accept this and avoid damaging both the party and any lingering prospect he might (yet) have of leading it one day.

(Denham and Dorey, 2006:40)

Table 16:   Support for Candidates in Conservative Party Leadership Membership Ballot of 2005

	Votes	Percentage
David Cameron	134,446	67.7
David Davis	64,398	32.3
Turnout (77.8%)		

Source: Lynch and Garnett, 2007:333

In the subsequent postal ballot of party members, Cameron, secured his expected victory. A sense of euphoria engulfed the Conservative Party. They sensed that a new era of Conservatism was about to commence. Moreover, Conservatives sensed that the party would unify successfully in the aftermath of the party leadership election. Eight years earlier Clarke had refused to serve under Hague in the 1997 to 2001 shadow cabinet having been defeated. Four years earlier, Clarke would again refuse to serve in the Duncan Smith shadow cabinet after his second electoral rejection. On both occasions Clarke had been less than praising of his newly elected party leaders. The immediate reaction to Cameron being elected was different. Davis was dignified in defeat and fulsome in his praise of his new party leader.

Table 17:   Comparative Mandates to Lead the Conservative Party

		Parliamentary Mandate (%)	Membership Mandate (%)
1965	Edward Heath	49.3	
1975	Margaret Thatcher	52.9	
1989	Margaret Thatcher	84.0	
1990	John Major	49.7	
1995	John Major	66.3	
1997	William Hague	56.1	
2001	Iain Duncan Smith	32.5	60.7
2003	Michael Howard	no ballot	no ballot
2005	David Cameron	45.4	67.7

Source: Adapted from Quinn, 2005:812-813

Moreover, as table seventeen suggests, the mandate to lead that Cameron possessed more than stood comparison with any of his predecessors in the formal democratic era. The level of support that victors had acquired in the final parliamentary ballot, under the 1965 to 1998 party leadership election procedures, ranged from the 49.3 per cent that Heath secured, (which was sufficient to negate the need for a confirmatory ballot as the defeated candidates withdrew, whilst procedurally being entitled to contest the confirmatory ballot), to the 84 per cent that Thatcher secured in the unequal contest of 1989. Cameron's acquisition of the party leadership was confirmed by his 67.7 percentage share of the party membership. However, his parliamentary figure, at 45.4, is a relatively impressive performance especially if we acknowledge that it was in effect the penultimate ballot, rather than the final ballot. If a final ballot amongst parliamentarians alone had occurred then Cameron's parliamentary mandate would have been far stronger.

This interpretation is partial as we are utilising statistical information for elections conducted under alternative procedures. That being the case, a more appropriate comparison, may be that between Duncan Smith and Cameron. Duncan Smith was perceived to possess a disputed mandate (having secured the party leadership through his 60.7 percentage share of the party membership), whilst Cameron was perceived to have an undisputed mandate, despite a marginal difference with the figure that Duncan Smith secured (60.7 to 67.7). How can this difference of perception relating to their mandate be explained?

We can argue that there are four explanations. First, Cameron came first amongst the party membership *and* amongst Conservative parliamentarians. Due to this dual endorsement, Cameron was not to suffer the accusations that were levelled at Duncan Smith; i.e. that his party membership endorsement was not shared by Conservative parliamentarians. Critics of Duncan Smith regularly reflected on the fact that one vote going to Portillo instead of Duncan Smith would have ensured that Portillo and Clarke were presented to the party membership rather than Duncan Smith and Clarke. Whereas the parliamentary screening that led to Duncan Smith being presented to the party membership was as tenuous as was procedurally possible, Cameron was clearly the preferred option of the Conservative parliamentarians.

Second, Cameron secured the support of nearly half of Conservative parliamentarians, whereas Duncan Smith was only able to garner the support of one-third of Conservative parliamentarians. Had their respective parliamentary ballots been followed by a further parliamentary ballot, rather than a party membership ballot, then Cameron's strength relative to Duncan Smith's immediately becomes evident. Cameron had ninety votes at the second parliamentary ballot in 2005, with Davis securing 57 and Fox 51. Had a further parliamentary ballot been conducted Cameron would only need to secure a further ten votes from the freed Fox endorsers, in order to win. Or to put it another way, Davis would have needed to add an additional forty two onto his second ballot return of 57 in order to deprive Cameron of victory. Given that Davis had lost support between the first and second ballots it would seem unlikely that he could have secured the additional votes from Fox. Whereas Cameron had a lead of thirty-three at the end of the parliamentary voting stage, Duncan Smith was second and trailing Clarke by five votes. In a hypothetical additional parliamentary ballot, Clarke would have needed to secure an additional twenty-four votes to claim a majority (i.e. 83 votes) of the 53 Portillo supporters, whereas Duncan Smith would have needed to secure twenty-nine of those freed Conservatives. Cameron was virtually certain to have triumphed in a hypothetical final parliamentary ballot, whereas Duncan Smith was a possible, rather than a probable victor. Due to these interpretations, Cameron could realistically claim a parliamentary mandate, Duncan Smith could not.

Third, the disputed nature of the Duncan Smith mandate to lead stemmed from the limited nature of his appeal to Conservative parliamentarians. From his limited parliamentary support base, Duncan Smith only had supporters of a pure Thatcherite persuasion. His endorsers were exclusively economic liberals, Eurosceptics, and social conservatives. His elevation to the party leadership made economic wets, Europhiles and social liberals, already a minority with the party, feel excluded further from the party. His elevation was a symbol of the ideological factionalism of the post-Thatcherite era and an impediment to unity. The comparison with Cameron is illuminating. Cameron had a broad-based parliamentary appeal. Both economic liberals and wets endorsed him; both Europhiles and Eurosceptics endorsed him, and both social conservatives and social liberals endorsed him. He was as inclusive as Duncan Smith was exclusive. He was a symbol of pragmatism and unity after the symbolic dogmatism and disunity of Duncan Smith.

Finally, Cameron was able to appear as the undisputed new leader of the party because of the reaction of Conservatives to his election. Conservative parliamentarians uniformly accepted the idea that Cameron had been legitimately elected as the new party leader. This ensured that he possessed the necessary authority over the parliamentary Conservative Party. Central to his capacity to claim his legitimate right to lead and demand authority was the reaction of elites within the parliamentary party. When Duncan Smith (and Hague) claimed the party leadership, their defeated opponent, Clarke, refused to serve in the shadow Cabinet. His refusal to serve reinforced the perception of division, and provided disaffected Conservatives of a wet, Europhilic, liberal persuasion, with an alternative figurehead on the backbenches. Cameron was more astute and fortunate than Hague and Duncan Smith. He astutely invited Davis to remain in the shadow Cabinet as shadow Home Secretary and Davis agreed to this request; whilst Fox remained in the shadow Cabinet as shadow Defence Secretary. To intensify the symbolism of unity Cameron drew into the shadow Cabinet, Hague, as shadow Foreign Secretary; and found roles for Duncan Smith and Clarke in forums designed to consider the strategic direction of Conservatism in the Cameron era.[15] A pervasive sense of unity and optimism engulfed the party, the like of which Conservatives had not experienced in a generation. The Conservatives had elected a non-Thatcherite endorsed candidate, for the first time in the turbulent post-Thatcherite era.

10.5   Explaining the Modernizers Triumph

When the Conservatives lost the general election of May 2005, there were two assumptions about the party leadership: first, that Howard would cease to be party leader, and second, that Davis was his most likely successor. As the candidature of Davis attempted to establish unstoppable momentum, few showed interest in the possibility of a candidature from Cameron, who at this juncture was a virtual political unknown. Yet, by the end of the parliamentary ballots, the momentum surrounding the candidature of Davis had collapsed, and now Cameron appeared to be unstoppable. Unlike four years earlier, Conservative parliamentarians had given a clear and unambiguous lead to the party membership, who duly followed their lead. The traditionalists had been defeated and the modernizers had triumphed. The key questions are how and why (Denham and Dorey, 2006:35).

The momentum of the Davis candidature can be seen to unravel due to a combination of circumstance and the limitations of Davis as a candidate. Circumstances clearly conspired against him. Being the overwhelming favourite in a rapid succession process is advantageous, just as it had been to

Howard two years earlier. A rapid succession process ensures that your momentum will put other candidates off the idea of standing. Being the overwhelmingly favourite, however, in a delayed contest, (almost a pre-contest contest), was seriously disadvantageous to Davis.[16] This required that he sustain that momentum through that ambiguous four month pre-election period, (between May and October), as well as through the official election contest between October and December. This gave ample opportunity for the Davis candidature to implode (i.e. make mistakes), and for an alternative young candidate (i.e. Cameron), to build his profile with fellow Conservative parliamentarians and the party membership (Denham and Dorey, 2006:36).

Clearly, to suggest that the Davis candidature imploded due to circumstance alone, would be erroneous. His candidature was undermined by a combination of complacency and strategic ineptitude (Montgomerie, 2005:2). The parliamentary Conservative party were predominantly economic liberal, Eurosceptic and socially conservative in their ideological disposition (see Hill, 2007). This was fertile ground for a candidate of his Thatcherite credentials, and he failed to maximise his support base in advantageous circumstances. He was unable to maximise his vote from the Eurosceptic Thatcherite right due to the fact that the candidature of Fox ensured that the Eurosceptic Thatcherite right vote would fracture in two. The fact that the candidature of Fox proved to be more impressive than the Davis camp had predicted meant that Fox made deeper inroads in the 'assumed' Davis support than anticipated. Had Davis been able to initiate an arrangement with Fox to prevent him standing, it would have enhanced his chances considerably.[17] Breaking down the parliamentary ballots demonstrates this. The combined Davis / Fox vote was 104 (62 / 42) votes in the first ballot, and 108 (57 / 51) in the second ballot. The majority of the parliamentary Conservative Party identified with pure Thatcherite values, but the participation of Fox undermined Davis.

Further evaluation of the parliamentary ballots demonstrates that Davis hit a ceiling in terms of gathering declarations of support. His fellow Thatcherites detected a sufficient number of limitations in his candidature to prevent them from endorsing him. Those limitations stemmed from assumed failures of leadership credibility. The turbulence of the post-Thatcherite era had been traumatic for the Conservative Party. The experience of electing Duncan Smith, whose parliamentary career had been defined by his disloyalty to Major, acted as a lesson to Conservatives of the dangers of disunity and disloyalty. When Duncan Smith had demanded that his Conservative parliamentarians 'unite or die', he looked hypocritical and Conservatives realised that death was a serious possibility. The need for a unifying political leader, not an ideologue, was clearly demonstrated. Whilst Davis did not have the habitual rebelliousness of Duncan Smith in his political resume, he did not represent a unifying political presence. Accusations abounded surrounding his serial disloyalty to Hague, Duncan Smith and Howard, all of whom were rumoured to be contemptuous of him (Montgomerie, 2005:2). His excessive ambition, and the methods that he had deployed to further his political career, had served to alienate many natural Thatcherite allies. That he had numerous political enemies[18] provided scope for the fledging campaign of his fellow Thatcherite, Fox, to gain credibility and converts (Montgomerie, 2005:2).

Moreover, the Davis campaign managed to antagonise the Eurosceptic Thatcherite right within the parliamentary Conservative Party by their desire to promote their candidate as a big tent candidate. In order to be an effective party leader, Davis wanted to present himself as a candidate of broader appeal. Whilst his campaign strategists were attempting to garner endorsements from the Europhile Tory left of the parliamentary Conservative Party, the Fox campaign claimed that their candidate was the true candidate of the right, and were thus able to claim defectors from Davis (Montgomerie, 2005:3). Davis had managed to depress his potential support base by the execution of a perfectly reasonable strategy of presenting himself as broad based candidate. Complacency regarding the viability of the Fox candidature would enable Thatcherite right votes to drift away from Davis. Meanwhile, his attempt to appeal outside of his natural Eurosceptic Thatcherite right constituency had limited success, as only a small number of traditional Europhile Tory left Conservatives gravitated to him (Denham and Dorey, 2006:36).

If demonstrating a reputation for unity was deemed to be a key leadership skill, then the need to demonstrate competent communication and presentational skills was also essential. The ineptitude of the Davis candidature did more than just embrace his poorly received conference speech, although this was clearly problematic and caused potential supporters to look elsewhere.[19] The Davis camp had also caused offence to many at the annual party conference, by having young female supporters attend the conference wearing tight t-shirts emblazoned with 'it's DD for me'[20] (Isaby, 2005:4). The divisiveness and weak communication and presentational skills of Davis were amplified by the unifying presence and presentational proficiency of his younger rival. As such, a symbiotic relationship exists between the implosion of the Davis candidature and the upwards trajectory of the Cameron candidature.

Cameron offered two crucial commodities that had been lacking in post-Thatcherite Conservative Party politics - electoral appeal and the capacity to unify. None of his rivals in the succession race could offer both. Clarke had electoral appeal, but Conservatives had already rejected him twice as he was not a unifying presence. Fox managed to overcome his political lightweight tag during the course of the campaign. However, his narrow ideological base suggested that he would struggle to secure centrist votes, and he would antagonise the minority Europhile Tory left within the parliamentary party. Davis suffered from a similar problem. His reputation for decisiveness and his pure Thatcherite credentials suggested that he would find internal party management problematic. This conjured up images of the Duncan Smith era, and this also applied to his communication and presentational limitations.

Cameron could unify the Conservative Party. This was demonstrated by the broad base of support that his candidature had. Conservative parliamentarians commonly associated with the Europhile Tory left (Stephen Dorrell, John Gummer and Andrew Lansley) and the Eurosceptic Thatcherite right (Bernard Jenkin, John Redwood and Peter Lilley) were all endorsing Cameron (Denham and Dorey, 2006:38-39). His capacity to straddle the Europhile Tory left and the Eurosceptic Thatcherite right demonstrated his capacity to unite a historically ideologically fractious party, and contrasted sharply with the narrow, sectional, ideologically based candidatures of his rivals. Moreover, Cameron had electoral appeal, or to put it in modern terms, he appeared to have the X-factor. He had demonstrated that he was charismatic and had the capacity to appeal to the electorate, most notably to disaffected former Conservative voters and floating voters (Montgomerie, 2005:5). He was a photogenic modern political operator, who appeared to be well versed in the skills of communication and presentation.[21] To a Conservative Party starved of electoral appeal and in need of centrist votes, Cameron was very appealing.

In offering both electoral appeal and the capacity to unify, Cameron was the candidate to transcend the legacy of Thatcherism. After a decade and a half of internal ideologically motivated divisions over the legacy of Thatcherism, a sufficient number of Conservatives, both parliamentarians and party members, recognised the need to disassociate contemporary Conservatism from its Thatcherite past. Endless debates about Thatcher and Thatcherism had engulfed Conservative Party leaders in the post-Thatcherite era, to such an extent that it was plausible to ask whether the Conservative Party was ungovernable. Her calculated endorsements of Major, Hague and Duncan Smith, had served to impede their party leadership, rather than assist them. Successive post-Thatcherite party leaders had all assumed the party leadership through their associations with the Thatcherite ideology. Major was elected as the most-Thatcherite when compared to Heseltine and Hurd. Hague had emerged as the best positioned Thatcherite to prevent Clarke from assuming the party leadership. The situation was the same with Duncan Smith, after the Thatcherite right rejected Portillo for deviating from the traditional orthodoxy of Thatcherite ideological thought. Obsessing about the ideological positioning of the candidates vis-à-vis Thatcherite ideology had not provided the Conservatives with what they desired most: power.

Cameron was able to exploit an altered mentality amongst Conservative parliamentarians and party members. The need to secure power was more important than the ideological purity of the candidate (Denham and Dorey, 2006:41). The majority of the parliamentary party were pure Thatcherites; the majority of party members we also pure Thatcherites. They were willing to put aside their ideologically motivated preference for the candidature of the likeminded Davis, to endorse the less ideologically acceptable candidate, Cameron, simply because of his enhanced capacity to appeal to the electorate. In doing so, they were willing to allow Cameron to reposition the Conservative Party on the centre ground of British politics, rather than the right-wing positioning of the Thatcherite and post-Thatcherite era.

The triumph of the modernizers represented a symbolic break with the Thatcherite past of the Conservative Party. Thatcher was no longer the yardstick by which evaluate the party leadership capabilities of a candidate. Cameron did not want to be compared with Thatcher; he wanted to be compared to Blair, as Denham and Dorey explain:

> derided by his critics for being policy lite – and thus redolent of a young Tony Blair – for his supporters and many of those who voted for him there was nothing wrong with this. Comparisons with Blair were indeed instructive, but should be construed positively, not negatively. Cameron's supporters recalled how Blair transformed his party's electoral fortunes, partly through his repeated emphasis on modernization (whilst eschewing specific policy commitments) and partly through sheer political energy and boundless optimism.
>
> (Denham and Dorey, 2006:41)

10.6   Conclusion

The manner in which Cameron acquired the party leadership mirrored the election of Heath forty years earlier. The Heath versus Maudling contest was characterised by the lack of bitterness, the limited impact of ideology as a voting determinant, the weaknesses of the pre-contest favourite Maudling being exposed during the campaign, a victor who espoused the nebulous mantra of modernisation, and an outcome that seemed to settle the issue of the succession for a generation. This notion of a Conservative Party coming full circle in terms of their party leadership could be extended further, to the man that Heath had replaced in becoming the first democratically elected leader of the Conservative Party. As an Etonian, Douglas-Home was seen as socially unrepresentative and an electoral impediment to electoral recovery. It was somewhat ironic that Cameron, the first Etonian leader since Douglas-Home, was elected for his ability to connect with the aspirations of the ordinary elector.

The triumph of Cameron and the modernizers was clearly unexpected. Cameron was the least experienced candidate by a considerable margin and his message of modernisation was a potentially dangerous campaign strategy given the rejection of Portillo four years earlier. It was a remarkable achievement for an unknown, inexperienced candidate to achieve such a complete electoral victory. He was the clear choice of Conservative parliamentarians across a broad ideological spectrum and he was the clear choice of the Conservative party membership. His campaign platform and his behaviour in the early stages of his party leadership tenure, suggests that he intends to exploit that undisputed mandate to reposition and repackage Conservatism and the Conservative Party (Gamble and Wright, 2006:1-2). The default status of Major, Hague and Duncan Smith contributed to the erosion of their authority. Cameron did not acquire the party leadership with these impediments or the poisoned endorsement of Thatcher. The disputed question of legitimacy (and thereby authority) in the post-Thatcherite era is now solved, and perhaps for a generation (Denham and Dorey, 2006:35).

It had been feared that the race to succeed Howard would degenerate into a protracted and bitter struggle that may produce a disputed outcome, in the manner of the election of Duncan Smith. Instead, the leadership election of 2005 demonstrated that the era of ideological categorisation being the leading determinant for mobilising support for *or* against candidates appeared to be ending. Conservatives gravitated towards the ideologically nebulousness of Cameron and the rhetoric of modernisation because perceptions of voter appeal and leadership style transcended the ideological certainties of the Thatcherite candidature of Davis. It suggested that Conservatives were finally learning from the mistakes of the past. The era of ideology was ending and Conservatives were re-engaging with the merits of pragmatism in the pursuit of power. The question is whether Cameron and the modernizers can deliver?

CONCLUSION

In the forty-two year period between 1922 and 1964 the Conservative Party would occupy power, either singularly or in forms of coalition, for thirty-three years. Their exclusions from high office were limited to less than nine years, of which six comprised the immediate post-war Labour governments. Although this four decade period was traumatic and turbulent, successive leaders of the Conservative Party could claim to have secured their primary objective. They had managed to maintain proximity to power. All seven leaders of the Conservative Party (Bonar Law, Baldwin, Chamberlain, Churchill, Eden, Macmillan and Douglas-Home) in this time period would also serve as Prime Minister. Yet, all of the seven aforementioned leaders had acquired the party leadership through the customary processes of consultation amongst party elites. The process may have been undemocratic but it secured its primary outcome, i.e. the emergence of a party leader who maintained the electoral hegemony of the Conservative Party. As such, its continuance could be justified. Only when a rigged and disputed process resulted to a disadvantageous outcome in the shape of Douglas-Home, and the Conservatives subsequently lost office, did they consider establishing formal democratic procedures for electing their party leader.

At the time of writing a further forty-two years have passed since the last leader to be determined by the magic circle, Douglas-Home, led the Conservative Party to defeat at the general election of October 1964. That forty-two year period broadly coincides with the process of democratisation within the Conservative Party vis-à-vis their party leadership. Since then they have contested twelve general elections, in which they have won five and have been defeated in seven. They have occupied power for twenty-two years of that time period, which is a considerable decline on their record in the 1922 to 1964 period. In that aforementioned period all seven party leaders were also Prime Ministers. Since the resignation of Douglas-Home there have been seven party leaders, of which only Heath, Thatcher and Major have also managed to be Prime Minister. Prior to the inception of internal democracy, the transference of the party leadership regularly coincided with the office of Prime Minister, given the electoral hegemony and governing dominance of the Conservatives. Since the inception of formal internal democracy for electing the party leader, Major is the only leader to acquire the office of Prime Minister simultaneous to their acquisition of the party leadership. What unites Heath, Thatcher, Hague, Duncan Smith and Cameron is that they all acquired the party leadership within one year of a Conservative electoral defeat. Howard acquired the party leadership just over two years after the preceding electoral reverse, but only after the first option, Duncan Smith, had been brutally removed from the party leadership.

The shift to internal democratisation and the electing of the party leader has actually coincided with a period in which all leaders of the Conservative Party, with the notable exception of Thatcher, have been unable to manufacture viable forms of statecraft. Statecraft comprises two basic objectives: first, the art of winning elections and second, the art of governing effectively. The immediate pre-Thatcherite Heath era would witness three election defeats in four elections over eight years, and a one-term administration derided for incompetence and incoherence. The post-Thatcherite era has seen the Conservative Party implode. The cumulative effect of the governing incompetence of the Major administration, and a fratricidal ideological struggle between Europhiles and Eurosceptics, has led to three successive electoral defeats, two of which justify the term landslide. Manufacturing a viable form of statecraft and narrating a new form of Conservatism that transcends Thatcherism and provides appeal has been beyond the competency of Hague, Duncan Smith and Howard. Whether Cameron can reconfigure Conservatism and obtain a level of political argument hegemony to construct a winning electoral strategy, whilst maintaining intra-party unity, remains to be seen.

Therefore, it is clear that leadership instability has intensified within the Conservative Party, most dramatically during the post-Thatcherite era. The level of that instability has destroyed the credibility of the oft-used cliché that the Conservatives secret weapon has been loyalty. Conservatives have developed a cultural predilection for assassinating their party leader or threatening to assassinate. Moreover the democratic procedures that have variously deployed, have since 1975, served to feed that predilection. The scale of leadership turbulence within the Conservative Party has not been matched by the Labour Party. Since 1965, the Conservative Party have conducted nine leadership elections and have had seven party leaders. In the same period, the Labour Party had only six leadership elections and six party leaders.[1] Moreover, the Labour Party has nothing that comes close to matching the three most intriguing leadership crises since the inception of internal democracy. They cannot match the disloyalty of the removal of Thatcher, who was assassinated despite winning three elections in succession and wishing to continue. They cannot match the absurdity of Major resigning the party leadership, only to declare immediately that he was a candidate in the vacant party leadership election. They cannot match the brutality of the eviction of Duncan Smith, who they removed from the party leadership before he had even had the opportunity to present himself to the electorate in a general election.

When comparing the Conservative Party to their own history, by examining the forty-plus year period prior to internal democracy to their most recent past, or by comparing their recent past over the last forty-plus years with their Labour counterparts, it is clear that the level of leadership instability that they have suffered from is alarmingly high. From this historical perspective a rather unwelcome pattern has emerged. The process of democratisation, which should be construed as an inherently noble and modern idea, appears to have been disadvantageous to the Conservative Party. We should not react to this interpretation by arguing that internal democracy is inherently bad and that the secretive magic circle was actually superior. Rather we can argue that the previous chapters have demonstrated the significance of the following three key themes when analysing the Conservatives since the age of Macmillan:

1. Generations of Conservative elites have been inept when devising their leadership election procedures. They have seemed incapable of agreeing on a stable method of electing their party leader. They have repeatedly felt the need to debate and adapt those leadership election procedures after identifying flaws in the existing procedures. This amounts to a *failure of process*.

2. Those failures of process have been matched by numerous unsatisfactory outcomes. A successful outcome constitutes a party leader who has legitimacy flowing from their method of acquisition, and who can enhance their authority over the parliamentary Conservative party by demonstrating their unifying capabilities, their electoral appeal and their governing competence. The book has demonstrated that in the post-Thatcherite era, the Conservatives have managed to repeatedly elect unexpected party leaders whose legitimacy as party leader has been questioned due to the method of acquisition. These crises of legitimacy have undermined their authority, thus reducing their leadership credibility and thereby the electoral appeal of the Conservative Party. The propensity for electing what we will define as default leaders in the post-Thatcherite era has demonstrated a *failure of outcome*.

3. When addressing party leadership selection Conservatives have demonstrated their obsession with ideology. When debating who their party leader should be, the Conservative parliamentarians (and latterly party members), should have been guided by one over-riding objective: which Conservative candidate being presented to them is the best equipped to

acquire and retain power. The candidate demonstrating the greatest evidence of electoral appeal and governing competence should have prevailed. Rather than adhere to this outward looking consideration of what would appeal to the electorate the most, Conservatives have often been overly influenced by what was most acceptable to themselves first. That growing obsession with ideology, from the dispute between the wets and dries by the 1980s, to the ruinous conflict between the Europhiles and the Eurosceptics in the late 1980s and 1990s, to the struggle between social liberals and social conservatives in the late 1990s and early part of the millennium, has loomed too large over their decision-making when faced with succession contests. This amounts to a *failure in selection criterion.*

These emerging themes – failures of process, outcomes, and selection criterion – require further elaboration. The first concluding comment relates to fact that the Conservatives have demonstrated that they have been inept when constructing, (and subsequently tinkering with), their electoral procedures. Their ineptitude when formulating their election procedures has ensured that the position of the incumbent party leader has since 1975 been increasingly insecure. The adaptations to the original 1965 prototype served to accentuate this correlation between process and leadership insecurity and instability. We can make a plausible case for stating that the formulation of the leadership rules have lacked clarity and have been driven by immediate short-term considerations; these adaptations have then created solutions that caused further dissatisfaction, which then in turn stimulated the rationale for further procedural adaptation (Garnett and Lynch, 2007:332-333).

The original democratic procedures for electing the party leader were established in 1965, as a reaction to the failure of the magic circle in determining the succession to Macmillan. Those party leadership election procedures were utilised only once, when Heath defeated Maudling for the vacant party leadership in July 1965. Despite being widely praised at the time of their first deployment, it would become apparent that there was a procedural flaw inherent within these original democratic procedures: i.e. the complete inability to remove a stubborn but discredited incumbent.

The absence of leadership ejection procedures contributed to the procedural adaptations permitting annual elections. The insertion of annual elections, confirmed in 1975, into the leadership selection procedures, (or more specifically leadership ejection procedures), was an act of political expediency driven by the short term need to find a procedural mechanism through which to remove Heath. This procedural mechanism designed to remove Heath in opposition, would then be utilised to remove Thatcher in government. This demonstrated the lack of clarity in the framing of the leadership election / ejection procedures, or the way in which those leadership procedures were interpreted by some Conservative parliamentarians. Thatcher herself believed that there was an unwritten convention that the leadership eviction procedures, that she had deployed against Heath in opposition, were not to be activated when in government and against an incumbent Conservative Prime Minister. This demonstrates the failings of the leadership selection and ejection processes: the security of an incumbent Conservative Prime Minister should not have been assumed to exist on the basis of an unwritten convention. It should have been explicitly and unambiguously stated that an incumbent Conservative Prime Minister could or could not have been challenged. The unwritten convention assumption was unhelpful. That Thatcher was then evicted, so forcibly against her will and with such ideologically motivated recrimination, was against the best interests of the party. It also created a precedent that intensified the insecurity of her successor, Major.

The misplaced assumption that it would not be deployed against an incumbent Conservative Prime Minister was destroyed and created the rationale for further procedural tinkering. Again that procedural tinkering was a short-term measure. The minor shift in 1991 involved tightening the rules on nominations for challengers, by demanding that 10 per cent of Conservative parliamentarians must request an annual election, rather than two nominees (Alderman, 1999:262). The motivation for tightening the challenging procedures (and placing restrictions on the timescale in which challengers could be initiated[2]) was to create more protection for incumbents. However, the experiences of the Major era demonstrated the inbuilt flaw in their procedural tinkering. Raising the hurdle to ten per cent, aligned to the precedent of Thatcher's removal, meant that Major's party leadership was virtually immobilised by *speculation* surrounding whether his critics would be able to mount a challenge in each of autumns of 1992, 1993 and 1994 (Alderman, 1999:262; Quinn, 2005:802).

The recriminations surrounding the leadership election and ejection procedures that removed Thatcher could not be resolved whilst in government. The dual nature of their increasing ideological polarisation, and the instability surrounding how Major acquired the party leadership in 1990, and retained it in 1995, led to the biggest institutional reform of the party leadership election and ejection procedures in 1998. The subsequent initiation of parliamentary screening, and then a two way ballot for the party membership to decide the party leadership, resulted in Iain Duncan Smith acquiring the party leadership. That he acquired the party leadership through a party membership mandate, but was devoid of a mandate within the parliamentary Conservative Party, fatally undermined his party leadership tenure. His subsequent removal became viewed as a referendum by Conservative parliamentarians on the new party leadership procedures. His successor, Howard, then initiated an attempt to partially reclaim the primacy of Conservative parliamentarians in selecting the party leader, but the fledgling constitutional apparatus of the party prevented him from doing so. Procedural tinkering can therefore be defined as the norm (Quinn, 2005:806).

Having considered the first concluding theme, that of the instability (or failure) of process, we can now turn our attention to the second concluding theme, which relates to the fact that they have demonstrated a continued capacity for returning unexpected party leaders, many of whom were to suffer from crises of legitimacy and accusations that they were default leaders. Such occurrences demonstrate failures of outcome.

The expectation was that Maudling would have been the successor to Douglas-Home, rather than Heath. Few anticipated that Thatcher would succeed Heath. It was widely assumed that the best placed successor was Whitelaw. Over a decade later the charismatic outsider, Heseltine, was deprived the party leadership, as the unheralded Major was elected as the successor to Thatcher. Of the candidates for the succession to Major, attention had focused on Heseltine and Portillo, but their unavailability created an open field, in which the favoured political heavyweight Clarke was rejected in preference to the younger and less experienced Hague. A sense of déjà vu characterised the post-Hague succession race, as Clarke was again favoured alongside the resuscitated and revisionist Portillo, only for the inexperienced and divisive Duncan Smith to acquire the party leadership to the bemusement of most moderate Conservatives. The ineptitude of the Duncan Smith leadership tenure, which necessitated his eviction via a confidence motion, enabled Howard to claim the party leadership via ritual acclamation. This amounted to a remarkable political recovery for a politician who had finished last in the parliamentary ballots that ultimately had handed the party leadership to Hague six years earlier. Finally, in the post-Howard succession race, the youthful and charismatic Cameron dramatically snatched the party leadership from the pre-contest favourite, Davis.

Table 18:   The Conservatives Unexpected Party Leaders

Leadership Change	Expected Party Leader	Selected Party Leader
1963	Butler	Douglas-Home
1965	Maudling	Heath
1975	Whitelaw	Thatcher
1990	Heseltine	Major
1997	Portillo, Heseltine or Clarke [1]	Hague
2001	Portillo, Clarke	Duncan Smith
2003	Howard	Howard
2005	Davis	Cameron

[1] Portillo was unable to contest the succession as he lost his parliamentary constituency in the 1997 general election. Heseltine was unable to contest the succession due to concerns surrounding his health.

When analysing this procession of the unexpected party leaders, it has been implied that some of them have been default party leaders – i.e. negatively induced candidates elevated due to the unacceptability of other candidates, rather than positively endorsed candidates who were propelled to the party leadership on a positive premise. This default party leadership thesis applies especially to three party leaders in the formally democratic era – Major, Hague and Duncan Smith – whose party leadership tenures coincide with the implosion of Conservative statecraft in the post-Thatcherite era.

This ties neatly into the third main concluding theme that has emerged from the preceding chapters: i.e. the Conservatives growing obsession with ideology, from the dispute between the wets and dries in the 1980s, to the conflict between the Europhiles and the Eurosceptics in the late 1980s and 1990s, to the struggle between social liberals and social conservatives in the late 1990s and early part of the current decade, all of which have, as the preceding chapters have demonstrated, loomed too large over the decision-making of Conservatives.

In assessing this, we can argue that there should be three over-riding leadership selection criterion which feed into the traditional Conservative statecraft model. First, Conservatives need a party leader who can unify the party; i.e. a party leader must then be deemed to be ideologically acceptable. This equates to the first dimension of statement, as a unifying party leader should enhance the probability of securing effective internal management. Second, Conservatives need a party leader who is an electoral asset to the party rather than an electoral liability. This equates to the second dimension of statecraft, which refers to the formulation of a winning electoral strategy. Third, Conservatives need a party leader who can demonstrate administrative capability, relative to their political rivals. This equates to the third and fourth dimensions of Conservative statecraft, i.e. securing political argument hegemony for the party (i.e. dominance of elite debate) and governing competence (Stevens, 2002:119; Hickson, 2005:181).

Table 19:   Party Leadership Criteria and Comparative Strength of Candidates

| Leadership Election | Internal Unity (Acceptable) | Strongest Candidate | | Chosen Leader |
		External Appeal (Electability)	Governing Credibility (Competence)	
1963 [1]	Douglas-Home	Hailsham	Butler	Douglas-Home
1965 [2]	Heath or Maudling	Heath	Heath or Maudling	Heath
1975 [2]	Whitelaw or Thatcher	Whitelaw	Whitelaw or Thatcher	Thatcher
1989 [2]	Thatcher	Thatcher	Thatcher	Thatcher
1990 [2]	Major	Major or Heseltine	Hurd	Major
1995 [2]	Major	Major	Major	Major
1997 [2]	Hague	Clarke	Clarke or Howard	Hague
2001 [3]	None	Clarke or Portillo	Clarke or Portillo	Duncan Smith
2003 [4]	Howard	Howard	Howard	Howard
2005 [3]	Cameron	Cameron	Clarke	Cameron

Source: Adapted and updated from Stark, 1996

[1]   Emerged via the magic circle or processes of elite consultations
[2]   Elected via ballot of Conservative Members of Parliament
[3]   Elected via dual franchise of first, ballot of Conservative Members of Parliament to screen candidates and then, second, leading two face ballots of Conservative Party members
[4]   No ballots conducted as one candidate standing

When observing the three leadership selection criterion, it is clear that the external criteria – of electoral appeal and governing competence – should take precedence over the internal criteria of ideological acceptability. If Conservatives decide that the ideological acceptability criteria is their dominant consideration then they are turning inwards upon themselves, when they should be projecting themselves outwards towards the electorate.

The war of the Macmillan succession saw a classic illustration of the Conservatives talking to themselves rather than the electorate. If competence was the criteria, then Butler was the primary candidate; if electoral appeal was the criteria, then Hailsham was the primary candidate. Conservatives should have restricted their succession considerations to these two, but as chapter two outlined, they opted for Douglas-Home on the supposed unifying capabilities that he offered (which proved to be ironic given the refusal of

Powell and Macleod to serve him). The post Douglas-Home succession battle saw Heath marginally better positioned than Maudling in all three leadership selection criteria, with his elevation to the party leadership devoid of significant ideological relevance as chapter three demonstrated.

Assessing the rise of Thatcher according to these three criteria is potentially problematic. On the electability criteria Whitelaw was the best positioned candidate. Stark implies that Whitelaw was also superior than Thatcher on the other two criteria: acceptability and competence. We can dispute this. In terms of competence, few disputed the administrative and political capability of Thatcher, and we can argue that on this criterion, she was the equal of Whitelaw. Stark positions Whitelaw as the most acceptable candidate, which he determines on the basis that Thatcher had assumed the party leadership on a wave of anti-Heath sentiment (Stark, 1996:127, 132). If we accept the revisionist accounts of her annexing of the party leadership, we can argue that Thatcher represented a viewpoint within the Conservatives at the time which suggested that a change of policy direction was required. To facilitate that change of policy direction, Thatcher was an acceptable option to the Conservatives.

The dramatic events of the autumn of 1990, which saw Conservative parliamentarians evict an incumbent Conservative Prime Minister, against her instincts and the wishes of the party membership, created a poisoned chalice of a political inheritance. Economic damp Europhiles embraced Heseltine as a means to remove an economic liberal Eurosceptic incumbent, in a dramatic attempt to change the policy and political direction of the Conservatives in order to retain their electoral appeal. Their attempted coup succeeded in slaying their ideological nemesis, Thatcher, but did not succeed in handing the party leadership to the economic damp, Europhilic wing of the party. The revenge of the Heathite economic damp Europhile Tory left was impeded by the mobilisation of the Thatcherite economic liberal Eurosceptic Conservative right, who gravitated to Major under the misplaced assumption that he was as Thatcherite as they were.

In the vacant second ballot, Major triumphed because he was sufficiently acceptable to the ideologically motivated Thatcherite Eurosceptics, (although he was their second preference after Thatcher), and centrist loyalists who felt that the unity of the party would be easier to reclaim under Major, rather than the instigator of the attempted coup, Heseltine. Major was thus the most acceptable candidate and this was a prime factor in his elevation to the party leadership. Heseltine and Major vied for the status as the candidate with the most electoral appeal. However, it should be noted that polling had demonstrated the appeal of Heseltine as an alternative party leader for almost five years, whereas Major gained appeal rapidly through the novelty of being a relative unknown. On the competence criteria, Hurd was perceived to be a competent and experienced senior Cabinet minister, having served in

Northern Ireland to 1985, the Home Office from 1985 and the Foreign Office since 1989. Heseltine had seven years worth of Cabinet experience, without occupying one of the three main offices of state. Major may have occupied the Foreign Office briefly and had recently been elevated to the Chancellorship, but his Cabinet experience was limited and spent mostly as number two to Nigel Lawson at the Treasury as the economy overheated and began to the journey towards economic recession.[3] Hurd was the most competent and experienced, followed by Heseltine, then Major. Heseltine was competitive with Major on the electoral appeal criteria. However, despite not being the most competent, experienced and being neck and neck on the electoral appeal criteria, Major was swept to the party leadership on the acceptability criteria. He won because he was not Heseltine and he was not Thatcher.

The extent of the ideological fratricide that engulfed Conservatism in the post-Thatcherite era was demonstrated by the Major versus Redwood party leadership election five years later. Major was clearly more competent and experienced than Redwood, and possessed greater electoral appeal than the rather austere former Welsh Secretary. However, when making these claims it is worth noting that the best alternatives to Major were Michael Portillo and Michael Heseltine, and not Redwood. Both wished to enter a hypothetical second ballot when Redwood had inflicted enough damage upon Major to force him to resign. Heseltine was not going to be the stalking horse for someone else again, whilst Portillo also felt that avoiding entry at the start was strategically in his best interests. Participants in the subsequent electoral ballot were thus engaging in game theory. Europhiles who wanted Heseltine had take care when voting that they did not end up facilitating a Eurosceptic takeover of the party under Portillo. Alternatively Eurosceptics who wanted Portillo did not want to end up with the Europhile Heseltine as their party leader. The fear of something worse (for both Europhiles and Eurosceptics) inflated the Major vote and enabled him to hold onto the party leadership. Conservatives viewed Major as the least worst option. He was the most acceptable, most unifying candidate, despite the fact that unity under the Conservatives had collapsed in the five years of his party leadership. That his victory was hailed as a success demonstrated how bad things had got for the Conservatives. The ideological disputes would rage on.

Tragically for the Conservatives ideology would be the dominant determinant in the post-Major succession election. On the electability criteria, Kenneth Clarke was clearly the best candidate for the succession. On the competence criteria, Clarke was again clearly the best candidate. Clarke had been a cabinet member for twelve years, and had served as Home Secretary (1992 to 1993) and Chancellor (1993 to 1997) with distinction. The only real contender on the competence and experience criteria was Michael Howard, who had served as Home Secretary between 1993 and 1997. Hague was clearly inferior to Clarke in terms of voter mobilisation and clearly lacked the experience of Clarke, having only served in the Cabinet for two years. However, the merits of Clarke, in terms of voter appeal and political competence, were outweighed by his ideological unacceptability to the Thatcherite Eurosceptic right. In the absence of Portillo, the Thatcherite Eurosceptic right were tactically disorganised, meaning that four candidates of their persuasion entered the succession contest. After the more credible articulators of the Thatcherite Eurosceptic message (Howard, Lilley and Redwood) had knocked each other out, Hague was left as the only remaining Eurosceptic, who could prevent Clarke assuming the party leadership. At the instigation of Thatcher herself, Conservatives gravitated to Hague on his perceived acceptability, despite his evident limitations when compared to Clarke. Just as Macmillan had obsessed about Butler not obtaining the party leadership, so Thatcher would obsess about Clarke.

This anti-Clarke obsession would contribute to a virtual repeat outcome four years later. At the parliamentary stage, Conservative parliamentarians had the option of two candidates who could broaden the electoral appeal of the Conservatives (Clarke and Portillo) and two candidates who offered considerable ministerial experience and competence (Clarke and Portillo). At this juncture, Conservative parliamentarians were also offered Iain Duncan Smith, who could not broaden the electoral appeal of the party, and who had no ministerial experience whatsoever. At the parliamentary stage, the social liberalism of Portillo was deemed unacceptable and he was knocked out, leaving the party membership to decide between Duncan Smith and Clarke. Here the Europhilia of Clarke was deemed unacceptable (as Thatcher reminded party members) and Duncan Smith was elected as the new party leader. Duncan Smith had emerged as the new party leader, despite the fact that two-thirds of the parliamentary Conservative Party had rejected him. The post-Hague succession crisis represents the nadir of the post-Thatcherite era of crisis. There was no candidate standing who was deemed as truly acceptable: in a moment of complete absurdity the disloyal Duncan Smith was now presented as the unifying compromise option, much to the chagrin of Major.

There by default stood Duncan Smith, vulnerable to eviction should he fail. That he proved to be politically out his depth as party leader led to his political execution and the old style emergence of Howard as the new party leader. In the 2001 to 2003 period Howard had performed admirably as Shadow Chancellor and the quality of his political conduct was magnified by the ineptitude of Duncan Smith and the lack of talent in the Duncan Smith shadow cabinet. Clarke and Portillo were no longer viable options. At the moment when Duncan Smith had the knife plunged into his back by his parliamentary colleagues, Howard was on the ascendant. He was clearly perceived as competent. Although he did not really offer electoral appeal he did offer political credibility in a manner sadly lacking in Duncan Smith. He was also viewed as acceptable to Conservative parliamentarians who coalesced around him so quickly that other candidates realised disputing his accession would be futile.

Although the Howard party leadership tenure would ultimately end in electoral rejection and failure, there is an argument that can be made to suggest that the Conservatives began their political recover through his accession to the party leadership. After five divisive and bitter party leadership contests in fourteen years, the Conservatives had elevated Howard to the party leadership in a manner that enhanced perceptions of their unity and would make it harder for Conservatives to use the question of the party leadership as a mechanism to further their ideological objectives. His legitimacy was undisputed and his authority was enhanced because of this. The Howard era led to a more harmonious Conservative mindset and Cameron would benefit from this in the post-Howard succession election. Cameron was clearly inferior to Clarke and to a lesser extent Davis and Fox (who had junior ministerial experience) on the competence and experience criteria. However, what sealed the party leadership for Cameron was to be the other two criteria. First, he received the proactive endorsement of both the left and right. Economic dries and wets endorsed him, Eurosceptics and Europhiles endorsed him, and although he was social liberally, social conservatives eventually began gravitating to him by the party membership stage. His ideological non-categorisation was appealing to a party that wanted to end the ideological factionalism of the previous decade and a half. Second, what really made Cameron seem like an attractive option to Conservatives was that his pragmatism seemed to make him attractive to the wider electorate. Conservatives seemed to be regaining an appreciation of the merits of pragmatism and unity in the pursuit of power. They realised that an ideologically nebulous leader in Cameron was a better option than an ideological pure Davis. He was the first party leader in the post-Thatcherite era, not to be endorsed by Thatcher, and this suggested that Conservatives were ending their self-destructive obsession with ideology.

These three concluding themes – failures of process, failures of outcome and the obsession with ideology – represent the central issues that emerge from analysing the history of Conservative Party leadership elections from Heath to Cameron. At this juncture, however, it is worth recalling that the rationale for the book stemmed from a desire to address a gap in the academic literature on party leadership elections and the history of the Conservative Party. In attempting to address the gap, the book has aimed to challenge two of the main arguments advanced by Stark.

Stark makes two intriguing claims about party leadership elections within British political parties: first, he argues that the leadership election and ejection procedures do not seriously impact upon the outcome of who becomes party leader; and second, identifying the re-election of Major in 1995 as a prime example, he argues that internal party leadership elections are beneficial processes (Stark, 1996: 124-172). This book challenges the Stark assumptions. It believes that the rules governing party leadership elections do matter to the outcome; and it also believes that intra-party leadership contests are potentially divisive rather than curative processes.

Let us consider the argument that rules governing party leadership do not matter to the outcome. The Stark implication is based across the three main political parties in the 1963 to 1995 time period (Stark, 1996:131-138). Stark concludes that an alternative method would have only affected the outcome in 1963, in which Butler would have won in a parliamentary ballot; and in 1975 when Whitelaw would have emerged through the magic circle. The post-Douglas-Home succession battle would still have resulted in Heath winning the party leadership, whilst if the magic circle had prevailed Thatcher would not have been able to have been challenged in 1989 or 1990, nor would Major have been able to initiate his put up or shut up strategy in 1995.[4]

The argument made here is that the Conservatives circumstances need to be disentangled from the Labour Party and the Liberal Party / Liberal Democrats. Moreover, the assertion needs to be tested against more recent developments, both by considering the four post-1995 party leadership elections, and considering the extension of the franchise in 1998 that impacted upon the 2001 and 2005 party leadership elections. By this we can construct a more detailed appraisal of the 1963 to 2005 party leadership succession battles and assess the likely outcomes,[5] according to three different methods of party leadership determination: first, the magic circle; second, a parliamentary ballot alone; and third, a party membership ballot.

Table 20:   Party Leadership Election Systems and Impact upon Outcomes

Leadership Election	Magic Circle	Parliamentary Ballot	Party Membership Ballot
1963	**Douglas-Home**	Butler	Hailsham
1965	Maudling	**Heath**	Heath
1975 [1]	Whitelaw	**Thatcher**	Whitelaw
1990 [2]	Hurd	**Major**	Major
1997	Clarke or Howard	**Hague**	Clarke
2001	Clarke, Howard or Portillo	Clarke	**Duncan Smith**
2003 [3]	**Howard**	Howard	Howard
2005	Davis	Cameron	**Cameron**

[1]   Assumes succession contest initiated after the voluntary resignation of Heath
[2]   Assumes succession contest initiated after the voluntary resignation of Thatcher
[3]   Assumes succession contest initiated after the voluntary resignation of Duncan
       Smith

What can actually be argued is that although the party leadership succession battles in other parties may not have been influenced by the leadership election procedures, for the Conservatives, the means of party leadership selection has been more significant than Stark admits. Stark acknowledges that Douglas-Home could only have emerged via the magic circle. However, contravening the view of Stark that Heath would have emerged regardless, it would be more plausible to suggest that Maudling would have emerged via the magic circle.[6] Had Heath voluntarily resigned from the party leadership in early 1975, Whitelaw clearly would have been the chosen successor of the Conservative establishment, and of the party membership.[7] Similar to the rationale for Whitelaw, Hurd would have been best positioned to assume the party leadership via the magic circle in the autumn of 1990, had Thatcher voluntarily resigned. More unifying that the maverick Heseltine, he was more experienced than the youthful Major, and thus under the criteria of the magic circle, Hurd would have been the logical successor. We can postulate that in a party membership ballot, party members would have moved for Major, due to the limited electoral appeal of Hurd, and the divisiveness associated with Heseltine for resigning from the Thatcher government.

The challenge to the Stark argument becomes more pronounced in the opposition era since 1997. The magic circle would have gravitated towards the two most senior candidates when Major resigned: i.e. Clarke as the recently departed Chancellor, and Howard, as the recently departed Home Secretary. Hague as a junior member of the Major Cabinet would not have been a realistic leadership contender. As chapter seven indicated, all polling at the time suggested that Clarke would have triumphed in a party membership ballot, even though he failed to do so four years later. In the post-Hague party leadership struggle, the magic circle would have tilted towards the most experienced and competent Conservatives, thus aiding the chances of Clarke and Portillo, and also Howard (even though he did not enter the contest). Had a final parliamentary ballot occurred, after the elimination of Portillo, Clarke would have probably secured a marginal endorsement (despite his pronounced Europhilia) at the expense of Duncan Smith. The elevation of Duncan Smith was clearly a by-product of the unique combination of rules and the circumstances that existed in 2001. Finally, in the post-Howard era, Cameron emerged via the dual endorsement of Conservative parliamentarians and party members, although the magic circle would probably have gravitated towards the more experienced Davis.

Having queried the Stark assumption that process does not impact upon outcome, the book can conclude with one further challenge to the assumptions laid down by Stark. Using the Major re-election of 1995 as a prime example, Stark concluded that party leadership elections were beneficial to the party (Stark, 1996:171). This book disputes this assumption and argues that the excess of party leadership elections has had negative consequences or political 'costs' for the Conservatives in three different ways: first, financial costs; second, disunity costs; and, third, what we can call decision costs (Quinn, 2005:795-796).

Prior to 1998 the Conservatives incurred limited financial costs through their party leadership elections. The electorate of the parliamentary Conservative Party was small and the contests were conducted inside a few weeks, thus making party leadership elections relatively inexpensive (Quinn, 2005:802). The shift to one-member, one-vote ballots amongst the party membership has created a financial cost to the Conservatives. The balloting expenses of the mass membership franchise, was one of the factors that contributed to the coalescing around Howard in 2003 simply to avoid the financial and time implications of a long-drawn out succession battle.

The second cost associated with party leadership elections is the disunity costs. During party leadership elections candidates can condemn the leadership credentials, policy positions and ideological beliefs of their rivals. The image of the party can be damaged if rival candidates ritually belittle each other during the course the campaign. That can leave an inedible impression of disunity and mutual hostility at elite level within the party. Given that the electorate tends to punish divided parties, then leadership elections can be seen as a symptom of the failings of the party, rather than showcasing the talents and ideas that exist within the party. The Heath versus Maudling contest; the Howard succession, and the Cameron versus Davis contest were relatively harmonious and were conducted with dignity and minimal rancour, thus limiting the disunity costs for the party. However, the six intervening party leadership succession battles from the Thatcher versus Heath contest to the Duncan Smith versus Clarke face off, all carried with them disunity costs to the Conservatives (Quinn, 2005:795).

The third and final cost associated with party leadership elections relates to what Quinn defines as the decision costs. It is inevitable and necessary for political parties to change their party leaders. However, an excess of party leadership elections and party leaders, is a symptom of failure within a party. On each occasion that the party conducts an internal party leadership election it incurs a decision cost. The decision to engage in an internal leadership election means that considerable time and effort will be devoted to looking politically inwards rather than outwards (Quinn, 2005:806). They should be looking outwards to the electorate by critiquing their Labour opponents and formulating policies that can appeal to the electorate and persuade them to endorse the Conservatives. Leadership elections compel them to look inwards and to the merits and demerits of their own leading parliamentarians.

Therefore, relative party leadership stability is usually an indication of the political success of a party. Thatcher held the party leadership for over a decade and a half and secured three successive elections victories. During her party leadership tenure, the Labour Party had four party leadership elections in 1976, 1980, 1983 and 1988. Blair held the Labour party leadership for nearly as long as Thatcher and has secured the same number of electoral endorsements. Since Blair assumed the leadership of the Labour Party, Labour have assumed the status as the natural party of government, whilst the Conservatives have had five different party leaders and have overseen five different leadership elections, in 1995, 1997, 2001, 2003 and 2005. During this time successive Conservative party leaders have been groping around, desperately searching for a viable statecraft strategy: i.e. a core belief that can unite the party and provide the basis for electoral appeal (the politics of support) and the basis for governing capability (the politics of power).

A renewed Conservative Party is emerging under the party leadership of Cameron. Despite the rhetoric on modernisation, much of the Cameron approach is derived from traditional Conservative political conduct: it is ideologically pragmatic in the pursuit of power, with an emphasis on broadening the appeal of the Conservative Party, whilst maintaining a greater degree of internal unity than evident in the previous two decades. Meanwhile, the retirement of Blair suggests that the pendulum on party leadership stability may be about to turn. If Cameron does become the next Conservative Prime Minister toward the end of this decade, then it will be the Labour successor to Blair, Gordon Brown, who will be desperately attempting to maintain his hold on the leadership of the Labour Party. Conservatives would no doubt welcome this, whilst political historians would welcome the opportunity to examine the history of Labour Party leadership elections. But what if Cameron fails and the Conservatives suffer their fourth successive electoral reversal?

NOTES

Chapter One

1   Blake, R. (1998) *The Conservative Party from Peel to Major*; Charmley, J. (1996) *A History of Conservative Politics 1900-1996*; Evans, B. and Taylor, A. (1996) *From Salisbury to Major: Continuity and Change in Conservative Politics*; Gilmour, I. and Garnett, M. (1998) *Whatever Happened to the Tories: The Conservative Party since 1945*; Ramsden, J. (1998) *An Appetite for Power: A History of the Conservative Party since 1830*.

2   Fisher, N. (1977) *The Tory Leaders: Their Struggle for Power*; Shepherd, R. (1991) *The Power Brokers: The Tory Party and Its Leaders*; Bogdanor, V. (1994), 'The Selection of the Party Leader', in Seldon, A. and Ball, S. (eds) *Conservative Century: The Conservative Party since 1900*.

3   Punnett, R. M. (1992) *Selecting the Party Leader: Britain in Comparative Perspective*; Stark, L. P. (1996) *Choosing a Leader: Party Leadership Contest in Britain from Macmillan to Blair*; Watkins, A. (1998) *The Road to Number 10: From Bonar Law to Tony Blair*.

4   The earlier 1975 party leadership election utilised the research of Cowley and Bailey to explain the influence of ideology on voting behaviour. Here the authors utilised the Norton typology, and findings, as the most appropriate way of determining the ideological disposition of the parliamentary Conservative Party in 1975 (Cowley and Bailey, 2000:599-629).

5   Tracing the voting behaviour of Conservative parliamentarians, and their ideological commitments, in the 1965 party leadership election was more problematic for two reasons. First, obtaining lists of the voting behaviour of Conservative parliamentarians in this leadership election was complicated by the fact this generation of Conservative elites was considerably more secretive and less inclined to reveal their voting behaviour, so fewer detailed listings were available. Second, the nature of ideological conflict at that juncture was less identifiable, given that it was the era of pragmatism, in which loyalty was to the party rather than to ideology.

Chapter Two

1   Punnett argues that these examples demonstrated the merits of the informal processes that the Conservatives possessed for determining the succession. These processes of consultation were so informal that an heir apparent could be

elevated to the party leadership with minimal disruption and delay (Punnett, 1992:32).

2   Balfour was concerned that having a peer as Prime Minister, in a Cabinet already overloaded with peers, might be problematic given that the Parliament Act of 1911 had moved the centre of political gravity to the House of Commons (Blake, 1998:213).

3   The vast majority of the national press predicted that Butler would emerge as the next party leader and Prime Minister (Fisher, 1977:85).

4   The succession crisis began with Lord Home as Foreign Secretary and ended with the peerage-less Alec Douglas-Home as Conservative party leader and Prime Minister. For the sake of simplicity the text for this chapter refers to Lord Home as Douglas-Home throughout.

5   The cataclysmic events of the Cabinet purge of July 1962 redefined perceptions of Macmillan. Political journalists ceased to define him as 'supermac' as had been the case in the late 1950s. They now dubbed him 'Mac the knife' (Ramsden, 1996:167). In the days after the cull, Butler joked about 'feeling his neck from time to time to make sure that his head was still on his shoulders' (Ramsden, 1996:168).

6   John Profumo, the Minister of War, admitted to lying to the House of Commons with regard to his relationship with Christine Keeler, who was also conducting a relationship with a Soviet Naval attache. Labour insinuated that Macmillan had been negligent over national security and that he was gullible for having accepting the original denial of Profumo (Gilmour and Garnett, 1998:181).

7   In July 1963, Conservative backbencher, Humphrey Berkeley advocated a system for electing Macmillan's successor via a ballot of Conservative MPs. He argued that 'a secret ballot would lessen the atmosphere of conspiracy and intrigue displayed on two occasions earlier in this century when the Conservative Party changed its leader' (Stark, 1996:16).

8   There was no need for Macmillan to announce his resignation prior to his operation. He could have delayed announcing it until after the operation and after the annual conference. Or he could have assessed after the operation whether he needed to resign at all. He later regretted having resigned (Ramsden, 1996: 197-198; Charmley, 1996:173). Butler was of the opinion that it was Douglas-Home who persuaded Macmillan to resign and extracted an immediate resignation statement from him (Howard, 1987:310).

9   Pearce notes that Butler did not realise how much Macmillan hated him (Pearce, 1997:116). Watkins observes that towards the end of 1962 Butler had observed that: 'I don't think Macmillan is ever going to go. You know what he said to me last weekend? "I don't see why I should make way for you, old cock"' (Watkins, 1998:70).

10   Three months before Macmillan resigned Butler had been informed by Major John Morrison, Chairman of the 1922 Executive Committee, that he [Butler] could not assume the party leadership as 'the chaps won't have you' (Bogdanor, 1994:77).

11   Lord Curzon in 1923 and Lord Halifax in 1940 had seen their prime ministerial ambitions stymied because they were peers (Shepherd, 1991:151).

12 The Act provided a window of opportunity for existing peers to disclaim their hereditary titles. They were permitted to renounce provided that they did so within a year of the passage of the Act (Blake, 1998:290).

13 Morrison, as Chair of the 1922 Executive Committee, had consulted with the then Lord Home in July 1963, and advised him that the demands of party unity would mean that Douglas-Home should make himself available for the party leadership, by disclaiming his peerage. Douglas-Home's response that 'I will see my doctor' indicates that as early as July he was contemplating positioning himself for the succession (Bogdanor, 1994:77). On the basis of this Gilmour and Garnett have argued that the actions of Douglas-Home between July and October 1963 indicate that he wanted the party leadership and that he covertly positioned himself for the succession. If he genuinely did not want the party leadership he would not have responded in the way that he did to Morrison's communiqué (Gilmour and Garnett, 1998:187).

14 Butler did inform Macmillan that there would be complications in a peer emerging as the next party leader. It would involve a delay, (in renouncing the peerage and finding and winning a parliamentary constituency), but Butler also expressed concern about 'the psychological impact such a step would have in the country' (Fisher, 1977:107).

15 Douglas-Home would explain why he made this statement to Cabinet in his memoirs. He would claim that he offered to assist Dilhorne on the basis that 'at that time (October 8th) the question of my succession to Macmillan, had simply not crossed my mind' (Home, 1976:181). Douglas-Home simply glosses over his July discussions with Morrison in this interpretation (Gilmour and Garnett, 1998:189).

16 Maudling was widely criticised for the delivery of his speech and his failure to inspire undermined his credibility as a serious candidate for the succession. Whilst not generating the same level of criticism as Maudling, Butler also offered a pedestrian and mundane speech, whereupon he was afforded a dutiful rather than a rapturous response (Gilmour and Garnett, 1998:193). Stark argues that Butler could have utilised his conference speech better by 'emphasising his extensive service to the party and to make the case that he, as deputy prime minister, was Macmillan's natural successor.' His inability to decisively make a claim for the party leadership was a strategic miscalculation (Stark, 1996:106, 212). Hailsham would defend his overly aggressive campaigning approach by arguing that he was encouraged to do so by Macmillan, who had advised him to utilise his conference speech to make the case for himself assuming the party leadership (Hailsham, 1990:352). Douglas-Home offered a well-received speech which commenced with the observation: 'I am offering a prize to anyone this morning who can find a clue in my speech that this is Lord Douglas-Home's bid for the leadership.' Such reluctance succeeded in deftly drawing attention to the notion of him assuming the party leadership whilst feigning not to seek it (Gilmour and Garnett, 1998:192).

17 Hailsham was criticised for the theatrical manner in which he claimed he was renouncing his peerage and, according to Leonard, for the way in which he paraded himself around the conference with his baby daughter and her bottle in his arms (Leonard, 2003:508). Thorpe argues that many traditionalist Conserva-

tives were appalled by this conduct, and argued that 'the proper person to be dispensing such attention was the nanny – and in private' (Thorpe, 1996:525).

18   When a Conservative backbencher suggested to Macleod during the conference that Douglas-Home could be drafted as a compromise candidate, Macleod responded by saying: 'don't be so bloody ridiculous, Alec told us in Cabinet that he wasn't a runner' (Fisher, 1977:104).

19   The concept of one parliamentarian, one vote did not appeal to Redmayne. When identifying the strength of feeling within the parliamentary party, he did not give equal weighting to the opinions of individual Conservative parliamentarians. He admitted that his calculations were based on the fact that greater consideration was given to 'people on whose opinion one would more strongly rely on than others', which meant that experienced parliamentarians tendered towards Douglas-Home (Redmayne, 1963:1013).

20   According to Berkley, Macmillan told the Whips' Office that 'I want Douglas-Home. Somehow or another you have got to devise a way so that I can say the party wants Douglas-Home' (Stark, 1996:18).

21   Gilmour and Garnett are critical of the notion of Douglas-Home emerging as a 'compromise' candidate. They argue that 'as there was no formal voting mechanism, there could never be a deadlock that would require a compromise candidate' (Gilmour and Garnett, 1998:194).

22   If we accept that these re-allocated preferences were an accurate reflection of parliamentary opinion it is worth considering the following hypothetical scenario. Suppose these figures, Douglas-Home 113, Butler 104 and Maudling 66, amounted to the second ballot findings in a democratic ballot of Conservative parliamentarians. In this scenario, Maudling would have withdrawn and a final parliamentary ballot would have occurred in which the freed Maudling endorsers (all 66 of them) would have with their preferences re-allocated. Given that Maudling and Butler were identifiable with the left and Douglas-Home with the right, we can hypothecate that enough Maudling supporters would have switched to Butler to ensure his election and the rejection of Douglas-Home. An interesting little exercise to consider, which can be neither proved, nor disproved.

23   The *Spectator* article that Macleod penned, was actually a book review of the recently published book by Randolph Churchill, entitled 'The Fight for the Tory Leadership'. Based on interviews with Macmillan, Churchill defended the process through which Douglas-Home had acquired the party leadership and the premiership. Churchill concluded that 'never in the history of the Tory party, have such full and diligent enquiries been made in the selection of a new leader…everyone in the party had had an opportunity to make his or her views felt, and the result of the canvass had been decisive…it was Tory Democracy in action' (Churchill, 1964:134). It was within this review article that Macleod introduced the term the magic circle (Stark, 1996:19).

24   Another absurd aspect of the Dilhorne figures was the assertion by Dilhorne that Hailsham would refuse to serve if Butler assumed the party leadership and premiership. However, Hailsham would form part of the stop-Douglas-Home, pro-Butler movement towards the end of the succession crisis, and apparently told Butler 'you must don your armour, my dear Rab, and fight'. Given this, it seems an implausible argument on behalf of Dilhorne (Gilmour and Garnett, 1998:200).

25 In advocating Douglas-Home, Macmillan wrote in his memorandum to the
    Queen that: 'Douglas-Home is clearly a man who represents the old governing
    class at its best and those who take an impartial view of English history know
    how good that can be. He is not ambitious in the sense of wanting to scheme for
    power, although not foolish enough to resist honour when it comes to him'
    (Gilmour and Garnett, 1998:197).

26 Macmillan was disdainful of their efforts. He found the coming together 'of all
    the unsuccessful candidates somewhat distasteful' (Gilmour and Garnett,
    1998:200). Butler was of the opinion that it was wrong for Macmillan to ignore
    the powerful objectives that at least seven Cabinet figures had to the emergence
    of Douglas-Home (Butler, 1971:248).

27 Mirroring the Powell view, Macleod argued that Butler's supporters had 'put the
    golden ball in his [Butler's] lap, if he drops it now it's his own fault' (Shepherd,
    1991:158).

28 Douglas-Home disclaimed his peerage on October 19th upon becoming Prime
    Minister. He did not secure a parliamentary constituency until winning a by-
    election on November 8th. This meant that for three weeks the Prime Minister
    did not have a seat in either Houses of Parliament (Fisher, 1977:111).

29 It is worth noting that neither Powell nor Macleod refused to serve under
    Douglas-Home in opposition to the system of consultation itself, it was merely
    the outcome. For example, Macleod would comment of the meeting involved
    himself, Powell, Hailsham, Maudling and Butler, in which they all agreed to serve
    under Butler, that 'the succession was resolving itself the right way' (Stark,
    1996:18). Only later did Macleod amend his position and come to argue that
    formal election rules needed to be utilised (Stark, 1996:186).

30 Fisher implies that Macleod's refusal to serve under Douglas-Home fatally
    undermined his party leadership ambitions. Noting that Macleod was more
    experienced and a far better debater and television performer than Heath, Fisher
    speculates that had Macleod agreed to serve he would have more than likely
    acquired the shadow Chancellorship ahead of Heath, when they entered
    opposition in October 1964. Given that Heath used the shadow Chancellorship
    as the basis for demonstrating his party leadership credentials between October
    1964 and July 1965 (when Douglas-Home resigned), it can be argued that
    Macleod simply handed the keys to the party leadership to Heath, at his own
    expense (Fisher, 1977:111).

31 This fact was even admitted by Macmillan, who later realised that Douglas-Home
    was not voter friendly. He admitted to his miscalculation with breathtaking
    arrogance: 'that illness was a sad blow for me. Without being conceited, it was a
    catastrophe for the party' (Clark, 1998:399).

32 Shepherd observed that Douglas-Home was 'plainly out of his depth on the
    economy; an earlier self-deprecating confession that he had to do all of his
    economic calculations with the help of a box of matches seemed all too evidently
    true. It made a pitiable contrast to Wilson's command of statistics and talk of the
    white heat of the technological revolution' (Shepherd, 1991:160).

33 Macmillan would observe that legislation permitting Lords to renounce their
    peerages had been a pivotal aspect of the succession crisis. Had the legislation
    not passed 'all of our troubles would have been avoided…[as]… neither Lord
    Hailsham nor Lord Douglas-Home could in practice have been considered for

the premiership. Butler must have succeeded, almost without challenge' (Watkins, 1998:73).

Chapter Three

1   Campbell has argued that the electoral defeat of October 1964 fatally undermined the credibility of Douglas-Home as party leader. He argues that it 'effectively disabled [him] as a long-term leader, confirming him as a stop-gap leader who was bound to give way sooner or later' (Campbell, 1993:166).

2   Blake would observe that Douglas-Home's limitations as leader of the opposition raised serious concerns amongst Conservatives. He would observe that 'his defects as a parliamentarian were now far more damaging than in office. He was too much of a specialist and he lacked the speed of repartee or the ability to coin phrases which enable a politician to cut a figure in the House of Commons' (Blake, 1998:297).

3   Definitive implied that the candidate who emerged as the new party leader must have been able to secure a level of support that was sufficient to preclude the emergence of determined opposition to their party leadership (Bogdanor, 1994:81).

4   Although it was generally accepted that there was a need to formulate some recognised electoral process, there was some contention surrounding the recommendations that were put forward. For example, Clark notes that one dissenter argued that it 'was unwise to give an exactly equal vote in choosing a potential Prime Minister to a senior Cabinet minister and to the newest recruit in the parliamentary party' (Clark, 1998:408).

5   The provision for allowing new candidates to enter at the second ballot stage was deliberate and framed by the traditional Conservative need that the party leader must not be a divisive figure, but a unifying figure. The scope for entrants to a second ballot would allow compromise candidates to emerge if two ideologically divisive first ballot candidates would be unable to secure consensus if either of them emerged as the new party leader (Bogdanor, 1994:81).

6   Garnett has speculated that Douglas-Home had hoped that this cosmetic and symbolic adaptation to the rules of succession would enhance his position: i.e. the new procedures would 'make the party look more democratic without the necessity of changing its leader' (Garnett, 2005:197).

7   Although certain candidates for the succession, such as Macleod and Powell, believed that they had nothing to gain from an early contest, an immediate shift was seen as the preferable option for advocates of Maudling and Heath (Shepherd, 1996:291).

8   Fisher observes that 'Heath in no sense actuated the campaign against Douglas-Home, but he must have known of it, [although] he did not encourage their activities, he did not discourage them' (Fisher, 1977:120).

9   In response to the speculation that over one hundred Conservative parliamentarians were actively endorsing Heath, Douglas-Home publicly acquitted Heath of any wrong doing. At a private lunch that both attended, Douglas-Home observed that Heath had an empty chair next to him and quipped: 'for one of your one hundred men, I suppose?' (Roth, 1971:184).

10   In a Sunday Times leader comment (18th July), William Rees-Mogg, argued that it was 'the right moment for change...[as]... it is hard to resist the widespread

view that the Conservatives will not win a general election while Alec remains their leader' (Fisher, 1977:121).

11 Gilmour and Garnett argue that the movement to destabilise Douglas-Home was a mistake. They suggest that 'Home should not have got the job, but neither should he have been pushed out of it. Despite his majority of two, Wilson was highly unlikely to be forced into an election. He would call one at a time of his own choosing when he was virtually certain to win. The party would have done better to go down to honourable defeat with Home than to impose that burden on a new leader' (Gilmour and Garnett, 1998:219).

12 When deciding to resign Douglas-Home was quoted as saying 'I didn't see why, after being Foreign Secretary and Prime Minister, I should, so to speak, have to fight for the position as leader of the opposition. It didn't attract me....If I'd been ten years younger, I'd have seen it through' (Fisher, 1977:122).

13 Butler retired from politics in 1965 and assumed the position of Master of Trinity College, Cambridge.

14 Four other potential names were mentioned without gathering sufficient momentum to justify announcing their candidature: they were Peter Thorneycroft, Christopher Soames, Quentin Hogg (Lord Hailsham) and Selwyn Lloyd. Thorneycroft and Soames were put forward as potential compromise candidates who could emerge in a hypothetical second or third ballot. The appeal of Hogg and Lloyd could have directed at those who may have wished to ensure that their leader was from a traditional Tory background (Campbell, 1993:177).

15 Evans and Taylor note that Heath was to be party leader in an era of ideological turbulence, characterised by the waning credibility of one-nation Conservatism and a surge in neo-liberal thinking within the parliamentary Conservative Party. Heath was to display a volatile type of pragmatism that seemed to be lacking in clear and consistent principle. He entered the decade as a progressive interventionist modernizer and ended it seeking to enter power as an advocate of the free market. The language of Selsdon and the Quiet Revolution was then abandoned in preference for a pseudo-corporatist advocacy of governance by tripartite concentration of the state, business and trade unions between 1972 and 1974. He was to enter the General Election of February 1974 as a class-based, anti-union advocate, and having been marginally defeated would morph into an advocate of national unity and promoter of coalition. Post-1975 two principles remained firm: first, his attachment to the intregrationist European project; and, second, personal pique towards his successor, Margaret Thatcher (Evans and Taylor, 1996:146-147).

16 The Heath campaign proved to be far more accurate in their predictions. They estimated that Heath would secure a first ballot return of just under 160 votes, which was only slightly over his eventual return of 150 (Gilmour and Garnett, 1998:220).

17 Roth argues that Douglas-Home favoured Heath over Maudling and in the ensuing ballot he voted for Heath (Roth, 1971:186).

18 Walker had earlier being attempting to advance the claims of Macleod. Once he realised that Macleod was not a viable contender, he transferred his allegiances to Heath (Fisher, 1977:125). He would become a pivotal player in the Heath era, and showing amazing political longevity, was to serve as a member of the Thatcher Cabinet until his voluntary retirement in 1990.

19 As campaign manager for Heath, Walker assigned Keith Joseph to ensure that Thatcher switched her allegiance from Maudling to Heath. The subsequent success that Joseph secured in transferring Thatcher to the Heath camp was seen as an exemplar of the operational effectiveness of the Heath campaign (Campbell,1993:179,181).

20 The insights of Fisher indicate how badly Maudling damaged his own prospects. He decided not to even canvass support from his shadow Cabinet colleagues. The consequence of that was that three quarters of the shadow Cabinet endorsed Heath. Backbenchers then became aware of the fact that the shadow Cabinet was gravitating towards Heath; this may well have influenced the decisions of the undecided, especially those new entrants to the parliamentary Conservative Party (Fisher, 1977:125, 127).

21 Norton and Aughey suggest that Heath secured the party leadership as the party was looking for their own version of Wilson (Norton and Aughey, 1981:144).

22 Evans and Taylor note that the candidature of Powell constituted a 'foretaste of the alliance Thatcher successfully constructed to win the leadership…[through]…a combination of free market enthusiasts, [and] traditional right wingers concerned about immigration' (Evans and Taylor, 1996:145-146).

23 An illustration of an economic libertarian, who gravitated away from Powell and to Heath, rather than Maudling, would be Geoffrey Howe (Shepherd, 1996:293).

24 Douglas-Home would admit that on this point they 'hadn't discussed it much' or 'thought a great deal about it at the time' (Hutchinson, 1970:138).

Chapter Four

1 Ramsden makes an interesting point about the notion of seeking confidence in his leadership, which would have prompted a leadership election. He notes that Heath had decided, 'with the convoluted logic of a trapped man', that 'he did not intend to fight a leadership contest because he wanted to stay on to resist the right wing', but this 'only made sense if he thought he would *lose* a contest' (Ramsden, 1996:435).

2 Herein lay a crucial difference between the 1965 and 1975 party leadership elections. In 1965, the 1922 Executive Committee remained neutral, having defended Douglas-Home, albeit without amazing enthusiasm. In late 1974 it was evident that the 1922 Executive Committee was clearly agitating for the removal of Heath (Watkins, 1998:187-188). On the notion of Du Cann assuming the party leadership, it is worth noting that his rumoured ambitions would have been swiftly disregarded by the magic circle system of consultation by elites. Without Cabinet experience they would have regarded him as of insufficient political standing to justify having leadership aspirations (Stark, 1996:95).

3 During this meeting, the Conservative backbencher, Kenneth Lewis, memorably noted that 'the party leadership was a leasehold, not a freehold' (Ramsden, 1996:438).

4 The offer of a shadow Cabinet berth for Du Cann was an attempt by Heath to disarm a dangerous political opponent. However, Fisher notes that it was hardly surprising that having been ignored for eight years, Du Cann should decline what seemed an oddly timed promotional opportunity (Fisher, 1977:160-161).

5 There was ambiguity surrounding whether these new leadership evictions procedures relating to when the Conservatives were in office. There was an implicit assumption that they were intended only for opposition, a view that Thatcher certainly believed. Watkins argues, however, that if this had been so, then the rules would have clearly stated that they provided for a challenge to the party leader only when the Conservative were out of office (Watkins, 1998:189).

6 This provision made it harder for Heath to secure a first ballot victory. It became known as 'Alec's revenge', given the assumption that Heathites had campaigned for his removal as party leader a decade earlier (Ramsden, 1996:440). Heath deeply opposed this amendment as he realised it undermined his chances of survival, but also because he felt that they would weaken the position of any incumbent Conservative Party leader (Heath, 1998:530). It was this procedural adaptation that would necessitate a second ballot in the 1990 Conservative Party leadership election and lead to the resignation of Margaret Thatcher. Heath appears to have been less concerned about this procedural amendment when it affected Thatcher than when it affected himself.

7 Given the subsequent defenestration of Heath this provision is intriguing. Heath retained the overwhelming support of the extra-parliamentary party, but such views, whilst supposedly formalised, were completely disregarded by Conservative parliamentarians, just as they were to be for Thatcher fifteen years later (Shepherd, 1991:169; Stark, 1996:30).

8 The provision for annual elections was damaging to Heath, even if he did retain the party leadership in the immediate short-term. Given that the general election may not occur until the autumn of 1979, the new rules meant that Heath could have been subject to further challenges in the autumns of 1975, 1976, 1977 and 1978. Given that he had party leader for over a decade we can argue that if the first attempted assassination failed, (i.e. the initial one in the first six months of the October 1974 convened Parliament), he would stand more vulnerable to a challenge before the next general election than a newly elected successor.

9 The two candidates who had opposed Heath ten years ago were no longer potential candidates. Enoch Powell had refused to stand as a Conservative candidate in the February 1974 general election and had become an Ulster Unionist parliamentarian at the October 1974 general election. Reginald Maudling had seen his political career descend into financial scandal in the interim period and was no longer viewed as viable candidate.

10 Clark offered the following observation of Joseph's method of public speaking: 'he gestured wildly, often (literally) beating his breast during a speech; and glared at his audience' (Clark, 1998:456).

11 Thatcher appeared to believe this herself. On October 15th 1974 she announced that: 'I think that it would be extremely difficult for a women to make it to the top' (Thatcher, 1995:262).

12 This culminated in a parliamentary rejoinder to Chancellor Healey, himself an impressive parliamentarian, which delighted Conservative parliamentarians. Thatcher noted of Healey: 'some chancellors are microeconomic. Some Chancellors are fiscal. This one is just plain cheap' (Thatcher, 1995:274-275).

13 The most ironic illustration of this was Michael Heseltine. He was an advocate of Whitelaw, and fearing that a second ballot may not occur, he was persuaded by Thatcher campaigners, notably, Norman Tebbit, that unless he voted for

Thatcher, there would be no opportunity for Whitelaw to emerge through the second ballot (Tebbit, 1988:141).

14   To prevent the need for a second ballot, the winning candidate needed to secure a majority plus a lead of fifteen per cent over the fifteen per cent (i.e. 159 votes). As Thatcher was short of the fifteen per cent threshold, a second ballot was scheduled for a week later on 11th February 1975.

15   The Heath camp had predicted that their candidate had 129 firm pledges, plus an additional seventeen Conservatives whom they thought would probably endorse him. Walker optimistically predicted a return between 138 and 144 (Ramsden, 1996:450).

16   Fraser also withdrew but without as much attention as Heath.

17   Whitelaw realised his chances of emerging with the party leadership on the second ballot were limited, but he did think that he could prevail via a third ballot. However, he was worried by the consequences of this scenario on his leadership authority and legitimacy. He feared that people (i.e. both Conservative parliamentarians and the electorate) might think it was odd that Thatcher had come first in two ballots, but would be defeated by second preferences votes on the third ballot (Fisher, 1977:176). Given the implications of similar scenarios for the authority and legitimacy of William Hague in 1997 (see chapter seven) and Iain Duncan Smith in 2001 (see chapter eight) these were genuine concerns.

18   To secure victory in the second ballot, the leading candidate needed to secure a simple majority of the parliamentary Conservative Party (i.e. 139 votes).

19   Although a valid argument relating to the conduct and outcome of the second ballot of the Conservative Party leadership election of 1975, it is worth noting that the logic underpinning this argument did not work for Michael Heseltine in the second ballot of the Conservative Party leadership election of November 1990 (Wickham-Jones, 1997: 82). This is explored in detail in chapter five.

20   Crewe and Searing observe that 'many Conservative MPs who voted for Mrs Thatcher as leader in February 1975 did so to get rid of Mr Heath and had no idea that she was about to hatch a new ideology and behind it march the party off to the right' (Crewe and Searing, 1988: 371).

Chapter Five

1   The incremental repositioning of the Conservative Party in opposition coincided with the implosion of the Labour Government. The IMF crisis of 1976 and the Winter of Discontent in 1978 / 1979 destroyed their governing credibility and authority, and the image of excessive trade union influence gave crucial political ammunition to the Conservative Party.

2   Thatcherism has been open to a myriad of interpretations Academics agree that Thatcherism constituted a distinctive strategy but there is little agreement on what exactly it entailed. For detailed reviews on the literature on Thatcherism see Jessop et al, 1988:22-51 and Evans and Taylor, 1996:219-246.

3   There was speculation throughout 1975 that Thatcher might face a Heathite based challenge that autumn but none was forthcoming (Stark, 1996:30).

4   Whilst serving as her Defence Secretary (1983 to 1986) Heseltine and Thatcher disagreed on the handling of Westland, a struggling helicopter manufacturer. Heseltine proposed a European based solution involving integrating Westland and British Aerospace with Italian and French companies, Thatcher favoured

merging Westland with an American company. Heseltine resigned from the Cabinet in January 1986 in protest at the style of Cabinet management that Thatcher adopted when handling this matter. He believed that Thatcher had prevented him from presented the case for the European backed rescue package to the Cabinet and resigned in protest. He remained on the backbenchers thereafter but was assumed to be positioning himself to succeed her as Conservative Party leader and Prime Minister should an opportunity arise.

5   The political media had long salivated at the prospect of a political 'rumble in the jungle' between the two heavyweights of Conservative politics: the Iron Lady and Tarzan (Norton, 1990b:259).

6   Heseltine was not party to the talks that resulted in the Meyer challenge (Shepherd, 1991:7).

7   One of the abstaining Conservative parliamentarians had been Heseltine (Crick, 1997:316).

8   As part of their re-election campaign, George Younger, informed Conservative parliamentarians that 'the Prime Minister expected all good Conservatives to do their duty' (Watkins, 1998:191).

9   Thatcher herself believed that the 'procedure for electing the Tory leader was, by *unwritten convention*, not intended for use when the Party was in office' (Thatcher, 1993:829). Clark observes that it is 'unclear' what the basis of this assertion was. Furthermore, he notes that in politics 'where crude power is at stake', it cannot be safe to rely on the strength of an 'unwritten convention' (Clark, 1998:487). Three years after her removal from office, Thatcher would argue that the Conservatives party leadership election / ejection procedures should be amended to make it impossible for an incumbent Conservative Prime Minister to be removed from office (Stark, 1996:32).

10 Their ideological falling out was symbolic. It demonstrated the fracturing of the Thatcherite ideological project, as Lawson and Howe had previously been seen as key players in the implementation of Thatcherism.

11 Baker noted that Onslow tried to persuade Thatcher against holding the ballot whilst she was at the European Summit. It would prove to be advice that Thatcher would wish she had acted upon (Baker, 1993:389).

12 The political impact was immediate. One Conservative MP observed that Howe' speech: 'tore away the veils…it showed that the talk about divisions in the party was true and that it wasn't the poll tax, it wasn't Michael Heseltine, it wasn't Europe, it was her' (Shepherd, 1991:1).

13 Various rumours abounded at the motivations of Howe. Theory one argued that Howe was acting with Heseltine (although given that his intervention undermined the Heseltine strategy this seems unlikely). Theory two was that he was acting alone but wanted to aid the chances of Heseltine assuming the party leadership (although as implied in theory one he succeeded in undermining the chances of Heseltine). Theory three was that he was using Heseltine. This assumed that Heseltine would challenge and lose but cause collateral damage to Thatcher. She would then be forced to stand down at some stage in the future, thus enabling Howe to assume the party leadership. This theory is undermined by the fact that Howe himself knew that his chances of succeeding Thatcher were now limited. Perhaps the following theory is the most plausible and articulated by Shepherd. He argues that Howe did not realise the full potential of his speech:

'the assassin was motivated not be guile but by a characteristically dogged determination to set out the facts fully and argue a reasoned case, whatever the political consequences' (Shepherd, 1991:3).

14 Heseltine was however, a reluctant challenger. It was rumoured that his immediate reaction to the Howe resignation speech was: 'well, I've got to, haven't I?' (Crick, 1997:344).

15 Having decided to formal challenge Thatcher, Heseltine requested that Howe publicly endorse him. Although Howe did subsequently vote for Heseltine, he could not bring himself to publicly endorse him, as he 'was determined to remain innocent of any charges of conspiracy' (Watkins, 1998:218).

16 Given this she concluded that 'if they were not already persuaded, there was not much left for me to persuade them with' (Thatcher, 1993:837).

17 William Whitelaw, (by now Lord Whitelaw), observed that if one third of the parliamentary Conservative Party failed to endorse her (i.e. 124) her position would be untenable (Baker, 1993:382, 384).

18 The result demonstrated the peculiarity of how political insiders interpret party leadership elections. Thatcher had come in first place and had a majority of over fifty votes over the defeated candidate Heseltine. However, her performance was viewed as having made her increasingly vulnerable to defeat. Heseltine, meanwhile, secured a minority and fifty plus fewer votes but was portrayed as having won the contest on points, rather than by a knockout (Shepherd, 1991:28).

19 Although Hurd signed her nominations papers for the second ballot, (albeit reluctantly), Thatcher was immensely upset by the attitude of Major. Her Chancellor had been recovering from a wisdom tooth operation as the leadership crisis had evolved. He was convalescing in his constituency home when Thatcher telephoned him, and asked him to sign her nomination papers and return to London to campaign for her. His hesitation in confirming his willingness to sign the nomination papers was then compounded by his non-committal reply to the request to campaign for her. Major said 'I will think about it' (Watkins, 1998:225, 228).

20 Committed Thatcherite, Alan Clark, recalled the excitement that her fight to win message provoked amongst the Heseltine camp. He noted in his diaries, how Hampson reacted to the news that Thatcher was still standing: 'We've made it. We can't lose now' (Clark, 1993:364).

21 With the benefit of hindsight, the appointment of Renton as Chief Whip was a misjudgement from Thatcher, given that Renton had a long standing political association with Howe (Watkins, 1998:217).

22 This was an issue that framed the attitude of Garel-Jones. He argued that if Thatcher won the second ballot 187 to 185 she could claim victory according to the electoral procedures for a second ballot. This would be a pointless exercise her argued; in effect she was finished (Watkins, 1991:11).

23 Watkins was puzzled by the drafting in of Wakeham. He would note that Wakeham had already decided that if Thatcher had failed to win outright in the first ballot, in was in the best interests of the party that she did not contest the second ballot: as such he was more of an undertaker than a campaign manager (Watkins, 1991:5-6).

24 Jeffreys argues that 'by way of atonement many MPs felt it important to vote for Major as Thatcher's preferred candidate' (Jeffreys, 2002:252).

25 Technically, the party leadership election of 1990 was never completed. Onslow simply decided that there would be no third ballot, even though Major had not secured the required majority. He revealed: 'I've cancelled it. I'm sure I've broken the rules, but what does it matter? What's the point in holding a ballot when there is nothing to decide? This is supposed to be the common-sense party' (Stark, 1996:215).

26 Two Conservatives with considerable experience in the Whips' Office, Tristan Garel-Jones and Richard Ryder, volunteered their services to the Thatcher campaign, (for the first ballot), but were informed by Morrison that their help was not required (Shepherd, 1991:22).

27 Younger had acted as the campaign manager to the Thatcher campaign the previous autumn. He agreed to serve in a similar capacity but did so reluctantly due to his altered circumstances – i.e. he had left government and had assumed a new position as Chairman of the Royal Bank of Scotland. He agreed to do so only because he feared that if he did not then it would be assumed that he did not support Thatcher any longer, and he knew that such assertions would carry political symbolism (Stark, 1996:110, 213).

28 Thatcher reluctantly admitted as much in her memoirs by saying the 'serene optimism which made Peter so effective at cheering us all up was not necessarily so suitable for calculating the intentions of that most slippery of electorates – Conservative MPs' (Thatcher, 1993:837).

29 Only in anticipation of the second ballot did Thatcher personally seek to canvass support. When she did so she was staggered by the response she received. She detected that even her supporters were complaining that her campaign team did not seem to be fighting (Thatcher, 1993:850).

30 Of the Cabinet, Thatcher observed that what 'grieved me, was the desertion of those I had always considered friends and allies and the weasel words whereby they transmuted their betrayal into frank advice and concern for my fate' (Thatcher, 1993:855). Gilmour and Garnett have added an intriguing rejoinder to this interpretation. They defend her Cabinet colleagues by stating: 'just why an honest estimate that she was going to lose should amount to betrayal, she does not explain' (Gilmour and Garnett, 1998:347).

31 Through a combination of published lists of declared supporters and direct contacts with the campaign teams and individual Conservative MPs, Cowley and Garry constructed a methodological robust data set of the voting behaviour of Conservative MPs. Each Conservative MP was then (where possible) attributed their ideological categorisation (wet or dry, Europhile or Eurosceptic, liberal or conservative). On the basis of knowing both the ideological categorisations of Conservative MPs, (from the Norton typology), and their voting behaviour, Cowley and Garry were able to conclude that the Thatcherite right (dry, sceptic, conservative) tended towards Major and the Tory left (wet, Europhile and liberal) tended towards Heseltine and Hurd (Cowley and Garry, 1998:473-499).

Chapter Six

1 For an appraisal of the crisis of legitimacy that Major suffered for the duration of his party leadership tenure, which includes a detailed analysis of the Conservative

party leadership of 1995, see Heppell, (2007) *Contemporary British History*, Vol. 21, No. 4. [copyright Taylor and Francis].

2   The Conservatives had entered the general election of 1992 with two clear messages underpinning their economic policy stance: first; membership of the Exchange Rate Mechanism as a counter-inflationary discipline; and second; an unequivocal commitment to reduce taxation when economically viable and with this a specific pledge had been made not to extend the imposition of Value Added Tax (Stephens, 1996:283).

3   Enforced withdrawal emboldened Eurosceptic sentiment within the parliamentary Conservative Party. Eurosceptics had argued that membership of the Exchange Rate Mechanism had prolonged the economic recession, whilst its failure, and the assumption that membership of the Exchange Rate Mechanism was a prelude to Economic and Monetary Union, intensified doubts about closer European integration (Denver, 1998:19-21).

4   The destruction of their reputation for low taxation was absolute. The cumulative impact of the indirect and direct increases in taxation initiated in the two budgets, amounted to the largest percentage annual tax increase in post-war British history: it amounted to the equivalent of three per cent of Gross Domestic Product out of the economy (Thompson, 1996:180; Seldon, 1997:409).

5   Major went as far as writing a script for a resignation broadcast. He also tipped off his preferred successor (Clarke) that he should prepare for a party leadership election (Seldon, 1997:321; Stuart, 1998:303). Major would later argue, however, that 'the weight of pressure was to stay, not to depart' but would admit that 'I was never certain that it was right, nor I am I now' (Major, 1999:336).

6   Tactically, Heseltine could not realistically challenge an incumbent Conservative Prime Minister twice. Over and beyond such tactical considerations was the health of Heseltine. He suffered a heart attack in 1993 which raised doubts about his political ambitions. The death of the Labour Party leader, John Smith, in 1994, who had earlier suffered a heart attack himself, appeared to reinforce doubts about the idea of Heseltine as a future party leader.

7   In the autumn of 1994 there was widespread speculation that Major would be subject to a leadership challenge from a stalking horse candidate from within the Thatcherite Eurosceptic right. As the deadline for nominations approached it was rumoured that Norman Lamont and Edward Leigh, two dismissed ministers, had assembled twenty-five of the necessary thirty-four names to initiate a challenge. The deadline for nominations coincided with a crucial vote on European Union budgetary contributions. Potential Eurosceptic critics who were contemplating not supporting the government on increasing contributions were warned that they would have the Conservative whip withdrawn. If they had the whip withdrawn then they would not be permitted to have their names included when initiating a leadership challenge. Eight Conservatives failed to support the government in the ensuring contributions motion and had the Conservative whip withdrawn. Those eight were critical to the capacity of Lamont and Leigh to reach the leadership election initiation threshold. Without them the critics of Major were unable to initiate a challenge and Major survived (Norton, 1998a:100).

8   Watkins noted that back in 1922 Andrew Bonar Law refused to become Prime Minister until he had formally acquired the position of leader of the Conservative

Party. Major was now resigning as leader of the Conservative Party but was deciding to remain as Prime Minister. Enoch Powell was one of the few political commentators to discuss this issue. Powell felt that the two positions, that of Conservative Party leader and Prime Minister, did not amount to separate or separable positions: Powell argued that 'one or other of them could not be renounced at pleasure without affecting the other' (Watkins, 1998:234, 239).

9   Major had famously been caught off camera referring to his Eurosceptic cabinet colleagues as bastards. The bastards within the Cabinet were assumed to be Michael Portillo, Peter Lilley and John Redwood. Eurosceptic backbenchers appeared to take the term as a badge of honour. Teresa Gorman would later write an overview of the passage of the Maastricht Treaty and entitle it *The Bastards* (Gorman, 1993).

10 Lamont famously referred to the Major government as given the impression of 'being in office, but not in power...[and of]...too much short termism, too much reacting to events, not enough shaping of events' (Seldon, 1997:378).

11 The incumbent Foreign Secretary, Douglas Hurd, announced that he would be standing down once the party leadership election was completed. Howard was to be disappointed as Malcolm Rifkind was appointed in succession to Hurd (Seldon, 1997:588).

12 Portillo had to cope with the embarrassment of being exposed installing extra telephone lines into the home of one his supporters, presumably as a potential campaign headquarters for his entry into the succession contest, once Major had been ousted (Barber, 2003:13).

13 Once Redwood declared and the campaign began, Lilley privately expressed the view that he wished he had resigned after all (Williams, 1998:113).

14 The press conference at which Redwood announced his candidature was widely seen as undermining, rather than enhancing, his prospects. Williams observes that the impression was 'that of a coup launched by a group of dissident Latin-American lieutenant-colonels who had just taken over the local airport and cancelled all flights' (Williams, 1998:105).

15 Crick denies a deal, Gove implies that a deal was arranged. Redwood argues the acceptance on Heseltine's part of his interdependence with Major arguing 'I think that it is possible for two very sophisticated politicians to do a deal without actually expressing the words of the deal... I think they understood each other perfectly well and so it would have been possible for hints to be made and the necessary steps taken' (BBC, 1999). Crick's argument about the promise about the succession seems plausible. It would be impossible for Major to 'simply deliver the leadership to Heseltine. If he had stepped down, then under party rules other candidates would have been entitled to stand, and Heseltine would almost certainly have faced opposition from Redwood and Portillo' (Crick, 1997:419).

16 The fact that Redwood had been regarded as a credible challenger rather than a stalking horse candidate aided Major. Stark argues that: 'the presence of a strong challenger helped Major by effectively lowering the threshold he needed to surpass; it is unlikely he would have remained leader had he received only two-thirds of the votes against a stalking horse candidate' (Stark, 1996:171). Gilmour and Garnett would later expand upon the Stark interpretation and argue that: 'almost certainly, Redwood garnered few, if any more votes than a non-entity

would have received. So by making Major's victory seem considerable against a former Cabinet Minister, Redwood had salvaged the Prime Minister' (Gilmour and Garnett, 1998:372-373).

17 The volatility of the third hurdle had become more profound in the closing days and hours of the contest. Major supporter, Andrew Bowden, argued that he 'would have to seriously reconsider his position' if he were to lose the support of a quarter of the party (i.e. he must obtain 246 votes). Steven Norris suggested Major would be 'in difficulties if he gets less than 230' (i.e. if 99 fail to endorse him). Some figures within the Major campaign briefed that an arithmetic victory, by overcoming the two necessary stipulations, would in itself constitute a political victory, and the artificial third hurdle was an unnecessary and distorting stipulation. Conflicting and disputed figures emerged primarily because the figure that would represent a sufficient vote of confidence was psychological / political rather than arithmetic / technical (Alderman, 1996:325).

18 Furthermore, their decision to accede to Major's request that no challenge would be permitted in November 1995 was also advantageous to the Prime Minister.

19 For a discussion of the troublesome Cabinet reshuffle of July 1995 see Seldon, 1997:597-600

20 When evaluating the leadership contest and the subsequent reshuffle, Gove observes that 'division within the ranks of the right had denied a numerically more powerful faction the influence it might have wielded' (Gove, 1995:341).

21 The high risk strategy that Major had adopted in challenging his critics to put up or shut up had derived benefits with regard to his security of tenure: it prevented a challenge from occurring in autumn 1995 and flowing from this Major was able to obtain the compliance of the 1922 Executive Committee in preventing a challenge from occurring in autumn 1996. The compliance of the 1922 Executive Committee ensured that Major could only be removed from the party leadership if he wished to resign or was persuaded to resign: he could not be forcibly evicted from the party leadership by his critics within the parliamentary Conservative Party before the general election (Williams, 1998:157).

22 Identification of Redwood supporters starts with the twenty-eight who were publicly declared Redwood supporters prior to the contest. The remaining base of the Redwood vote can be determined by the following sources: first, Conservatives who declared in the immediate aftermath of the vote; second, Conservatives who revealed during the 1997 Conservative Party leadership contest that they had supported Redwood two years earlier; and third, Conservatives who although they did not state their voting behaviour, the Redwood camp claimed that they were amongst their voters.

23 The research concluded that of the 329 Conservative parliamentarians, 98 were Europhiles, 39 were party loyalists / agnostic, and 192 were Eurosceptic. The breakdown of the Major vote was 96 pro-Europeans, 35 party loyalists, and 87 Eurosceptics. Redwood had the following breakdown from his 89 votes: 0 pro-Europeans, 2 party loyalists and 87 Eurosceptics. The failure of the Redwood candidature stemmed from only securing 87 of the 192 Eurosceptic votes. Major survived having secured more pro-European endorsers than Eurosceptic endorsers (Heppell, 2000:427-428).

24 This is an assertion that has been advanced by the following academics. Norton has argued that if Thatcher had remained as party leader then her approach to

European policy would have increased the possibility of an irrevocable split (Norton, 1994:104). Baker et al have argued that had Thatcher been replaced with either Hurd or Heseltine (rather than Major) than a more pro-European policy would have been pursued and a formal split could have resulted (Baker et al, 1993:420-434).

Chapter Seven

1 Williams would observe that Eurosceptic and Europhilic Conservatives were at last allied – in common humiliation (Williams, 1998:183).

2 Alderman notes that some within the parliamentary Conservative Party were ready to accept the notion of a caretaker party leader, who would give the Conservatives some breathing space in which to evaluate their political predicament, before considering the means of electing a new party leader and determining who that party leader should be (Alderman, 1998:3).

3 However, some Conservatives rejected the notion of attempting to revise the party leadership election procedures given the succession contest had effectively begun. Attempting to amend the rules of that contest could prove to be highly divisive, as 'any reforms introduced in this atmosphere would be doubted by one faction or another as a means of advancing a particular person's cause' (Alderman, 1998:4).

4 A Gallup Poll stated that Clarke was the preferred candidate of both Conservative voters (Clarke first with 30 per cent and Hague second with 19 per cent) and all voters (Clarke first with 27 per cent and Hague second with 12 per cent) (*The Daily Telegraph*, 25th May 1997) Clarke also came first in a poll of constituency chairman, peers and members of the European Parliament. In the poll of constituency chairman, Clarke was backed by 269 chairs and Hague by 178, with Howard trailing in last with the support of only 10 chairs. All seventeen Conservative members of the European Parliament supported Clarke (Norton, 1998b:12).

5 Clarke also was able to attract the highest number of fellow Conservative elites to his candidature. Of the remaining members of the Major Cabinet, who were not themselves candidates, Clarke secured the public endorsements of Michael Heseltine, Stephen Dorrell, John Gummer, George Young and Douglas Hogg (Norton, 1998b:12; Alderman, 1998:9).

6 Lilley also attempted to persuade Hague not to run but to endorse his candidature instead. Hague was offered the position of Shadow Chancellor in a Lilley led Conservative Party Shadow Cabinet, plus an insurance that in the next Conservative Party leadership campaign Lilley would endorse the candidature of Hague. Hague resisted the overtures of the Lilley campaign, just as he had those of the Howard campaign (Alderman, 1998:5).

7 Cowley argues that the Widdecombe quote made such an impact that it would be guaranteed an entry in all half decent dictionaries of political quotations (Cowley, 1997:92).

8 Given the emotions aroused by Widdecombe's speech, Lilley dropped her as part of his campaign team (Alderman, 1998:15).

9 Any candidate who secured 95 votes on the first ballot would have been immediately elected – i.e. an absolute majority plus a majority of fifteen per cent (Norton, 1998b:12).

10   The failure of any of the candidates to secure thirty per cent in the first ballot was unprecedented in the history of Conservative Party leadership elections.

11   Any candidate securing 83 votes on the second ballot would have been immediately elected – i.e. an absolute majority (Norton, 1998b:12).

12   This tactical alliance was simultaneously described as a dream ticket and a nightmare ticket (Norton, 1998b:12). Those with memories of the previous party leadership election in 1995 recalled how Clarke claimed that the Conservatives would never win an election in a thousand years on the policy platform that Redwood believed in (Williams, 1998:106).

13   It was assumed that the existing sixty-four votes for Clarke would remain intact as would the existing sixty-two for Hague. All Clarke had to achieve from the pact with Redwood was nineteen of the thirty-eight Redwood votes. It was a misplaced assumption as some existing allegiances to Clarke were lost and Redwood could not carry his supporters as had been assumed (Williams, 1998:220-222).

14   What is intriguing about the Clarke-Redwood alliance is that it did provoke some positive responses from political commentators. Indicative of such interpretations was that of Hugo Young of the *Guardian*. Young noted that the Conservatives seem 'on the brink of showing it is not dead...here at last is an early sighting of the Conservative Party we used to know and fear. Ideas, it turns out, [may] matter less than hatred' (Williams, 1998:222).

15   Redwood argued that the was attracted to the alliance with Clarke as it was imperative to end the 'balkanisation' of the Conservative Party and that only Clarke offered an approach which was 'inclusive' enough to achieve this. By adopting a free vote on the hypothetical question of a parliamentary division of the single European currency advocates of the Clarke-Redwood alliance suggested that this was more inclusive and unifying than the stance that Hague had shifted towards; i.e. his insistence that members of his shadow cabinet would have to endorse his negative stance on the hypothetical question of the single Euro-pean currency (Alderman,1998:12).

16   However, if this was so obvious why make the accommodation during the party leadership election. Surely a pact agreed before the commencement of the party leadership election would have seemed more intellectually plausible. That it occurred in the manner that it did, and when it did, suggests that it was an act of mutual expedience that Redwood and Clarke were propelled into, given the way in which the leadership election had evolved.

17   Reflective of the condemnation was the view of Conservative parliamentarian, Peter Tapsell, who viewed the unholy alliance as 'one of the most contemptible and discreditable actions by a senior British politician that I can recall during thirty-eight years in the Commons' (Watkins, 1998:197).

18   The alliance between Clarke and Redwood did place many Thatcherite Euro-sceptics in a quandary and the intervention of Thatcher probably aided them. Their dilemma was should they support the political heavyweight (Clarke) who has the 'wrong' agenda on Europe or should they support the political light-weight (Hague) who was now increasingly claiming to have the 'right' agenda on Europe (Alderman, 1998:13).

19   Despite having acted as the campaign manager for the Redwood candidature, Duncan Smith also rejected the Clarke-Redwood alliance and voted for Hague

and emerged as a member of the Shadow Cabinet days later. Duncan Smith was pivotal in co-ordinating the defections from Redwood to Hague rather than to Clarke-Redwood (Taylor, 2003:234).

20 As the political academic and seasoned analyst of party leadership elections, Philip Cowley, observed: 'in every leadership contest, much is made of the supposed virtues of the various candidates, such as their charisma, intelligence, debating skills, and electoral appeal (or lack thereof). Yet what is striking about the 1997 contest – and, indeed, about most Conservative leadership contests, is how little these factors seem to affect people's voting. Instead, most of the voting is driven by ideology' (Cowley, 1997:93-94).

21 The viability of the Howard-Hague joint ticket, that the Howard campaign sought to create, was that should Howard assume the party leadership with Hague as his deputy, then the Thatcherite Eurosceptic right would have the 'lineage' on the party leadership. This theory assumed that it was inevitable that the Conservatives would lose the next general election but that Hague would be well positioned to be the next leader but one of the Conservatives (Nadler, 2001:9).

22 All 164 Conservative parliamentarians were situated on the European policy ideological divide and evaluated on the basis of a range of indicators – e.g. division lists, early day motions, membership of party groups, and public comment. All were then defined as Europhile, Eurosceptic or centrist loyalist. The research that included division lists and early day motions was predominantly derived from the behaviour of Conservative parliamentarians from the 1992 to 1997 Parliament. Those entering Parliament in May 1997 were located primarily through public comment and membership of party groups. The research identified 13 pro-Europeans, 11 agnostics and 140 Eurosceptics (see Hill, 2004, 2007).

23 Alderman notes that the three candidates most identifiable with the Thatcherite Eurosceptic right (i.e. Redwood, Lilley and Howard) were effectively engaging in a primary for the support of the Thatcherite Eurosceptic right in the first ballot (Alderman, 1998:10).

24 Hague won the party leadership through the final ballot endorsements of the Eursceptics. Of his 92 votes, 81 were from known Eurosceptics (see Hill, 2004, 2007).

25 Garnett is critical of the photo-opportunity in front of the assembled press in which Thatcher endorsed Hague. He notes that 'she kept repeating the name of her little known champion, giving the impression that she might forget it herself without coaching her memory…Hague stood beside his voluble patroness with a fixed smile' (Garnett, 2003:58).

26 When winning the party leadership election that made him Prime Minister, Major had spent £20,000. In winning the party leadership, but only the position of leader of the opposition, Hague had spent £80,000. The remaining four defeated candidates incurred combined costs of around £170,000 (Alderman, 1998:15).

Chapter Eight

1 Garnett and Lynch suggest that his party leadership tenure can be split into two sections. The initial stage was the compassionate Conservative stage, between 1997 and 1999, when he attempted to reach out to the uncommitted centrist

voters. This was then followed by the core vote stage and the common sense revolution rhetoric between 1999 and 2001. Garnett and Lynch note that 'in the first stage, Hague repeatedly referred to the unappealing reactionary image of the party and pledged to improve it; in the second, he seemed to embody that image, appearing to be intolerant and even xenophobic' (Garnett and Lynch, 2003:4).

2   The party leadership credibility of Hague was also undermined by his weak public profile. For example, tactics that were deployed in an attempt to portray him as a youthful political leader, in touch with modern society (e.g. the baseball cap imagery, the attendance at the Notting Hill carnival, and the reference to alcohol consumption in his youth) backfired badly (Garnett and Lynch, 2003:3).

3   Hague became the only the second leader of the Conservative Party who failed to became Prime Minister. The other one was Austen Chamberlain who was leader of the Conservative Party between March 1921 and October 1922 (Cowley and Quayle, 2001:46).

4   Four senior figures within the Conservative Party (Andrew MacKay, Ann Widdecombe, Iain Duncan Smith and Lord Strathclyde) attempted to persuade Hague not to resign immediately. They requested that he delay his decision to resign to allow the party time to reflect upon the reasons for their electoral defeat before they were asked to determine the succession. Hague was not persuaded by their arguments (Walters, 2001:2-3).

5   No confidence motions had been initiated against Hague during his four year tenure (or in the three years since its inception in 1998), although rumours and conspiracies against his party leadership were omnipresent given the Conservatives flat-lining in the opinion polls. These rumblings of discontent were ratcheted up in 1999 after the parliamentary return of Portillo (Garnett and Lynch, 2003:4).

6   The observations of Quinn relating to the non-candidature of Widdecombe are illuminating. Quinn notes that the parliamentary party were effectively screening the type of candidates that they would allow to be presented to the mass membership. This can stop the mass membership for voting for candidates that they most admire. This created a dilemma for Widdecombe. She was popular amongst the party activists and may well have been able to perform well if presented to them. However, she lacked a support base amongst her parliamentary colleagues so standing was futile (Quinn, 2005:804).

7   The appearance of Duncan Smith, which resembled Hague, led to suggestions that he was 'Hague Mark Two' or 'Hague without the jokes' (Walters, 2001:225). It also led to crude jibs about Duncan Smith looking like Hague's father (Norton, 2001:13). The inferior version of Hague argument was emphasised by the Clarke campaign. As one Clarke supporter observed: 'what can Duncan Smith bring to the party that Hague didn't other than the word "never" [over the single currency]?' (Norton, 2001:13).

8   That an ideologically repositioning had occurred was evident from Portillo's resignation from the Thatcherite 'No Turning Back' group of Conservative parliamentarians.

9   Upon his return to Parliament in the Westminster by election of November 1999, which followed the death of the incumbent, Alan Clark, Portillo had been appointed as Shadow Chancellor. Rather than restrict himself to his economic portfolio, Portillo would articulate an agenda way beyond his portfolio

responsibilities. His primary concern was that the electorate thought that the Conservatives were 'uncaring about unemployment, poverty, poor housing, disability, and single parenthood', and that they were associated with 'greed and the unqualified pursuit of the free market' (Taylor, 2005:147). Portillo wanted to address these electoral impediments and create a new modernised Conservatism based around 'different ages, social types, ethnic groups and cultures' (Taylor, 2005:147).

10 The Conservatives were widely condemned for constructing party leadership election rules that made no provision for such an eventuality. Cowley and Green observe that it was odd that the party was subjected to so much criticism for this, when in reality, the obvious solution to the dilemma (and in the interests of the party) was for Ancram and Davis to withdraw themselves (Cowley and Green, 2005:3).

11 An illustration of the hostile briefing of the Portillo camp occurred during the leadership campaign when they described Ancram as a 'talentless, old duffer' (Carter and Alderman, 2002:578).

12 Portillo would later lament that 'I seem to unite people against me in antagonism' (Walters, 2001:207).

13 From this description Norton would appear to regard the Europhilia of Clarke as likely to create a reaction from the Eurosceptics that would disunite the party. It would also appear to suggest that the social liberalism of Portillo would not provoke a similar reaction from social conservatives as Clarke's Europhilia would from Eurosceptics.

14 This concern appeared to resonate with the party membership. Surveys of the party membership identified their concerns that with Clarke as party leader the party would have difficulties in presenting a unified message. Cowley and Green note that one survey revealed that sixty per cent of the party members feared that Clarke would split the party (Cowley and Green, 2005:4).

Chapter Nine

1 This interpretation would famously result in Theresa May (the then Party Chair) informing the Conservative annual conference of autumn 2002, that the Conservatives were perceived as the 'nasty' party (Cowley and Green, 2005:5).

2 The observations of Garnett and Lynch appear chime with those of Cowley and Green. They argue that the election of Duncan Smith over the ultimate symbol of Europhilia, Clarke, appeared to confirm that the Europhiles had finally been defeated. The defeat of Clarke, and the retirements from Parliament of leading Europhiles, such as Heseltine and Heath, meant that any remaining Europhile dissidence would generate less publicity (Garnett and Lynch, 2003:5).

3 His own personal ratings were uniformly disastrous. Whereas fifty-eight per cent of the electorate though Blair was a good leader, only fourteen per cent believed Duncan Smith was a good leader. That only eighteen per cent of the electorate believed that he would be effective Prime Minister was immensely worrying for Conservatives. Rumours abounded that Central Office staff 'kept the results of their focus groups from the leader, so damning was the public's view of him' (Cowley and Green, 2005:6).

4 In his defence Duncan Smith was less gaffe prone that his predecessor. Although he did cause himself considerable embarrassment when visiting a Sunderland

supporting part of County Durham, by praising their hated rivals, Newcastle United (Garnett and Lynch, 2003:8).

5   Garnett and Lynch observed that these moves, and the motivations that underlay them, suggested that the modernisation project had been terminated. They revealed how one anonymous Conservative believed that the sackings demonstrated Duncan Smith's 'utter paranoia that Portillo's people are trying to get him' (Garnett and Lynch, 2003:10).

6   In total, eight Conservatives rebelled against the voting instructions and a further thirty-five were absent from the division. They were assumed to be abstainers (Cowley and Stuart, 2004:357).

7   John Bercow had resigned from the Shadow Cabinet in order to oppose the stance that Duncan Smith was imposing (Cowley and Stuart, 2004:357).

8   In May 2003, Crispin Blunt was the first Conservative parliamentarian to publicly state that Duncan Smith should be removed via a confidence motion. He argued that 'we have the handicap of a leader whom Conservatives in Parliament and outside feel unable to present to the electorate as a credible alternative Prime Minister' (Cowley and Green, 2005:6).

9   An investigation by the parliamentary commissioner for standards completely exonerated the Duncan Smiths of any impropriety. By the time the investigation was completed Duncan Smith had been removed from the leadership of the Conservative Party (Norton, 2005:48).

10   Fisher observes that Wheeler had made substantial donations to the Conservatives in preparation for the 2001 general election. Wheeler, who opposed Clarke assuming the party leadership, was nonetheless unhappy with the performance of Duncan Smith as party leader. As a consequence, Wheeler made what were for him only small donations (totally £28,000) during the Duncan Smith era. Wheeler celebrated the removal of Duncan Smith by donating £500,000 to the party (Fisher, 2004:406, 409).

11   If Duncan Smith had triumphed it would be twelve months before another confidence motion could be activated.

12   His defeat ensured that he became the first Conservative Party leader since Austen Chamberlain in the 1920s not to contest a General Election as party leader (Heffernan, 2003:3).

13   Roth eloquently identified that Howard's 'complex character' made him a difficult politician to interpret. Roth notes that Howard possessed experience of his political craft and was an intelligent, urbane and subtle man. However this had to be measured against the fact that 'his driving ambition can sometimes make him play ruthlessly to the tabloid gallery or ride roughshod over colleagues' (Roth, 2004:362).

Chapter Ten

1   Kelly would observe that if Duncan Smith had acquired the party leadership on the tide of internal democracy, then Howard had acquired it as that tide turned. He notes constituency chairs seemed relatively comfortable with the notion that parliamentarians had 'taken matters into their own hands' and that by installing Howard at the expense of Duncan Smith, the 'party had finally come to its senses' (Kelly, 2004a:402).

2   Their suspicions about the capacity of Duncan Smith to embrace and sustain the modernisation agenda proved to be correct. As the previous chapter identified, his decision to impose the Conservative whip against the adoption of children by homosexual couples, demonstrated his socially conservative and traditionalist instincts, rather than his commitment to social liberalism and inclusive modernisation.

3   As suggested in the previous chapter, the dominant area of policy disputation for New Labour related to the Iraq War and specifically the legal basis for justifying military action (Seldon and Snowden, 2005:728).

4   Two illustrations of note were identified by Roth and Cowley and Green. Roth admired the manner in which Howard delighted Conservatives and dismayed Labour, with a 'masterfully sneering attack' on Blair. Howard skilfully reminded parliamentarians of Blair's previous boast that he had 'no reverse gear'. He taunted Blair by saying that MPs 'could hear the gears grinding as you came before us, lip quivering once again' (Roth, 2004:362). Cowley and Green were equally praising of how Howard handled Blair on education. Howard argued that 'as a grammar school boy he would be taking no lessons on education from a public school educated Prime Minister' (Cowley and Green, 2005:7).

5   Attempting to interpret their electoral rejection as a qualified success (i.e. that the recovery had commenced) was a sign of how bad things had become for the Conservatives, according to Cowley and Green. They argue that despite the increase in parliamentary representation, the Conservatives were still 158 parliamentary seats behind Labour; whilst their parliamentary representation was lower than the Labour representation in the 1983 general election, which was their electoral nadir. They conclude that the evidence of a Conservative revival was meagre (Cowley and Green, 2005:1).

6   By resigning Howard became the fourth Conservative Party leader to have unsuccessfully opposed Tony Blair, after Major, Hague and Duncan Smith. Moreover, he became the third successive party leader who had failed to become Prime Minister. Between 1881 and 1997 only one party leader, Austen Chamberlain, had failed to become Prime Minister. Inside eight years the Conservatives had added three more to the list alongside Chamberlain (Cowley and Green, 2005:2).

7   In the immediate aftermath of their general election defeat, Howard would reshuffle his shadow Cabinet, in a manner which was assumed to be designed to showcase the credentials of David Cameron, who was promoted to shadow Education Secretary, and Liam Fox, who was promoted to shadow Foreign Secretary. The fact that Howard catapulted George Osborne to the position of Shadow Chancellor, led to speculation that Osborne might be a candidate for the succession, but he choose not to stand, and backed his modernising ally Cameron instead.

8   Conservative Parliamentarians voted 71 to 29 per cent in favour of change; Voluntary activists voted 58 to 42 per cent in favour of change; and Conservative peers and Members of the European Parliament voted 63 to 37 per cent in favour of change. The overall figure was 61 per cent for change and 29 per cent change, thus falling short of the two-thirds majority required (Wintour, 2005:1).

9   To his critics his political lightweight credentials were intensified by the alleged and repeated references to his friendship with the pop singer and former Neighbours actress, Natalie Imbruglia (Jeffreys, 2005:1).

10   Fox had also developed a reputation for the near the knuckle humour, which could cause offence and potential embarrassment to the Conservatives should he acquire the party leadership. For example, he was once forced to make a public apology after describing the Spice Girls as 'three dogs and a blackbird' (Hall, 2002:1).

11   The repeated references in the academic literature to the notion of candidates putting down markers for future party leadership election bids is intriguing. Notable candidates who were assumed to be doing this were of course Powell in 1965, but also Prior and Howe in 1975. The future bids never did materialise, so it is bemusing that the Powell precedent is referred to so much, as it is precedent based on a record of failure.

12   Upon completion of the Conservative Party Conference, Howard formally tendered his resignation, and the Chair of the 1922 Executive Committee, Michael Spicer, initiated the procedures for the parliamentary stage of the party leadership contest.

13   The Davis conference speech badly undermined his party leadership chances just as poor conference speeches by R. A. Butler and especially Reginald Maudling had undermined their party leadership chances during the war of the Macmillan succession forty-two years earlier.

14   The impact of the conference speeches was immediate. It was so pronounced that the political analyst, Peter Kellner, admitted that 'he had never seen such a big change in such a short time in thirty-five years of reporting and conducting opinion polls' (Montgomerie, 2005:7).

15   Clarke was appointed to a Democracy task force, whilst Duncan Smith was appointed to a Social Exclusion task force.

16   The Davis camp felt that Howard engineered a delayed departure schedule in order to undermine their candidates' chances (Montgomerie, 2005:1-2).

17   This was unlikely given the antipathy that existed between Davis and Fox (Sparrow, 2005:5).

18   Montgomerie alleges that during the course of the party leadership election campaign it had been revealed that the Conservative Whips' Office had once selected Davis for the 'shit of the year' award (Montgomerie, 2005:2).

19   The Davis camp had spent weeks seeking his endorsement of Alan Duncan. They were scheduled to announce it hours after the conference speech, until Duncan decided to back out the minute Davis completed his soporific speech. He sent a lethal text to Derek Conway, an aid to Davis, which read: 'that was ABYSMAL…you will have to count me out' (Kite and Hennessy, 2005b:16).

20   Later on in the party membership stage of the contest, Davis managed to appear sexist again when he revealed in a radio interview that he preferred blondes to brunettes. The more astute Cameron avoided answering the question (Carlin, 2005:10).

21   The American political pollster, Frank Luntz, confirmed that his opinion polling had demonstrated that Cameron was 'exactly what swing voters are looking for in a Conservative leader' (Jones and Carlin, 2005:1).

Chapter Eleven

1   Parliamentary ballots saw James Callaghan elected as party leader and Prime Minister in 1976 after the voluntary resignation of Harold Wilson. Michael Foot succeeded Callaghan through a parliamentary ballot in 1980, by which time the Labour Party were in opposition. Neil Kinnock acquired the party leadership following the resignation of Foot in 1983. Kinnock was elected through the electoral college system which had replaced the parliamentary ballot system. He would withstand a challenge by Tony Benn five years later to retain the party leadership. John Smith won the endorsement of the electoral college in 1992 after Kinnock resigned. Tony Blair secured the party leadership through the same electoral college system following the death of Smith in 1994.

2   The previous procedures stipulated that a challenge had to be initiated in the first four weeks of a parliamentary session, or the first six months of the parliament. These were reduced to two weeks and three months respectively (Quinn, 2005:801).

3   Stark disputes this assertion and positions Major and Hurd as jointly the most competent of the three leading candidates. If we factor experience into our competence criteria then clearly Major was less qualified to lead than either Hurd or Heseltine (Stark, 1996:132).

4   The basis of the Stark assumption that rules do not influence outcomes is derived primarily from the Labour Party and Liberal Party and allied succession contests. He concludes that Labour would still have selected Wilson, Callaghan, Foot, Kinnock, Smith and Blair irrespective of the party leadership election systems deployed. He notes that the Liberals would still have elected Thorpe and Steel; that the Social and Democratic Party would still have elected Jenkins and Owen, and the Liberal Democrats would still have elected Ashdown (Stark, 1996:133).

5   Such an undertaking can only be considered with qualifications. The actions of political elites are framed by the existence of the present and existing environment. Alternatives succession procedures may have altered their decision-making and will have affected the range of candidates wishing to position themselves for the succession. The exercise is hypothetical and requires the reader to understand this in order to appreciate the arguments advanced.

6   This argument is given fuel by the observations of Watkins who noted that Conservatives felt that the natural order of succession was Butler than Maudling (Watkins, 1998:187).

7   Thatcher herself admits that it would have been inconceivable that she could have emerged via the magic circle (Thatcher, 1993:832).

APPENDIX

Table 21   **Conservative Party Leadership Election Procedures: Parliamentary Ballots 1965 to 1998**

1a. Vacancies Only

Candidates required the backing of two Conservative parliamentarians to propose and second their candidatures. The names of those who proposed and seconded candidates remained confidential until 1990, but they were then revealed from 1990 onwards. Then onto contest – see section 2 below.

1b. Challenges Only

Between 1965 and 1975 there was no provision for a challenge to the incumbent.

Between 1975 and 1991 the nomination rules were the same as for vacancies. Annual elections were permitted. Challenges had to be conducted within four weeks of a new parliamentary session or within six months of the commencement of a new parliament.

Between 1991 and 1998 the nomination rules were the same as for vacancies. Annual elections were still permitted. However, activating a formal election now required ten per cent of the parliamentary Conservative Party to demand one by writing to the chair of the 1922 Executive Committee. The names of the ten per cent of Conservative parliamentarians requesting an election were not publicised. Letters requesting an election had to be received within two weeks of a new parliamentary session or within three months of the commencement of a new parliament.

2. All Contests

If only one Conservative declared an interest in the party leadership, then that candidate was announced as being elected the new party leader. If there was more than one candidate, then Conservative parliamentarians were invited to consult with their constituency associations, before they participated in a series of eliminative ballots. The series of ballots should be completed within two to four weeks.

First Ballot of Conservative Parliamentarians

To secure outright victory in the first parliamentary ballot the leading candidate had to secure a simple majority and hold a fifteen per cent lead over their nearest rival. Abstainers and ballot spoilers were included in these thresholds from 1975. Conservative parliamentarians voted for one candidate. If no winner then a second ballot called.

Second Ballot of Conservative Parliamentarians

Candidates who had contested the first ballot could seek re-nomination and continue on or they could drop out. New candidates were permitted to enter the election at the second ballot stage. To secure outright victory in the second parliamentary ballot the leading candidate needed to secure a simple majority of Conservative parliamentarians entitled to vote. Conservative parliamentarians voted for only one candidate. If no candidate elected according to these procedures, a third ballot will be called.

Third Ballot of Conservative Parliamentarians

No new candidates permitted to enter at third ballot stage. Until 1991 the three leading candidates from the second ballot competed to determine winner (alternative vote system). After 1991 only leading two candidates from second ballot allowed to proceed. To secure victory in the third parliamentary ballot the leading candidate needed a simple majority of Conservative parliamentarians who voted. A fourth ballot could be held if the third ballot ended in a tie.

Source: Adapted from Quinn, 2005:810

Table 22:   Conservative Party Leadership Election Procedures: Parliamentary and Party Membership Ballots 1998 to the present day

1.   Contests

Activated by the death of an incumbent, the resignation of an incumbent or the defeat of an incumbent following a confidence motion – see section 2 below

Candidates announce their intention to stand by an agreed deadline and they require the backing of two Conservative parliamentarians to propose and second their candidatures. Those who propose and second candidates will have their names made public.

If only one candidate puts themselves forward, then that candidate is duly elected as the new party leader.

If only two candidates put themselves forward, then the election progresses to a one-member, one vote ballot of party members with immediate effect.

However, if there are more than two candidates putting themselves forward, then a series of eliminative ballots will be held to reduce the number of candidates put to the party membership down to two. Participation in those eliminative ballots will be restricted to Conservative parliamentarians.

- In each parliamentary ballot, each Conservative parliamentarian will vote for one candidate and the bottom candidate will be eliminated.

- A series of eliminative ballots will be conducted until only two candidates remain

The two leading candidates will then present themselves to a ballot of the party membership. This will be a one member, one vote postal ballot. The winner requires a simple majority. The campaigning period for the party membership ballot will last two months.

2.   No Confidence Votes

A confidence motion will be initiated by the following means. Fifteen per cent of Conservative parliamentarians (names of whom remain confidential) need to write to the Chair of the 1922 Executive Committee requesting a vote of confidence should be held against the incumbent party leader. Or a confidence motion can be activated by the incumbent party leader, who is entitled to request one.

A motion of no confidence in the incumbent party leader can be activated at any time; there is no provision for annual elections.

When a confidence motion is initiated, (either by the fifteen per cent threshold being passed or by the incumbent party leader requesting it), Conservative parliamentarians alone participate in a ballot to indicate whether they continue to have confidence in the incumbent party leader or they do not. To overcome the confidence motion, the incumbent party leader needs to secure a simple majority of Conservative parliamentarians.

If the incumbent party leader overcomes the confidence motion, no further confidence motions can be called for another year. If the incumbent party leader is defeated in the confidence motion, then they are obliged to tender their resignation and a leadership election commences. The defeated incumbent party leader is barred from putting themselves forward as a candidate in that leadership election.

Source: Adapted from Quinn, 2005:810

BIBLIOGRAPHY

Alderman, K. (1996), 'The Conservative Party Leadership Election of 1995', *Parliamentary Affairs*, Vol. 49, No. 2, pp. 316-322.

Alderman, K. (1998), 'The Conservative Party Leadership Election of 1997', *Parliamentary Affairs*, Vol. 51, No. 1, pp. 1-16.

Alderman, K. (1999), 'Revision of Leadership Procedures in the Conservative Party', *Parliamentary Affairs*, Vol. 52, No. 2, pp. 260-274.

Alderman, K and Smith, M.J. (1990), 'Can British Prime Ministers be given the push by their parties', *Parliamentary Affairs,* Vol. 43, No. 3, pp. 260-276.

Baker, D., Gamble, A., and Ludlam, S. (1993), 'Whips or Scorpions? Conservative MPs and the Maastricht Paving Motion Vote', *Parliamentary Affairs*, Vol. 46, No. 2, pp. 151-166.

Baker, K. (1993) *The Turbulent Years: My Life in Politics* (London: Faber and Faber).

Barber, S. (2003), 'No Change, No Chance: Economic Failure and the 1995 Tory Leadership Crisis', *Conservative History Journal*, Autumn 2003.

Bartle, J. and Laycock, S. (2006), 'Elections and Voting', in Dunleavy, P., Heffernan, R., Cowley, P., and Hay, C (eds), *Developments in British Politics 8* (Basingstoke, Palgrave).

Baston, L. (2004) *Reggie: The Life of Reginald Maudling* (Gloucestershire: Sutton).

BBC, (1999) *The Major Years*, 5th October 1999.

Behrens, R. (1980) *The Conservative Party from Heath to Thatcher* (Farnborough: Saxon House).

Berkeley, H. (1972) *Crossing the Floor* (London: Allen and Unwin).

Blake, R. (1998) *The Conservative Party from Peel to Major* (London: Arrow).

Bogdanor, V. (1994), 'The Selection of the Party Leader', in Seldon, A. and Ball, S. (eds) *Conservative Century: The Conservative Party since 1900* (Oxford: Oxford University Press).

Brandreth, G. (1999) *Breaking the Code: Westminster Diaries* (London: Phoenix).

Brock, G. and Wapshott, N. (1983) *Thatcher* (London: Futura).

Broughton, D. (2004), 'Doomed to Defeat? Electoral Support and the Conservative Party', *Political Quarterly*, Vol. 75, No. 4, pp. 350-355.

Brown, C. (1997), 'Runners and Riders in Race to lead Party', *The Independent*, 6th May 1997.

Brunson, M. (2000) *A Ringside Seat: The Autobiography* (London).

Bulpitt, J. (1986), 'The Discipline of the New Democracy: Mrs Thatcher's Domestic Statecraft', *Political Studies*, Vol. 34. No. 1, pp. 19-39.

Butler, R. A. (1971) *The Art of the Possible* (London: Hamish Hamilton).

Butler, D. and Kavanagh, D., (ed.), (1997) *The British General Election of 1997* (London: Macmillan).

Butler, D. and Kavanagh, D., (ed.), (2001) *The British General Election of 2001* (London: Macmillan).

Butler, D. and King, A., (ed.), (1966) *The British General Election of 1966* (London: Macmillan).

Campbell, J. (1993) *Edward Heath: A Biography* (London: Jonathan Cape).

Campbell, J. (2003) *Margaret Thatcher. Volume Two: The Iron Lady* (London: Jonathan Cape).

Carlin, B. (2005), 'Davis's blonde moment upsets Tory women', *The Daily Telegraph*, 10th November 2005.

Carlin, B, Isaby, J, and Jones, G. (2005), 'Cameron surge puts Clarke at risk of early exit', *The Daily Telegraph*, 10th October 2005.

Carter, N. and Alderman, K. (1991), 'A Very Tory Coup: The Ousting of Mrs Thatcher', *Parliamentary Affairs*, Vol. 44, No. 2, pp. 125-139.

Carter, N. and Alderman, K. (2002), 'The Conservative Party Leadership Election of 2001', *Parliamentary Affairs*, Vol. 55, No. 3 pp. 569-585.

Charmley, J. (1996) *A History of the Conservative Party 1900-1996* (London: Macmillan).

Churchill, R. (1964) *The Fight for the Tory Leadership: A Contemporary Chronicle* (London: Heinemann).

Childs, S. (2006), 'Political Parties and Party Systems' in Dunleavy, P., Heffernan, R., Cowley, P., and Hay, C (eds), *Developments in British Politics 8* (Basingstoke, Palgrave).

Clarke, K. (2001) *The Conservatives need a leader who can win the General Election* (London: Andrew Tyrie).

Clark, A. (1993) *Diaries* (London: Wiedenfeld and Nicolson).

Clark, A. (1998) *The Tories: Conservatives and the Nation State 1922-1997* (London: Weidenfeld and Nicolson).

Cole, J. (1995) *As it Seemed to Me: Political Memoirs* (London: Weidenfeld and Nicolson).

Collings, D. & Seldon, A. (2001) Conservatives in Opposition, *Parliamentary Affairs*, Vol. 54, No. 4, pp. 624-637.

Cowley, P. (1996) 'How did he do that? The Second Round of the 1990 Conservative Leadership Election', in Broughton, D. (ed.), *British Election and Parties Yearbook, 1996* (London: Frank Cass).

Cowley. P. (1997), 'Just William? A Supplementary Analysis of the 1997 Conservative leadership contest', *Talking Politics*, Vol. 9, No. 4, pp. 91-95.

Cowley, P. and Bailey, M. (2000), 'Peasants' Uprising or Religious War: Re-examining the 1975 Conservative Leadership Contest', *British Journal of Political Science*, Vol. 30, No. 4, pp. 599-629.

Cowley, P. and Garry, J. (1998) 'The British Conservative Party and Europe: The Choosing of John Major', *British Journal of Political Science*, Vol. 28, No. 3, pp. 473-499.

Cowley, P. and Quayle, S. (2001), 'The Conservatives: Running on the Spot' in Geddes, A. and Tonge, J. (eds.), *Labour's Landslide II* (Manchester: Manchester University Press).

Cowley, P. and Stuart, M. (2003), 'The Conservative Parliamentary Party' in Garnett, M. and Lynch, P. (eds.), *The Conservatives in Crisis* (Manchester: Manchester University Press).

Cowley, P. and Stuart, M. (2004), 'Still Causing Trouble: The Conservative Parliamentary Party', *Political Quarterly*, Vol. 75, No. 4, pp. 356-361.

Cowley, P. and Green, J. (2005), 'New Leaders, Same Problems: The Conservatives', www.revolts.co.uk/two%/20leaders%/20same%/20problems.pdf .

Coxall, W. and Robins, L. (1998) *British Politics since the War* (Basingstoke: Macmillan).

Crewe, I. and Searing, D. (1988) 'Ideological Change in the British Conservative Party', *American Political Science Review*, Vol. 82, No. 2, pp. 361-381.

Crick, M. (1997) *Michael Heseltine: A Biography* (London: Penguin).

Critchley, J. (1994) *A Bag of Boiled Sweets* (London: Faber and Faber).

Denham, A. and Garnett, M. (2002) *Keith Joseph* (Chesham: Acumen).

Denham, M. and Dorey, P. (2006), 'A Tale of Two Speeches: The Conservative Party Leadership Election', *Political Quarterly*, Vol. 77, No. 1, pp. 35-41.

Denver, D. (1998) 'The Government That Could Do No Right', in King, A *et al*, *New Labour Triumphs: Britain at the Polls* (London: Chatham House).

Dorey, P. (1995) *British Politics since 1945* (Oxford: Blackwells).

Du Cann, E. (1995) *Two Lives: The Political and Business Careers of Edward Du Cann* (Upton upon Seven: Images).

Evans, B. and Taylor, A. (1996) *From Salisbury to Major: Continuity and Change in Conservative Politics* (Manchester University Press).

Fisher, N. (1977) *The Tory Leaders: Their Struggle for Power* (London: Weidenfeld and Nicolson).

Fisher, J. (2004), 'Money Matters: The Financing of the Conservative Party', *Political Quarterly*, Vol. 75, No. 4, pp. 405-410.

Foley, M. (1993) *The Rise of the British Presidency* (Manchester: Manchester University Press).

Foley, M. (2002) *John Major, Tony Blair and the Conflict of Leadership: Collision Course* (Manchester: Manchester University Press).

Fowler, N. (1991) *Ministers Decide: A Personal Memoir of the Thatcher Years* (London: Chapmans).

Gamble, A. (1988) *The Free Economy and the Strong State* (London: Macmillan).

Gamble, A. (1996) 'An Ideological Party', in Ludlam, S. and Smith, M. J. (ed.), *Contemporary British Conservatism* (London: Macmillan).

Gamble, A. and Wright, T. (2004), 'Conservative Rebirth', *Political Quarterly*, Vol. 75, No. 1, pp. 1-3.

Gamble, A. and Wright, T. (2006), 'New Conservative?' *Political Quarterly*, Vol. 77, No. 1, pp. 1-2.

Garnett, M. (2003), 'Win or Bust: The leadership gamble of William Hague' in Garnett, M. and Lynch, P. (eds.), *The Conservatives in Crisis* (Manchester: Manchester University Press).

Garnett, M. (2004) 'The Free Economy and the Schizophrenic State: Ideology and the Conservatives', *Political Quarterly*, Vol. 75, No. 4, pp. 367-372.

Garnett, M. (2005), 'Planning for Power', in Ball, S. and Seldon, A. (eds) *Recovering Power: The Conservatives in Opposition since 1867* (Basingstoke: Palgrave).

Garnett, M. and Lynch, P (2003), 'The Tribulations of a Quiet Man: Iain Duncan Smith and the Conservative Party', *Political Studies Association Annual Conference*, April 2003, www.psa.ac.uk/journals/pdf/5/2003/Mark%20Garnett.pdf .

Garnett, M. and Lynch, P. (2007) *Exploring British Politics* (London: Longman).

Gilmour, I. and Garnett, M. (1998) *Whatever Happened to the Tories: The Conservative Party Since 1945* (London: Fourth Estate).

Goodhart, P. (1973) *The 1922: The Story of the 1922 Committee* (London: Macmillan).

Gorman, T. (1993) *The Bastards: Dirty Tricks and the Challenge to Europe* (London: Pan).

Gove, M. (1995) *Michael Portillo: The Future of the Right* (London: Fourth Estate).

Hall, S. (2002), 'Fox retreats from Abortion Ban Demand', *The Guardian Unlimited*, http://society.guardian.co.uk/health/news/0,,431893,00.html, 1st February 2002.

Hailsham, Lord (1990) *A Sparrow's Flight* (London: Collins).

Hayton, R. (2006), 'Conservative Party strategy in Opposition: A Strategic-Relational Anaylsis, *Political Studies Association Annual Conference*, April 2006, http://www.psa.ac.uk/journals/pdf/5/2006/Hayton.pdf .

Heath, E. (1998) *The Course of My Life: My Autobiography* (London: Hodder and Stoughton).

Heffernan, R. (2003), 'Beyond Iain Duncan Smith: The Conservative Party under Michael Howard', in Dunleavy, P. *et al, Developments in British Politics 7* (London: Palgrave), http://www.palgrave.com/politics/dunleavy/update2.htm webpage update.

Heppell, T. (2000) *Prime Ministerial Leadership and Conservative Party Management 1992 to 1997* (Unpublished doctoral thesis, University of Newcastle).

Heppell, T. (2002) 'The Ideological Composition of the Parliamentary Conservative Party 1992-1997', *British Journal of Politics and International Relations*, Vol. 4, No. 2, pp. 299-324.

Heppell, T. (2006) *The Conservative Party Leadership of John Major* (Lampeter: Edwin Mellen Press).

Heppell, T. (2007), 'A Crisis of Legitimacy: The Conservative Party Leadership of John Major', *Contemporary British History*, Vol. 21, No. 4.

Heseltine, M. (2000) *Life in the Jungle: My Autobiography* (London: Hodder and Stoughton).

Hickson, K. (2005), 'Inequality', in Hickson, K. (ed) *The Political Thought of the Conservative Party since 1945* (Basingstoke: Palgrave).

Hill, M. (2004), 'Ideology and the Parliamentary Conservative Party Leadership Election of 2001', Politics Research Paper (Huddersfield: Centre for Democracy and Governance) (21st February 2004).

Hill, M. (2007) *The Parliamentary Conservative Party and the Party Leadership: The Elections of William Hague and Iain Duncan Smith* (unpublished doctoral thesis, The University of Huddersfield).

Hogg, S. and Hill, J. (1995) *Too Close to Call: Power and Politics: John Major in No. 10* (London: Little, Brown and Co.).

Horne, A. (1989) *Macmillan: 1957-1986, Volume II of the Official Biography* (London: Macmillan).

Home, Lord (1976) *The Way the Wind Blows* (London: Collins).

Howard, A. (1987) *RAB: The Life of R. A. Butler* (London: Jonathan Cape).

Howe, G. (1994) *Conflict of Loyalty* (London: Macmillan).

Hutchinson, G. (1970) *Edward Heath: A Personal and Political Biography* (Longman: London).

ITN News (2003), 'Duncan-Smith to Face Vote of Confidence', 28th October 2003.

Isaby, J. (2005) 'Spy: Conservatives in Blackpool' *The Daily Telegraph*, 4th October 2005.

Jeffreys, K. (2002) *Finest and Darkest Hours: The Decisive Events in British Politics from Churchill to Blair* (London: Atlantic Books).

Jeffreys, S. (2005), 'Tory Leadership: Runners and Riders' *The Guardian*, 6th May 2005.

Jessop, B., Bonnet, K., Bronley, S. and Ting, T., (1988) *Thatcherism: A Tale of Two Nations* (Cambridge: Polity Press).

Jones, G. (2005), 'Clarke and Fox fighting to stay in the race', *The Daily Telegraph*, 18th October 2005.

Jones, G. and Carlin, B. (2005), 'Forget the Speech, says straight-talking Davis', The *Daily Telegraph*, 11th October 2005.

Keegan, W. (1984) *Mrs Thatcher's Economic Experiment* (Harmondsmith: Penguin).

Kelly, R. (2004a), 'Tough times for the Tories' *Politics Review* Vol. 13, No. 3 pp. 2-5.

Kelly, R. (2004b), 'The Extra Parliamentary Tory Party: McKenzis Revisited', *Political Quarterly*, Vol. 75, No. 4, pp. 398-404.

King, A. (1992) 'The Implications of One-Party Government', in King, A. (ed.), *Britain at the Polls* (London: Chatham House).

King, A. (2005a), 'A Cameron-Fox contest is what most grassroots Conservatives want', *The Daily Telegraph*, 20th October 2005.

King, A. (2005b) 'Clarke has a clear lead, but do the Tories have the will to win', *The Daily Telegraph*, 3rd October 2005.

Kite, M. and Hennessy, P. (2005a), 'A Robot in the Headlights', *The Sunday Telegraph*, 9th October 2005.

Kite, M. and Hennessy, P. (2005b), 'War of the Daves: Heavyweight Tory Championship Bout, *The Sunday Telegraph*, 23rd October 2005.

Kumarasingham, H. (2005), 'Home Sweet Home: The Problematic Leadership of Alec Douglas-Home', *Conservative History Journal*, Vol. 5, pp. 13-15.

Lamont, N. (2000) *In Office* (London: Warner).

Leonard, D. (2003), 'Alec Douglas-Home: Right Man, Wrong Century?', *Political Quarterly*, Vol., 74, No, 4, pp. 504-512.

Macleod, I. (1964) 'The Tory Leadership', *The Spectator*, 17 January 1964.

Major, J. (1999) *John Major: The Autobiography* (London: Harper Collins).

Maudling, R. (1978) *Memoirs* (London: Sidgwick and Jackson).

McAnulla, S. (1999), 'The Post-Thatcher Era', in Marsh, D. et al, (eds.), *Post war British Politics in Perspective* (Cambridge: Polity Press) .

Montgomerie, T. (2005), 'How Cameron won…and Davis lost', http://conservativeblogs.com/toryleadership/2005/how_cameron_won. html .

Nadler, J. (2001) *William Hague: In his own right* (London: Politicos).

Norris, S. (1996) *Changing Trains: An Autobiography* (London: Hutchinson).

Norton, P. (1990a), 'The Lady's not for turning but what about the rest: Margaret Thatcher and the Conservative Party 1979 to 1989', *Parliamentary Affairs*, Vol. 43, No.1, pp. 41-58.

Norton, P. (1990b), 'Choosing a Leader: Margaret Thatcher and the parliamentary Conservative Party 1989-1990', *Parliamentary Affairs*, Vol. 43, No. 3, pp. 249-259.

Norton, P. (1992), 'The Conservative Party from Thatcher to Major', in King, A. (eds) *Britain at the Polls 1992* (Chatham, Chatham House, NJ).

Norton, P. (1994), 'Factions and Tendencies in the Conservative Party', in Margetts, H and Smyth, G. (eds.), *Turning Japanese? Britain with a Permanent Party of Government* (London: Lawrence and Wishart).

Norton, P. (1998a) 'The Conservative Party: In Office but not in Power', in King, A. *et al*, *New Labour Triumphs: Britain at the Polls* (London: Chatham House).

Norton, P. (1998b) 'Electing the Leader: The Conservative Leadership contest 1997', *Politics Review*, Vol. 7, No. 4, pp. 10-14.

Norton, P. (2001), 'The Conservative Leadership Election', *British Politics Group Newsletter*, Fall 2001, pp. 11-16.

Norton, P. (2005), 'The Conservative Party: The Politics of Panic' in Bartle, J. and King, A. (eds), *Britain at the Polls 2005* (CQ Press: Washington).

Norton, P. and Aughey, A. (1981) *Conservatives and Conservatism* (London: Temple Smith).

Parkinson, C, (1992) *Right at the Centre* (London: Weidenfeld and Nicolson).

Pearce, E. (1997) *The Lost Leaders: The Best Prime Ministers we never had* (London: Little Brown and Company).

Peele, G. (1998), 'Towards 'New' Conservatives? Organisational Reform and The Conservative Party', *The Political Quarterly*, Vol. 69, No. 2 pp. 141-147.

Prior, J. (1986) *A Balance of Power* (London: Hamish Hamilton).

Punnett, R. M. (1992) *Selecting the Party Leader: Britain in Comparative Perspective* (London: Harvester Wheatsheaf).

Quinn, T. (2005), 'Leasehold or Freehold? Leader-eviction rules in the British Conservative and Labour Parties', *Political Studies*, Vol. 53, No. 3, pp. 793-815.

Ramsden, J. (1996) *Winds of Change: Macmillan to Heath 1957-1975* (London: Longman).

Ramsden, J. (1998) *An Appetite for Power: A History of the Conservative Party since 1830* (London: Macmillan).

Redmayne, M. (1963) *The Listener*, (19.12.63), pp. 1013.

Rentoul, J. (2001) *Tony Blair: Prime Minister* (London: Warner Books).

Roth, A. (1971) *Heath and the Heathman* (London: Routledge and Kegan Paul).

Roth, A. (2004), 'Michael Howard: The First Jewish Prime Minister?', *Political Quarterly*, Vol. 75, No. 4, pp. 362-366.

Ridley, N. (1991) *My Style of Government: The Thatcher Years* (London: Fontana).

Seldon, A. (1997) *Major: A Political Life* (London: Weidenfeld and Nicolson).

Seldon, A. and Ball, S. (1994), 'Introduction' in Seldon, A. and Ball, S. (eds) *Conservative Century: The Conservative Party since 1900* (Oxford: Oxford University Press).

Seldon, A. and Snowden, P. (2005a), 'The Barren Years 1997-2005' in Ball, S and Seldon, A. (eds.), *Recovering Power: The Conservatives in Opposition Since 1867* (London: Palgrave).

Seldon, A and Snowden, P. (2005b), The Conservative Campaign', *Parliamentary Affairs*, Vol. 58, No. 4, pp. 725-742.

Shepherd, R. (1991) *The Power Brokers: The Tory Party and Its Leaders* (London: Hutchinson).

Shepherd, R. (1996) *Enoch Powell: A Biography* (London: Pimilco).

Sky News (2003), 'Duncan-Smith loses Vote of Confidence', 29th October 2003.

Smith, M. J. and Ludlam, S. (1996) 'Introduction' in Ludlam, S. and Smith, M. J., (ed.), *Contemporary British Conservatism* (London: Macmillan).

Sparrow, A. (2005), 'Fox: Out of the Race, but no longer a lightweight', *The Daily Telegraph*, 21st October 2005.

Stark, L. P. (1996) *Choosing a Leader: Party Leadership Contest in Britain from Macmillan to Blair* (London: Macmillan).

Stephens, P. (1996) *Politics and the Pound* (London: Papermac).

Stevens, C. (2002), 'Thatcherism, Majorism and the Collapse of Tory Statecraft', *Contemporary British History*, Vol. 16, No. 1, pp. 119-150.

Stuart, M. (1998) *Douglas Hurd: The Public Servant* (London: Mainstream).

Taylor, A. (2005), 'Economic Statecraft', Hickson, K. (ed) *The Political Thought of the Conservative Party since 1945* (Basingstoke: Palgrave).

Taylor, I. (2003), 'The Conservatives 1997-2001: A Party in Crisis?', Garnett, M. and Lynch, P. (eds) *The Conservatives in Crisis: The Tories After 1997* (Manchester: Manchester University Press).

Tebbit, N. (1988) *Upwardly Mobile* (London: Weidenfeld and Nicolson).

Thatcher, M. (1993) *The Downing Street Years* (London: Harper Collins).

Thatcher, M. (1995) *The Path to Power* (London: Harper Collins).

Thompson, H. (1996) 'Economic Policy under Thatcher and Major', in Ludlam, S., and Smith, M. J., (ed.), *Contemporary British Conservatism* (London: Macmillan).

Thorpe, D. (1996) *Alec Douglas-Home* (London: Sinclair Stephenson).

Walters, S. (2001) *Tory Wars: Conservatives in Crisis* (London: Politicos).

Watkins, A. (1991) *A Conservative Coup: The Fall of Margaret Thatcher* (London: Duckworth).

Watkins, A. (1998) *The Road to Number 10: From Bonar Law to Tony Blair* (London: Duckworth).

Wheatcroft, G. (2005) *The Strange Death of Tory England* (London: Allen Lane).

White, M. (1997), 'Widdecombe rounds on Contender Howard', *The Guardian*, 12th May 1997, p. 8.

Whitelaw, W. (1989) *The Whitelaw Memoirs* (London: Aurum Press).

Wickham-Jones, M. (1997), 'Right Turn: A Revisionist Account of the 1975 Conservative Party Leadership Election', *Twentieth Century British History*, Vol. 8, No.1, pp. 74-89.

Williams, H. (1998) *Guilty Men: Conservative Decline and Fall 1992-1997* (London: Aurum Press).

Wintour, P. (2005), 'Howard Defeated on Leadership vote change', *The Guardian Unlimited*, http://politics.guardian.co.uk/toryleader/story/ 0,,1579760,00.html , 28th September 2005.

Young, H. and Sloman, A. (1986) *The Thatcher Phenomenon* (London: BBC).

INDEX